L10-S

S0-BAB-047

PROTESTANTISM
AND
REPRESSION

PROTESTANTISM AND REPRESSION

A Brazilian Case Study

RUBEM A. ALVES

Translated by John Drury

Revised by Jaime Wright

ORBIS BOOKS
Maryknoll, New York 10545

The Catholic Foreign Mission Society of America (Maryknoll) recruits and trains people for overseas missionary service. Through Orbis Books Maryknoll aims to foster the international dialogue that is essential to mission. The books published, however, reflect the opinions of their authors and are not meant to represent the official position of the society.

First published as *Protestantismo e repressão,* copyright © 1979 by Editora Atica, S.A., R. Barão de Iguape, 110, São Paulo, Brazil

English translation copyright © 1985 by Orbis Books, Maryknoll, NY 10545

All rights reserved

Manufactured in the United States of America

Library of Congress Cataloging in Publication Data
Alves, Rubem, A., 1933–
    Protestantism and repression.

    Translation of: Protestantismo e repressão.
    Bibliography: p.
    1. Protestant churches—Brazil—Controversial
literature.   2. Protestantism—Controversial literature.
3. Evangelicalism—Brazil—Controversial literature.
I. Title.
BX4836.B8A4813   280′.4′0981   82-3594
ISBN 0-88344-098-9 (pbk.)

I speak of consistency in one sense only, limited to the correspondence between behavior and thought, to the inner harmony between general principles and their application. Therefore I consider a consistent man to be simply one who, possessing a certain number of general, absolute concepts, strives earnestly in all he does, and in all his opinions about what should be done, to remain in the fullest possible accord with those concepts.

Why should anyone inflexibly convinced of the exclusive truth of his concepts regarding any and all questions be willing to tolerate opposing ideas? What good can he expect of a situation in which everyone is free to express opinions that to his mind are patently false and therefore harmful to society? By what right should he abstain from using any means whatsoever to attain the goal he regards as correct? In other words, total consistency is tantamount in practice to fanaticism, while inconsistency is the source of tolerance.

. . . We must note that humanity has survived only thanks to inconsistency. . . . The race of inconsistent people continues to be one of the greatest sources of hope that possibly the human species will somehow manage to survive.

Lezek Kolakowski
"In Praise of Inconsistency"

CONTENTS

FOREWORD

Over the last twenty years, incredible changes have taken place in the Presbyterian Church of Brazil. In 1959, on the occasion of its centennial celebrations, this Church was acclaimed as the outstanding success story of Protestantism in Latin America; it was hailed for its vitality, its prospects for continued growth, and for the role it seemed destined to play in the life of that nation. Today, after fifteen years of domination by a small group of reactionary leaders, it has been decimated. Many who once spoke of its great promise now wonder how long it can survive. The word "Presbyterian" now calls to mind the destructiveness of religious fanaticism and repression.

Two decades ago, the future of Brazil's Presbyterian Church seemed assured because it had produced an extraordinary new generation of ministers and lay men and women: intellectually gifted, socially concerned, and dedicated to the service of Church and country. Most of them have long since been put out of the Church; those who remain are marginalized and isolated. Many of those trained as ministers were not only denied any opportunity to serve the Church; they were also forced to spend years re-orienting and re-training themselves professionally. In the early sixties, these young Presbyterians were the vanguard of a movement of theological revitalization and church renewal. Their thought and activity spawned new movements in Brazil and made a significant impact in wider ecumenical circles. Today, the Church to which they offered these gifts is a theological wasteland, dominated by the most narrow fundamentalistic Calvinism.

Ministers and lay persons of this new generation were acutely aware of their rootedness in their own culture and history, were deeply disturbed by the poverty and sufferings of their people, and were committed to working for social transformation. Their faith stance led them to enter various professions with a strong sense of vocation and to become involved in political movements for change. Today, if they still continue to pursue these goals, they do so in isolation. The Presbyterian Church, rather than sustaining this quality of life, is identified with the most reactionary political developments and does its part to legitimate a repressive order.

I lived in Brazil in the late fifties and early sixties and was in close contact with this new generation. Since that time, I have observed the course of events from a distance and have been deeply disturbed by what I have seen. I have been shocked to see how quickly a few men without scruple could destroy the hopes and wreck the lives of young men and women who dared to care about what was happening in the world around them. I still mourn the loss this has meant for the Protestant movement in Brazil and for that nation. Beyond all this, *I'm haunted by the suspicion that what happened in Brazil could also happen here.*

No one in the movement for renewal in Brazil twenty-five years ago imagined that such a drastic change could occur in the Presbyterian Church. We were confronted by declarations from the pulpit and statements in official church publications calling for the suppression of progressive theological thought and attacking those who took up the cause of social justice; but we paid little attention to them. We were sure that the future would be ours, not theirs. However, what we were doing undermined the position of the traditional church leaders and they fought ruthlessly to survive. Many middle-class lay men and women, whose whole system of values and way of life were called into question by what was happening in society at large, took refuge in a closed and absolute religious system, and supported those church leaders who provided such a system for them while using it for their own ends. We were completely unprepared for what happened and were thrown on the defensive by it.

In many ways, our North American social system and way of life is entering a period of crisis as profound as that experienced by Brazilians in the early sixties. As our traditional assumptions about America's place in the world, our economic order, our major institutions, and our value system are being called into question, many people are looking anxiously for a religious assurance that they are right after all. As our mainline Protestant Churches continue to decline, they become more rigid and demand greater conformity. As those in positions of leadership are thrown on the defensive, they too may fight desperately for survival.

You may feel that the fear I have expressed is totally unwarranted. Before you dismiss the possibility completely, however, I suggest that you give consideration to it in the light of recent Presbyterian history in Brazil, taking advantage of the publication in English of Rubem Alves's *Protestantism and Repression.* If anyone is prepared to analyze what happened there and to guide us in our reflection on its implications for North American Protestantism, that person is Rubem Alves.

Alves is one of the most outstanding and best-known contemporary Third World theologians. He has a brilliant mind and an extraordinary capacity to articulate his thought. His interest in and knowledge of Brazilian culture and history are matched by a thorough mastery of the Western philosophical and theological tradition. By identifying with and responding to historical developments in Brazil, he has been able to look at our Western heritage from new perspectives and to open new horizons for Christian thought. This is clearly demonstrated in his two books originally published in English, *A Theology of Human Hope* and *Tomorrow's Child.*

More recently, Alves has concentrated his attention on the study of religion, bringing to it his theological perspective, insights gained from sociology and psychology of religion, and his own personal experience. He belonged to the generation under attack, was himself forced to leave the Church early on, and has been profoundly affected by these developments. His autobiographical essay, "From Paradise to the Desert," published by Orbis Books in *Frontiers of Theology in Latin America*, portrays his re-examination of his religious experience and the evolution of his theology under these circumstances.

In *Protestantism and Repression*, he wrestles with the question, Why did all this happen? What is there, in the structure and logic of what he calls "Right-Doctrine Protestantism," that leads to repression under certain historical conditions? His analysis is thorough; his insights, profound; his conclusions, astonishing.

My conviction about the importance of this book is something that has grown on me as I have lived with it over several months. At first, I questioned its relevance to our own situation. Alves has no intention of presenting us with a blueprint of the shape of things to come in this country. Nor can we import his thought and apply it in the United States. Whatever the similarities between certain Protestant movements in Brazil and in this country, the process of historical development has been quite different. I was impressed by his argument but not entirely convinced by it. His logic is clear and profound; it may also be mistaken at certain points. (I have often been surprised by developments in religious movements which have defied the limits set by my own thought about them.) Thus I resisted Alves's argument.

Gradually, however, I began to read this book in a different way. As I got into the author's critical examination of religious institutions in Brazil, I found myself challenged to look at religious institutions in the United States from the same critical perspective, undertaking my own analysis and formulating my own conclusions. As I went about this task, I found Alves's insights and language helping to enlarge my vision, giving me a clearer sense of what needs to be done here, and encouraging me to take new initiatives.

I am convinced that *Protestantism and Repression* can help prepare the way for a long overdue reformation in North American Christianity, if we are willing to face and work through some of the major issues Alves raises for us. I want to call attention to four which I consider important:

1. Alves insists that we can understand a religious movement and how it functions only if we are aware of the question or questions it proposes to answer and the nature of the answer it provides. In other words, every religion addresses itself to certain specific human anxieties and offers a way of dealing with them. It structures a world for the believer; it organizes human experience in a particular way and thus makes sense out of life. Moreover, when that whole world of meaning is called into question, either by changes in society or by a new awareness on the part of groups within a religious

organization, it not only reaffirms the elemental logic of its position but defends itself vigorously against those in its midst who challenge it.

There is nothing new about this insight into the nature of religious movements. We need to be reminded of it because we so often ignore it when working for the renewal of the Church. We assume, for example, that if only we can help biblical Christians to see what the Bible teaches, they will accept it; that believers will be open to new insights and realities if they are presented in the right way. But those to whom we address ourselves are likely to accept biblical truths and new approaches only if they can be incorporated into the structure of meaning provided for them by their existing religious system.

Consequently, a religious reformation depends upon the transformation of the system as a whole. It can happen only with the articulation of a new set of questions about life, together with new answers: the creation of a new universe of meaning. Rational criticism of the irrationality of certain theological ideas and ethical prescriptions, or the demonstration, to those who emphasize the authority of the Bible, that they have carefully selected the particular texts to which they give this authority, will convince few; indeed it could push many to defend their position more vigorously. If we hope to contribute to change, then we must understand *why* certain theological ideas and ethical prescriptions are so important to those who hold them, how they speak to their anxieties and what sort of security they offer. We must also help them to see how the religious resources they cherish can provide them with another way of looking at and responding to the world that threatens them.

Alves has done a formidable job of exploring the structure of meaning within which Protestantism in Brazil has been operating, and uncovering its hidden presuppositions. Our engagement with his thought could contribute a great deal toward further exploration of these dimensions of religious movements in our society.

2. *Protestantism and Repression* presents a rigorous analysis of the constituent elements in Right-Doctrine Protestantism—that blend of Calvinist Fundamentalism and Pietism taken to Brazil a century ago by missionaries and repeated by each generation since then. This theology focuses on the anxieties of men and women unable to cope with the personal and social crises arising in a changing world. Rather than offering psychological and sociological explanations for and solutions to these crises, this type of Protestantism attaches ontological significance to them. They are spoken of theologically, in terms of sin, disobedience to God, guilt, etc. The answer offered is salvation through conversion. But conversion offers freedom from this intensified anxiety only if there is some guarantee that the anxiety will not reappear. That guarantee, says Alves, is provided by "absolute truth," which excludes all possibility of doubt. The Bible as an inerrant text—the words of God; an integrated system of doctrine accepted as the correct formulation of revealed truth; ethical norms conceived of as divine and immutable, together with the authority of the church institution and its

discipline—all these constitute a *new security system*. Within this system, the Protestant principle is negated, and the traditional Protestant concern for tolerance, freedom, and democracy goes by the board.

I think the time has come for us to look seriously at what is happening in American Protestantism in the light of Alves's thesis. We are living a moment in which the crisis of personal self-identity and the erosion of our system of values proceed apace. This creates great anxiety; it also awakens a tremendous longing for security. If Alves is correct, then Evangelical Protestantism is structured to respond to this anxiety by naming theologically and sacralizing the very values and structures which are being called into question. To sustain this position, while cultural crisis and social disintegration progress, will call for greater insistence on biblical inerrancy, more rigid doctrinal formulations, the absolutizing of certain prescriptive ethical norms, and tighter ecclesiastical discipline.

If this does happen, the distance between the Protestant myth and Protestant reality will widen. Certain Protestant groups will speak of a New Reformation, but function in bondage to the logic of the established institution. They will proclaim freedom while demanding conformity. They will make much of the Resurrection of Jesus but make no room for the surprises of faith or for the creation of anything new. Worst of all, they will use the language of transcendence to absolutize that-which-is; thus, the God they defend so passionately will be transformed into an idol.

I don't claim that this is inevitable. I do believe that Alves has put his finger on the logic by which much of Evangelical Protestantism functions here as well as in Brazil. I hope that the terms of his analysis of Right-Doctrine Protestantism will provide us with clues for perceiving better what is now going on in some of our religious institutions and what may lie ahead of us.

3. At a time when many Protestants in Brazil were becoming involved in social and political movements for change, and the Roman Catholic Church was beginning to provide a community of support for such individuals and movements in their midst, the Presbyterian Church and its leaders reacted vigorously against all this. They not only denounced this concern as a betrayal of the gospel; they eliminated from their communion pastors and lay persons whose faith led them to join in the struggle for liberation. When the military regime consolidated its power, members of the Roman Catholic hierarchy took a courageous stand against repression. The Protestant churches remained silent; in some instances, they gave the regime their support.

Alves is determined to uncover the fundamental reason why this occurred. His conclusion: The position taken by the leaders of the Presbyterian Church was the natural if not inevitable expression of the inherent logic of Right-Doctrine Protestantism. "A social ethic is not an essential part of the Protestant universe." In fact, it collides head-on with the presuppositions underlying the Protestant worldview. A religion of salvation of the individual soul, says Alves, has no place for concerns about social justice, the exploitation of the poor, or structural change. Its emphasis upon authority and security, combined with the doctrine of Providence, works against any conclusion that faith calls for social transformation. The human historical Jesus who "walked among us" has been pushed aside. In his place, Protestantism puts the Christ, the cosmic center of power for healing, the Savior who resolves the ontological problem of guilt.

This judgment on Alves's part may be too harsh. Not everyone in a religious movement functions according to its inherent logic. But recognition of that fact does not invalidate the thrust of his argument and should not keep us from seeing what is happening in our midst. For we are surrounded by abundant evidence that confirms his thesis. I would mention only the alliance of right-wing political leaders and Evangelical preachers and movements in attempts to defeat liberal Congressmen, in opposition to the Equal Rights Amendment, in movements to "defend the family" and "expose its enemies," in efforts to justify more military spending and revive the rhetoric of the Cold War. Unless we take seriously the possibility that these and other efforts are grounded in the universe of meaning of much Evangelical Christianity, we will not be prepared for what is likely to happen in the next few years.

I personally rejoice in the new social concerns now finding expression in many Evangelical groups, and see in them a sign of hope for the future. But Alves suggests to us that any significant and sustained breakthrough in this area will depend upon a major change, on the part of Protestants, in their overall understanding of their faith and its relation to the world. In other words, Christian social action will flower and play a creative role in our time only to the extent that it is part of a major theological renewal.

What Alves has to say about repression is, in my judgment, even more important for us. He claims that a certain type of Protestantism responds to threats to its continuity by stifling openness and free discussion and suppressing dissent. Any religion that reacts to change in this way cannot be expected to take a stand against repressive political regimes.

For years, I have been acutely aware of the fact that the United States Government has encouraged, supported, and trained those who have established repressive regimes in one Third World country after another—in order to guarantee the stability of an established order serving our economic and geopolitical interests. Gradually, I have come to the conclusion that those in power here will eventually resort to the same sort of repressive measures internally, as social unrest grows within a system incapable of solving our most pressing problems. The resurgence of right-wing movements in the last few years not only confirms this assessment, but suggests that the repression of dissent may occur much earlier than anticipated.

I have attempted to call attention to this danger in ecclesiastical circles, in the hope that the leadership of our mainline Churches would respond to it. Alves has convinced me that the response I hoped for will not be forthcoming. I am still convinced that there are many Christians whose faith compels them to expose this danger, to struggle for the creation of a more just and human social order, and to keep alive the belief that such transformation is possible. But if there is any likelihood that our religious institutions will themselves repress dissent, then we have no choice but to form small communities which can have a life of their own, independent of the present ecclesiastical structures. Only from such a base will concerned Christians sustain their faith, witness to the freedom of the gospel, and speak out for the most elemental human values in an authoritarian society.

Sooner or later, we may face here a situation similar to that which confronted German Christians at the time of Hitler. The struggle between repressive religion—allied with repressive political forces—and transformative faith is essentially a struggle about what belief in and obedience to Jesus Christ are all about in this time and place. German Protestantism had the capacity to respond to that challenge through the formation of the Confessing Church. How much longer will we wait until we begin to articulate a similar response?

4. Is a certain type of Protestantism, under certain historical conditions, destined to become repressive and follow the path of sclerosis and slow death, as has happened with the Presbyterian Church of Brazil? Or can a movement born in a Reformation reform itself once again in response to God's action in a changing world?

In *Protestantism and Repression*, Alves is more interested in understanding how Protestantism has functioned in the past than in showing what it can become in the future. In his concluding chapter, he suggests one alternative: a faith stance that embraces doubt; that sits loose to the past in order to find and speak a new word; that organizes life around aspirations for the future and sparks creativity. The experience of life and growth and the fulfillment that comes through change can then be so compelling that women and men no longer need the security provided by sacred authority and absolute truth.

Does such a redemptive process have a chance today? Can it emerge and survive in a repressive society? As Alves indicates, this new spirit appeared in Brazilian Protestantism in the late fifties and early sixties and spread rather widely, especially among young people. It did not survive in any institutional form. Why not? Granted, the suppression was thorough and ruthless. Yet the leadership of the Presbyterian Church of Brazil could do no more than throw those who represented this spirit out of the Church; they could not destroy the movement. In the past, many "heretical" groups have survived and grown under severe persecution. One reason why this movement was destroyed was that its members did not expect nor were they prepared for the drastic steps that were taken against them. They had no strategy worked out for the survival of their communities; those who were serving the Church professionally found themselves suddenly deprived of the only possibility they had of supporting themselves and their families.

If something like this happened in our Churches today, would we respond differently? I doubt it. Many of the ministers, seminary students, and lay persons I know who are most critical of what is happening—or not happening—in our religious institutions, have left the Church and given up. I know many clergy and lay people who feel certain that the religious institutions they serve are not only bankrupt but are slowly dying; I know of no network of persons who feel compelled to lay the foundations for a community of new life, who are exploring ways to free themselves for this task of community-building without depending on the Church for economic survival. I hope that closer acquaintance with what happened in the Presbyterian Church in Brazil will provide an added stimulus to concentrate on this task.

As one of those who were involved in the attempts to create an alternative to the traditional Right-Doctrine Protestantism in Brazil, I have given much thought over the years to the question of why our efforts failed. Prodded by Alves, I have come to a new conclusion. We rejected a religion based on absolute truth and unquestioned authority. We knew that we were living in a situation in which all absolutes were idolatrous and unworthy of our trust. We were searching for another way of ordering our lives and orienting our struggles. Our small communities of young people and students were beginning to provide the support for such a reinterpretation of our faith and the reordering of our lives. I now realize, however, how limited our whole approach was. Our neo-orthodox theology had lost its attraction, but we did not understand why. Our small student communities were sustained by their newly found social concerns and political activities more than by a compelling new experience of the power of the gospel. And we certainly had not articulated a new religious language capable of speaking either to the religious disorientation or to the personal anxieties of other people in the Church.

As I look at the religious scene in North America today, I do not see many groups that have gone beyond the limitations of the Brazilian experience of two decades ago. But we do have some distinct advantages: the advancing crisis of Western culture, together with developments in the feminist movement, are exposing much more sharply the bankruptcy of our conceptual systems and of the types of rationality which we have until recently taken for granted. We now know that each of us can make sense out of our world only as we cultivate the inner resources we need to order the unique historical experiences of unique personalities. We also know a great deal about the process by which such growth and transformation take place. As we free ourselves from abstract theological concepts and prescriptive ethical norms, we have a better chance to draw on and be empowered by our heritage of faith. When we do this, we may also discover that we are able to offer more traditional church members a new experience of faith, and that doing this makes much more sense than criticizing their inherited religious orientation—which may no longer be life-giving even for them.

We are on the threshold of a new historical era. The presence and influence of Jesus of Nazareth in our history has prepared the way for it. We may discover, in the coming decades, that the presence and influence of Jesus in a historical community of faith will also produce new religious movements capable of orienting and sustaining creative living in a time of transition. In that case, the aborted efforts of a small band of Brazilian Protestants will have their place in a larger history, and Rubem Alves's reflection on their struggle and his own will sharpen our insight, accelerate our process of response, and lighten our burdens.

—Richard Shaull

A PERSONAL WORD AT THE START

HOW I CAME
TO THIS SUBJECT

The explorations found in this book were provoked by the rigidly conservative behavior of a particular brand of Brazilian Protestantism. This conservative behavior has manifested itself on two distinct yet complementary levels.

The first level is circumscribed within the boundaries of the religious institution; it is intramural. It finds expression as resistance to any and all efforts of innovation. This resistance is given legitimacy by sacralizing forms of thinking and acting which have been inherited from the past; and it is effectively carried out by setting up control mechanisms which are designed to eliminate deviant forms of thought and behavior.

The second level of conservative behavior is not confined to the intramural life of the religious institution. It has to do with the relationship between the institution and its members on the one hand, and political reality on the other. It finds expression in the legitimation of the existing setup of power and authority, and in the absence of any sort of prophetic criticism.

This phenomenon presents a problem, for two basic reasons.

First, on the intramural level, the existence of mechanisms designed to control thought and repress behavior is clearly opposed to the classic ideological tradition of Protestantism, with its emphasis on freedom of conscience, free inquiry, and democracy.

Second, on the extramural level, there are indications that when Protestantism first set foot in Brazil, it presented itself as a revitalizing force. It did not pass itself off as a mere bowing to prevailing sociopolitical conditions. The democratic organization of its Churches, its efforts on behalf of liberal education, its secularizing efforts in favor of the separation of Church and state, its denunciations of Catholic domination of Brazil as a force for economic backwardness and political totalitarianism: all these things suggest that Protestantism at that time was looking for profound political, social, and economic transformations in the country.

The situation of the Catholic Church at that point was exactly the opposite.

It was fearful of any ruptures in the existing setup and completely in the camp of traditionalism. Committed to the past, it was hostile to modernity and to secularization and democratic pragmatism, which threatened the foundations of a sacral social order. The Catholic Church accused Protestantism of being a dangerous subversive force, going so far as to denounce Protestantism as an accomplice of communism, however witting or unwitting it might be of the fact.

Then around the middle of the decade of the fifties, when some were attempting to rethink Protestantism in its theological, institutional, and social aspects, mechanisms of control and repression were set in motion; eventually they ended up eliminating the new tendencies completely. Talk about freedom of conscience gave way to talk about obedience and conformity to the thinking inherited from the past. The repressive mechanisms found a powerful ally in the political and ideological transformations that ensued. As a result, religious reformism came to be identified with political subversion, and all possibility of prophetic proclamation was ruled out. Brazilian Protestantism stands out noticeably for its silence in this respect, and so it has not suffered any form of political oppression.

Now these phenomena become very intriguing when one makes a comparative study of what has been going on in the Catholic Church. For it has taken a very different, and quite surprising, course. Its internal structure is hierarchical, vertical, centralized, and legitimated by the dogma of papal infallibility. Again and again Protestantism has claimed that this structure accounted for the unity of the Catholic Church. The unity, in other words, was due to extremely efficient mechanisms of control. Yet this structure, surprisingly enough, has permitted the rise of a great diversity of differing theological positions and lifestyles. It is curious that such an apparently monolithic structure would display so much elasticity; that it would prove so capable of accepting "free inquiry" without schisms resulting. Moreover, on the external front, a Church once characterized by traditionalism, conservatism, and sacralization of the powers that be has now begun to display a prophetic style of life, denouncing the State and the rich, defending the poor and weak, and facing all the political consequences that this posture entails.

The empirical materials analyzed here do not allow me to extrapolate conclusions beyond the limits of the specific type of Protestantism that I studied. But the temptation is great. For many years I have been fascinated by the relationship which appears to exist between truth and intolerance. Inquisitions, religious and secular, old and modern, are always carried out by people who are convinced of the truth of their cause. And, conversely, there seems to exist a permanent relation between doubt and tolerance. Read this book, thus, as *one instance* of something which appears to be a *universal and constant temptation of the human spirit*. We are, all, guilty of the same original sin. Some Catholic friends, after reading the argument, remarked that this is an apt description of the same process that is operative within their own institution. And they could not understand why I described it with such a "romantic" term as I did.

Similar things could be said of other societies in which the *right doctrine* is at stake. I think, for instance, of the inquisitorial processes which one often finds in political parties, specially those which claim to have a monopoly of the true interpretation of the destiny of the world. The Soviet Communist Party and Joseph McCarthy are not, after all, as different as one could think. They are both moved by the same spirit. And even the scientific community, which often boasts about its tolerance, is always supicious of "preachers of new doctrines." Science also has its inquisitions.

Not very many will be interested in this almost insignificant object, a small group of Protestants, in Brazil. But we cannot ignore the fact that we all, without exception, live and move on the threads of a cobweb which is woven of truth and intolerance. And we are either spiders or flies. The object, insignificant as it is, is a mirror.

THE MORAL INTENTION
OF SCIENTIFIC DISCOURSE

---

*Philosophy . . . is a fight against the fascination
which forms of expression exert upon us.*

Wittgenstein a: 27

*Criticism has plucked the imaginary flowers on
the chain, not in order that man shall continue to
bear that chain without fantasy or consolation,
but so that he shall throw off the chain and pluck
the living flower. The criticism of religion disil-
lusions man so that he will think, act and fashion
his reality like a man who has discarded his illusions and regained his senses.*

Marx: 244

The vicissitudes of my biography have caused me to be deeply interested in
Protestantism. My interest is an ambivalent one, characterized by a mixture
of hate and love.

This is an initial confession which could be used to impugn the conclusions
I present in this book. A person who is emotionally involved with his or her
object, so the argument goes, cannot possess the serenity, impartiality, and
objectivity that characterize science. Only someone who never loved or hated
Protestantism can write about it with objectivity.

A very odd conclusion. Carried to its ultimate implications, it means that
we can only be objective about something which is devoid of interest insofar
as we are concerned. If I have a passionate interest in flowers, that passion
prevents me from knowing them scientifically. I would be better off devoting
myself to stones. If I detest pollution, then the results of my work will be
prejudiced by my emotional stance. I would do better to devote myself to
archaeology.

I don't think a science without emotion is possible. It is my affective relationship to an object, an object that allures or threatens me, that creates the conditions allowing me to concentrate my attention. The object which provoked my interest becomes the focal point of my eyes and mind while the rest of the world becomes a matter of only secondary importance. It was emotion that turned one particular object, amid the limitless multiplicity of possible objects, into the object of my cognition.

I agree with Gunnar Myrdal: "A 'disinterested' social science has never existed and, for logical reasons, can never exist" (Myrdal: 55). It is an illusion to think that scientific knowledge, as opposed to common-sense knowledge, is objective; that common-sense knowledge is distorted by emotions. As Alvin Gouldner puts it: "Sociologists must surrender the human but elitist assumption that *others* believe out of need whereas *they* believe because of the dictates of logic and reason" (Gouldner: 26). Whether we like it or not, says Myrdal, valuations are present in scientific thought just as they are in common sense. For centuries the social-science tradition has concealed the valuations behind the scientific approach. Now we must admit the fact that "on an elementary level the mechanism of biased research does not differ from the one operating in popular thinking" (Myrdal: 50).

What are we to do? "The only way in which we can strive for 'objectivity' in theoretical analysis is to expose the valuations to full light, make them conscious, specific, and explicit, and permit them to determine the theoretical research" (Myrdal: 55–56).

That is what I want to do. My starting point is a decision which can be expressed very simply: *Talk about social fact must itself be turned into a social fact.* Is this intention too pretentious? I don't think so. I accept, as my program, what lies implicit in our everyday talk. Our talk is motivated by a hope: the hope that talking will in some way have a real impact on the situation and alter it. There is no guarantee that my intention will meet with success. Its possible failure, however, does not annul it as an intention. I don't simply want to talk *about* some social fact. I want my talk to be intelligible to those participating in the situation which I am investigating—which is to say, to those *about whom* I am talking. Berger and Luckmann observe that the human world is sustained by the tenuous thread of conversation which articulates it (Berger and Luckmann: 152f.). I wish to become a partner in this conversation, so that the world will be changed.

I reject a disinterested discourse. Indeed I don't think such a discourse is possible: "Indeed, no social science or particular branch of social research can pretend to be 'amoral' or 'apolitical.' . . . Research is always and by logical necessity based on moral and political valuations" (Myrdal: 74). All theory and all research conceal a practical intention. They wish to do something with the real.

But disinterested thinking and talking have come to be regarded as the ideal of scientific language, as if they had no interest in the future of the object under scrutiny. It is against that kind of scientist that Nietzsche launched one of his most ferocious attacks in *Thus Spoke Zarathustra:*

"This would be the highest to my mind"—thus says your lying spirit to itself—"to look at life without desire and not, like a dog, with my tongue hanging out. To be happy in looking, with a will that has died . . . the whole body cold and ashen. . . . And this is what the immaculate perception of all things shall mean to me: that I want nothing from them, except to be allowed to lie prostrate before them like a mirror with a hundred eyes" [Kaufmann b: 234].

Nietzsche then proceeds to show the implications of such an attitude as far as he is concerned:

But this shall be your curse, you who are immaculate, you pure perceivers, that you shall never give birth, even if you lie broad and pregnant on the horizon [Kaufmann b: 235].

Disinterested talk, *talk about* that is not addressed to the object, talk *about an object* that is addressed to others rather than the object, may well seem to be an act of nobility. My talk should not intrude as an invader into the tenuous thread of conversation that sustains the world which I am investigating.

But perhaps we must subject such an intention to criticism. Suppose I articulate the results of my investigation in concepts, categories, and an overall style which are incomprehensible to those I am studying. Can I really assume that the object under investigation will remain virgin and undefiled if I use such an approach?

All scientific effort creates a body of knowledge. Let us raise a question: *For whom* was this knowledge created? I can try to protect those I am investigating by dressing my knowledge in words, categories, and a style inaccessible to them. If I do this, then I do not violate them directly with my knowledge. There is another side to the coin, however. The knowledge thus created was offered to others, but not to the participants in the situation. This poses a danger, since the knowledge *about them* may function in practice as knowledge *against them*.

Knowledge is power. It is necessary to know *to whom* such power is being given.

What happens when the knowledge produced by scientific work is not linked up with the language of the group under study? What happens when the scientist does not become an interlocutor within the tenuous thread of conversation which sustains the world? What happens when scientific knowledge is expressed in such a way that it cannot be appropriated by those who were the object of investigation? Let us consider the process.

First, the scientist *uses* human beings as raw material for his or her theoretical creation, for his or her knowledge. Second, the created knowledge takes on objective form as *talk about* the object, be it in the form of an article, a thesis, or a book. The object is left in its status as raw material. Third, we must ask ourselves: *For whom* is this knowledge produced? Who exactly are the people who are in a position to appropriate this knowledge? Obviously the knowledge is produced for someone, but not for the participants in the situation under study. Who, then? The elite who have command of the concepts, categories, and style with which the object under investigation was theoretically constructed. So we conclude that the resultant knowledge is handed over, not to the people which it discusses, but to other people. It is as if the scientist said to his or her object: "I am studying you. But through my discourse I will hide from you my knowledge about you." Fourth, if knowledge is power, then our conclusion must be that those who are in a position to appropriate it end up having *knowledge about*, and hence *power over*, the people under study, which the latter themselves do not have.

So I raise the question: Under these conditions is it not possible for scientific knowledge to assume a form of power against the human beings under study?

The knowledge produced must be a precise tool. But that is not enough. Besides being precise, the tool must be suitable for use. It is useless to make binoculars and microscopes for the blind. Their precision isn't worth a thing. When I make a microscope or a pair of binoculars, I have already made a decision: these tools can only be used by people who can see. In like manner, the concepts and categories we employ, and the style we use in our work, function in a deterministic way: they select in advance those who will be able to understand them, and hence use them; and thus they eliminate those who cannot.

It is understandable that scientific work should be written for the scientific community. It is particularly justified in the realm of the natural sciences, where language is not a tool of direct action on the real. Experiments are not carried out by means of magical words. Words do not alter the behavior of atoms and cells.

Things are different in society, however. Language helps to make the social world what it is. As Simmel noted, society is "my representation"—something dependent on my conscious activity—in a very different sense than the external world is (Natanson: 76). My thinking about nature does not alter nature, but my thinking about society does alter society. Language itself is a tool for direct interference in the social realm. Hence a scientific language which is not linked up with the spoken language of everyday life runs the risk of being something like a laboratory technique that has no way of interacting with the object under investigation.

Again it is Gunnar Myrdal who calls our attention to a disturbing fact: "The tendency in recent decades has been for social scientists to close themselves off by means of unnecessarily elaborate and strange terminology, often to the point of impairing their ability to understand one another—and perhaps occasionally even themselves" (Myrdal: 42).

Before we ask why they would make such an option, let us remember one thing. If scientists chose to write and speak *for* those they were studying, their language would have to be understood by those people; it would have to be understood outside academic circles. If, on the other hand, the scientific community is the "significant other" whom they are addressing, then the average person will have a hard time understanding them.

But why should they opt for abstruse language? There are reasons of a scientific nature. Common language is imprecise, lacking the rigor and the categories needed to comprehend the object. By the same token, however, this option is often taken for parascientific, almost ritual, reasons. One's initiation into scientific *gnosis* tends to be verified and affirmed by one's ability to articulate knowledge in terms of the esoteric idiom which is the monopoly of the scientific community. Hence simplicity is often taken to be simple-mindedness, and comprehensibility is regarded as superficiality.

Could we say that scientists are talking to the people? I leave that question unanswered.

I believe that there is a moral question which the social scientist must answer: Who are my interlocutors? To whom am I addressing myself? For whom am I producing knowledge? I recall the words of Max Weber: "Thus if we are competent in our pursuit . . . we can force the individual, or at least we can help him to give himself an *account of the ultimate meaning of his own conduct*" (Gerth and Mills: 152). We are in the service of moral forces, helping to produce self-clarification and a sense of responsibility.

Here I want to fashion a discourse about Protestantism that will be intelligible to Protestants. I am trying, as best I can, to shed light on Protestantism by using categories which are not alien to it. I don't want to create a parallel language. I am, to some extent, picking up a suggestion made by Wittgenstein:

> It is wrong to say that in philosophy we consider an ideal language as opposed to our ordinary one. For this makes it appear as though we thought we could improve on ordinary language. But ordinary language is all right. Whenever we make up "ideal languages" it is not in order to replace our ordinary language by them; but just to remove some trouble caused in someone's mind by thinking that he has got hold of the exact use of a common word [Wittgenstein a: 28].

I have tried to situate myself on the very inside of Protestant language. That language contains many implications which are obscured and even denied by its conscious articulation. I am looking for what Wittgenstein called "tacit conventions" (Wittgenstein b, section 4.002: 37). They are conventions which are found in language, but which are hidden by it.

In another work Wittgenstein defined the task of philosophy as "a fight against the fascination which forms of expression exert upon us" (Wittgenstein a: 27). The notion of fascination, of enchantment, is highly suggestive. To be fascinated or enchanted is to be under the power of something strange which dominates us without our knowing it, which is present without our seeing it. To regard language as a form of enchantment is to recognize that it holds and dominates us, making it impossible for us to take cognizance of the ultimate meaning of our conduct.

If I adopt this fight against the enchantment of language as my program here, what exactly do I mean by it?

First and foremost, we must divest language of its sacred vestments, of its pretensions to truth. Languages are *constructions* of reality. They are not copies of the real. Languages express our inklings, our *guesses*, about the world. So to fight against the enchantment of language is to fight against its dogmatic pretensions, which go by the name of orthodoxy in the realm of religion. The task of philosophy is marked by what Kolakowski called "an attitude of negative vigilance in the face of any absolute" (Kuncewicz: 326).

I see the task of philosophy as a fight against absolutes. This, then, is one of the objectives of my investigation: to shed light on the absolutes which lie buried inside the tolerance, democratic spirit, and free inquiry enunciated by the Protestant discourse.

Such a program cannot be carried out by constructing a parallel language to which those under the spell of enchantment would have to convert. What is the point of offering some supposedly "true" language to replace one I judge to be "false"? That would be nothing more than a substitution of idols, an exchange of absolutes. Besides, the relationship between a parallel "scientific" language comprehensible only to specialists and ordinary language would be about the same as that between the old Latin liturgy of the Catholic Church and the various representations of the common people's everyday religiosity. Enchantment is not dispelled simply by the *magical* power of "truth." Of course we can dream of creating a land of critical language, a utopian isle of knowledge, and hope that human beings will immigrate to it. But there is another alternative. We can take ordinary, everyday language and insert a critical question into it. We can thus turn it into a problem from within itself, subverting its certitudes, revealing the contradictions imbedded in it, and so undermining its bedrock consistency.

But that raises another question which must be answered: If I do insert my talk into the tenuous thread of conversation going on among the people I am studying, how am I to prevent my talk from being assimilated and neutralized by their discourse? Won't such a procedure make me the prisoner of the very discourse I am studying and abort my critical intentions? At this point I would like to cite a passage from A. N. Whitehead *(Modes of Thought),* since it sheds light on what I am trying to do here:

> Both in science and logic you have only to develop your argument sufficiently, and sooner or later you are bound to arrive at a contradiction, either internally within the argument or externally in its reference to fact. . . . Philosophy is the criticism of abstractions which govern special modes of thought [Kaufmann a: 170].

The job is not to create a new language, but to push it to its ultimate consequences. When that is done, one finds that it always contains contradictions. In our everyday use of language we do not take note of that fact. We are so caught up in it, so sure of its truth, so familiar with it, that we don't have the critical distance needed to see it as a precarious construct: "The validity of my knowledge of everyday life is taken for granted by myself and by others . . . until a problem arises that cannot be solved in terms of it. As long as my knowledge works satisfactorily, I am generally ready to suspend doubts about it" (Berger and Luckmann: 44).

The task of philosophy is to introduce doubt where there was only certainty, to point up inconsistency where only consistency was visible. As Hegel pointed out in *The Phenomenology of Spirit* (section 31): "Quite generally, the familiar, just because it is familiar, is not cognitively understood" (Hegel a: 18). Genuine knowing is directed against mere familiarity, against the representations that are presented to us in ideal terms.

By analyzing a discourse we can confront it with the elements which lie buried within it. They can be seen in the very process of speaking. What I want to do here is disentangle the tacit and unconscious conventions contained in the discourse of Protestantism. I want to push its argument to its conclusions, to reveal the inconsistency which lies buried within the consistency. As Findlay puts it in his study of Hegel: "Each inadequate form of consciousness must be given enough rope to hang itself: it must be allowed to ruin itself in doubt, and to break down in utter despair. Its view of the object, which seemed identical with the object as it is *in itself*, must be shown to be no more than the object as it is *for us*" (Findlay: 88).

Let me just say in passing that this program is a worthwhile one both for the average conscience and the scientific conscience. Within rather modest limits, I will be helping to fulfill the vocation which Weber envisioned for his science: helping people to give themselves an account of the ultimate import of their own conduct.

Of course such a program makes sense only if we assume that language helps to sustain and support the human realm. If the human realm is not sustained by language, if language is viewed as nothing more than the symbolic articulation of society's material relations, then there is no point in trying to alter society by a critique of language. If language is the symbolic effect of some material cause, then logically we cannot presume to alter the cause by altering the effect—just as a disease cannot be cured if one attacks nothing but its symptoms.

Let me bring in here Marx's attack on the Young Hegelians in *The German Ideology,* which has some connection with this point:

> Once upon a time a valiant fellow had the idea that men were drowned in water because they were possessed with the idea of gravity. If they were to knock this notion out of their heads, say by stating it to be a superstition, a religious concept, they would be sublimely proof against any danger from water. His whole life long he fought against the illusion of gravity, of whose harmful results all statistics brought him new and manifold evidence. This honest fellow was the type

of the new and revolutionary philosophers in Germany [Marx and Engels: 37].

The problem with the Hegelian system, held in different ways by both Old and Young Hegelians according to Marx and Engels, is that it pictures the real, material world of human beings as something produced by ideas and concepts:

Since the Young Hegelians consider conceptions, thoughts, ideas, in fact all the products of consciousness, to which they attribute an independent existence, as the real chains of men . . . it is evident that the Young Hegelians have to fight only against these illusions of consciousness. Since, according to their fantasy, the relationships of men, all their doings, their chains and their limitations are products of their consciousness [Marx and Engels: 41].

According to Marx, the Young Hegelians are under the illusion that the world is maintained by consciousness. If that were the case, then one would only have to alter consciousness to transform the world. Now if we accept Marx and Engels's formulation of the issue here, we would certainly have to agree with them. But the question is whether the laws of society are identical with the laws of nature—with the law of gravity, to use their specific example. It is clear that, in dealing with the Young Hegelians here, Marx and Engels are indulging in polemics and caricature. After all, Marx himself was the one who pointed out that theory had its place: "Clearly the weapon of criticism cannot replace the criticism of weapons, and material force must be overthrown by material force. But theory also becomes a material force once it has gripped the masses . . . when it demonstrates *ad hominem*, and it demonstrates *ad hominem* as soon as it becomes radical" (Marx: 251). At that point theory becomes an intellectual weapon, a weapon of the human spirit.

My position, then, is that language cannot be regarded merely as the effect of some cause, as the symbolic articulation of material relationships. As Ricoeur has pointed out, language is both infrastructure and superstructure; we are involved in a circular process, or a series of circles, where the terms embrace and move beyond each other:

Speaking leads to Doing, and Doing to Speaking; perceptual truth leads to scientific truth, which leads to ethical truth, which in turn leads back to perceptual truth, etc. There are "circles" but no "hierarchy," no infrastructure or superstructure in the global movement of history [Ricoeur a: 12].

On the one hand language cannot be regarded as *the* thing that sustains the world. On the other hand we cannot possibly understand its function if we do not realize that language does help to keep the world going. As Alvin

Gouldner points out: "The old society is not held together merely by force and violence, or expedience and prudence. The old society maintains itself also through theories and ideologies that establish its hegemony over the minds of men, who therefore do not merely bite their tongues but submit to it willingly" (Gouldner: 5).

All the arguments against this role of language fail, it seems to me, precisely because they are *framed in language*. If one does honestly feel that way, the only honest course intellectually is silence. People who teach and write on the subject accept a tacit convention: i.e., that by working in the area of language they are contributing to the transformation of the world. Frederick the Great of Prussia offered this devastating criticism of Holbach's *System of Nature:*

> After the author has exhausted all evidence . . . to show that men are guided by a fatalistic necessity in all their actions, he had to draw the conclusion that we are only a sort of machine, only marionettes moved by the hand of a blind power. And yet he flies into a passion against priests, governments, and against our whole educational system; he believes indeed that the men who exercise these functions are free, even while he proves to them that they are slaves. What foolishness and what nonsense! If everything is moved by necessary causes, then all counsel, all instruction, all rewards and punishments are as superfluous as inexplicable; for one might just as well preach to an oak and try to persuade it to turn into an orange tree [Cassirer b: 71].

So I myself reject the view that it makes no difference what one human being or even all human beings think: that what matters is *what is* and what human beings will be *forced to do by this reality*. I write because I believe, despite any arguments to the contrary, that language and thought, too, sustain the world; that by transforming them we are doing something to transform the world. If I did not believe that, I would stop teaching and writing.

PROTESTANTISM
AND
REPRESSION

INTRODUCTION

RIGHT-DOCTRINE PROTESTANTISM (RDP): AN IDEAL TYPE

> *For a society is not made up merely of the mass of individuals who compose it, the ground which they occupy, the things which they use and the movements which they perform, but above all is the idea which it forms of itself.*
>
> *Durkheim a: 422*

As I have already indicated, my aim is to offer an analysis of Protestantism. That points us in a certain direction, but it does not mean that I have defined the precise object of my analysis. The general, comprehensive term "Protestantism" does not refer to anything clearly defined.

History confronts us with a plurality of Protestantisms, and I see no way of reducing them to a common denominator. We must remember that the term crystallized in the midst of a polemical discourse. The Catholic Church used it to refer to all the movements which parted company with Catholicism from the early sixteenth century on; in one fell swoop it could thus define them all as heretical movements. On their side the dissenting movements used the same term in an equally polemical way to assert the existence of unity among themselves; but this unity manifested itself only in their confrontation with a common enemy, the Catholic Church. Apart from this polemical use, the unity suggested by the term "Protestantism" dissolves into a multiplicity of oppositions. There stand the Protestant *denominations*, and the oppositions among them are not superficial. Hence the term Protestantism, it seems to me, cannot be used as a scientific concept because it does not refer univocally to a specific object exhibiting behavioral constants.

So I cannot talk about Protestantism in general. To achieve the desired precision, we must work out a classification in terms of *types*. Here history would seem to come to our aid. It offers us a readymade typology crystallized in institutional organizations: i.e., the *denominations*. The adoption of a historical typology would greatly simplify my work. It would permit me to

1

point to specific social units that are clearly delimited in time and space, and often in terms of social classes as well. I would not have to *construct* any types. I could simply *assemble and employ* the types that history has placed before us. I would simply take the denominations—distinct and definite objects—as the point of departure for my work of analysis and explanation. I would then be dealing with such things as Lutheranism, Calvinism or Presbyterianism, Anglicanism, Methodism, the Baptist Churches, Pentecostalism, and Congregationalism.

Unfortunately when we take this typology offered by history and subject it to sociological analysis, it proves to be inadequate. For the denominations, separated by history, are grouped together again by sociological analysis on the basis of organizational and bureaucratic patterns that are common to various denominations. That is what Ernst Troeltsch did, to cite one example, when he reduced the multiplicity of denominations to two basic types: *churches* and *sects* (Troeltsch b: 331–42).

We must require of a type the same thing that is required of a theory in the natural sciences: the phenomena covered by it have to exhibit unity of behavior. If that is not the case, if organizations allegedly belonging to one and the same type do not behave similarly, then we are forced to conclude that the type is not adequate. Let me offer a concrete example here. Troeltsch's typology presupposes that the form of organization, the political and bureaucratic setup, is a determining factor in the behavior of the type. Churches exhibit specific behavioral uniformities that are different from the behavioral uniformities of sects. But certain behavioral peculiarities cannot be explained satisfactorily by a group's form of organization.

During the last twenty years or so in Brazil, the various Churches saw their inner ideological and theological unity broken. New, distinct, and different ways of articulating the faith surfaced within the Churches, as did new ways of understanding the world and new types of self-understanding. How did the various Churches react to this common phenomenon? Uniformly? Not at all. In some of them the new spirit did not produce any appreciable crisis. They did not feel that a new articulation of the faith jeopardized the identity of the community. The tensions did not provoke any new Inquisition or any schism. These Churches displayed considerable elasticity in keeping divergent intellectual stances within their ranks. In other Churches, however, the appearance of a new way of articulating the faith had catastrophic results. It produced panic. These Churches felt seriously threatened, and they acted forcefully to re-establish the authority and rule of their traditional ideological and theological discourse. This meant inaugurating inquisitional practices, the function of which was to eliminate the divergent discourses classified as heretical. Thus, in the first group of Churches mentioned above, doctrinal uniformity was not seen as essential to the unity and identity of the church community; that was not how their self-understanding envisioned the matter. In the second group of Churches, by contrast, intellectual unity became the fundamental mark of their unity and identity.

It seems to me, therefore, that a typology based on organizational criteria is not enough. Alongside it we must envision another typology that takes due account of the specific features of self-understanding which we find in the Churches. I think, in other words, that we have to elucidate the *spirit* of the social group in question, its *collective consciousness*. I don't think that this collective consciousness (or awareness) can be spurned as an explanatory factor. It cannot be dropped to concentrate solely on other factors of a purely material nature. I agree with Durkheim: "For a society is not made up merely of the mass of individuals who compose it, the ground which they occupy, the things which they use and the movements which they perform, but *above all is the idea which it forms of itself*" (Durkheim a: 422; my italics).

I maintain that the idea which a group has of itself is one of the fundamental concepts to be considered in trying to explain the behavior of the group. What is more, I don't think that this idea can be reduced to a mere reflex, however direct or indirect, of material relations—with the latter being viewed as the only factors that are really determining. As Durkheim put it: "Collective consciousness is something more than a mere epiphenomenon of its morphological basis, just as individual consciousness is something more than a simple efflorescence of the nervous system" (Durkheim a: 423–24). The same would apply to religious awareness. As he wrote about religion: "In showing that religion is something essentially social, we do not mean that it confines itself to translating into another language the material forms of society and its immediate vital necessities" (Durkheim a: 423). It is this idea which a group forms of itself, its collective consciousness, to which I am referring here in abbreviated form when I employ the term *spirit*.

Now the concept of *spirit* takes in more than the total content of the collective consciousness, if by the latter we are referring specifically to *conscious awareness*. The things of which we are *consciously aware* are merely a *partial product* of an *unconscious structuring activity*. The collective consciousness, which can be described by various methods of empirical investigation, contains only the real objects of knowledge for the group in question; it knows nothing of the possible objects of knowledge. To come to know the spirit of a group, it is not enough to make an inventory of the content of its consciousness at a given moment; we must also shed light on the collective unconscious principles by which the group constructs its reality. I thus accept the suggestion offered by the sociology of knowledge that reality is always socially constructed (see Berger and Luckmann, for example). And my aim here will be to make plain the principles by which *a certain Protestant spirit constructs its reality*.

But how am I to proceed in trying to make clear the spirit of the group in question? I will borrow a suggestion from Karl Mannheim:

It is . . . the nature of the dominant wish which determines the sequence, order, and evaluation of single experiences. This wish is the organizing principle which even moulds the way in which we experience time. . . . The innermost structure of the mentality of a group can never be as clearly grasped as when we attempt to understand its conception of time in the light of its hopes, yearnings, and purposes. On the basis of these purposes and expectations, a given mentality orders not merely future events, but also the past [Mannheim: 209].

Note that Mannheim sees the mentality of a group as a *structuring activity* on the one hand, and also as a *wish*. The group's reality is fashioned by the structuring activity, which in turn is grounded on the wish. So if we want to understand the spirit of a group, we must start with its foundational emotions. These founding emotions are the emotional matrix out of which the group organizes its time.

In the passage cited above Mannheim refers only to the time factor, but the reality which is socially constructed by the group is not limited to time. Their wish also constructs a geography. It fashions not only clocks and calendars but also maps and roadways. Both time and space have to be made meaningful: they cannot be separated. Reality is always a spatio-temporal synthesis. Space without time would confront us with a frozen, immobile reality. Time without space would confront us with empty movement. The world comes into being only in the linkup between space and time.

In trying to describe a particular spirit of Protestantism here, then, I shall try to cover both aspects mentioned by Mannheim. I shall try to shed light on its founding emotions, and I shall try to describe the world which is fashioned out of those emotions.

What materials will I use in executing this task? I am going to have recourse to language. Social consciousness exists only through language. Emotions and visions of the world which cannot be stated are ones which still lack the social prerequisites of expression. If something is not or cannot be stated, then it may be an individual reality but it certainly cannot be a social reality. What interests me here is the spirit of a group—i.e., a social reality. So I will make use of the language of this group as something revealing its spirit.

Let me summarize what I have said so far briefly. The concept of spirit prompts me to investigate the nature of the "dominant wish" in the group under investigation, and to make clear the principles underlying its construction of reality. I shall do this through an analysis of the language used by the group. So where do I go from here? How will I proceed from this point? I hope to make that clear to my readers by commenting briefly on the possibilities and problems of sociological sampling.

The simplest solution would seem to be this: to take a sample of the institution one wishes to analyze. On the basis of empirical data obtained from our investigation we could then proceed by way of inductive generalization, thereby arriving at some conclusion about the prevailing averages or means of the group. These averages would constitute normality for the group.

Though not a full portrait, they would represent at least a profile of the invisible thing we are seeking: the spirit of the group.

Let me picture this procedure visually. Let G^i be a given social group characterized by a specific institutional organization. And let us assume that G^i is unified by one and the same spirit. Now let A^i be a sample taken from within group G^i. How do we get from A^i to G^i? This step is possible only if we assume that continuity exists between A^i and G^i—i.e., that A^i is a microcosm of the macrocosm G^i. Once we accept this hypothesis, we proceed by way of inductive generalizations.

But now let us complicate this simple hypothesis by introducing another hypothesis into the picture. Let us assume that the institutional organization before us, which appears to be one object, does not contain only one uniform, homogeneous social group within it. Let us assume that it contains two or more groups within it, and that the relationship between them is one of conflict. If that is the case, we cannot use our initial working hypothesis. The institutional organization would have G^i1, G^i2, G^i3 etc., as opposing subunits; and their opposition would be masked and hidden by the apparent organizational unity. Let us represent the new schema as follows:

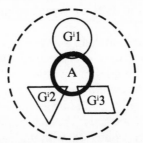

Note that the organization is now represented by a dotted line to indicate that its unity is only apparent. What is of interest are the various subunits, but they do not present themselves directly as specific objects. Their specificity becomes invisible within the overall organization, in which they all seem to participate in the same way. The dark circle A represents any given sampling.

What result would we get from sampling and inductive generalization in this case? Would those procedures reveal to us the specificity of the conflicting subunits? No. They could detect certain variations. But given the presupposition that the sample is a microcosm of a single macrocosm, those variations belonging to distinct and conflicting subunits and hence indicative of opposing spirits would be integrated into one and the same normal-distribution curve; they would be viewed as abnormal variations of that curve. The extremes could not be comprehended as expressions of specific, opposing spirits. The contradictions would disappear as contradictions, being viewed as aspects, nuances, and variations of *one and the same object, one and the same spirit*.

Our object, then, would be represented by one single curve as follows:

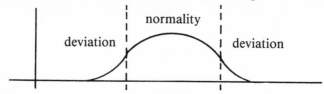

On the extreme left is the pathology of the left; on the extreme right, the pathology of the right. Both would be deviations referring to *one and the same object*. And what is the object in question? The normality found in the center of the curve. I recall here a remark made by Durkheim: "In order that sociology may be a true science of things, the *generality* of phenomena must be taken as the *criterion of their normality*" (Durkheim b: 74–75; my italics).

Now the problem here, as I have suggested, is that we can be led astray by taking the apparent organizational unity of our object as evidence of its inner unity. Using the method of inductive generalizations, which seems to have all the appearances of scientific rigor, we end up establishing a single false object when the reality in question is a series of distinct objects which happen to find themselves within the boundaries of one and the same organizational unit. Nothing guarantees that the unity of organization demarcates one and the selfsame spirit.

It seems to me, therefore, that there is no reason compelling us to conclude that a sample is a microcosm of one macrocosm. Does that mean I am trying to denigrate empirical techniques of investigation? Not at all. I am simply questioning a *theoretical assumption* underlying this type of empiricism. The data are not the starting point of the investigation. As Robert K. Merton noted: "One's concepts *do* determine the inclusion or exclusion of data. . . . *Data* are not 'given' but are 'contrived' with the inevitable help of concepts" (Merton: 108). Approaching the multiplicity of data in front of me, I must realize: (1) that though they may be fish caught in the same body of water, (2) not all the fish are of the same type. Some are prey, serving as food for other fish that hunt them. To interpret hunting fish and hunted fish as variations of one and the same type would be a great mistake. So even as I approach my data, I must bring along some criterion of discrimination.

The first criterion is provided by the object itself that I am trying to shed light on: i.e., the spirit of a group, its founding wishes, its structuring of reality. I shall try to discover that spirit by seeing how it makes its presence felt in language. While it is true that the relationship between sign and signification is arbitrary, it is also true that the connections between the signs are not. The latter connections are constant relations, which take on the character of a logical system. So here we have our first criterion: *it is not enough simply to juxtapose all the data at our disposal; we must proceed to discriminate between the data and organize them so that the constructed object presents a logical unity.* In terms of our specific object here, this means that we cannot include within it horizontal and vertical articulations in time, nor can we place a dogmatic concept of truth right alongside an existential concept of truth. They are not variations of one and the same object, whose truth is to be found in the normality of averages and midway positions. Instead they belong to different, opposed spirits.

That being the case, I must approach the empirical data with a criterion of discrimination which is prior to my sample. It is not the sample that will reveal the object to me through its midway ranges. Instead I need an ideal construct of the object to give me the criteria I need to seek out the sample that is meaningful for my purposes. In other words, I must make use of an *ideal type*.

How do we fashion an ideal type?

That is a tantalizing question. It is a mistake to think that the embarrassment is faced only by those who study the human being. I recall a statement attributed to Gauss: "I have had my solutions for a long time, but I have not yet figured out how I can arrive at them." I deny that there is a method for the construction of an ideal type. I also deny that there is a method for the construction of theories in the exact sciences. I think that Kuhn is quite right. He has pointed out that when science reaches a moment of crisis, when the old theories fall apart, it is not possible to construct a new theory by using methods borrowed from older theories. At such moments the scientist is confronted with a logical gap. His or her new theory will be fashioned with the help of inklings and intuitions that do not yet enjoy scientific respectability (see Kuhn).

What gives a theory or a type its status as a scientific instrument is not the fact that we can scientifically explain the process of its construction. It is the fact that, once constructed, such theories and types can be subjected to testing. Methods do not construct theories, but rather vice-versa. Theories construct methods. The validity of a theory or a type, however provisional it may yet be, is due to its ability to solve problems—both those already solved by competing theories and those which they could not solve. As Kuhn has pointed out, a theory is not accepted initially after having past the Cartesian test and demonstrated that it is *grounded on bases that are beyond all doubt.* Instead the scientist embraces a new theory because it promises to solve new problems and break new ground. In other words, the act in which the scientist embraces a new theory is an act of faith, a wager. It is only after this initial act that the scientist will devote himself or herself to testing the theory through experiments that may or may not corroborate it.

I am incapable of explaining the method which led me to construct the type that I am going to describe in the course of this book. Emotions, values, and biographical experiences are involved in the process. Many suggestions came to me from previous discussions of my subject. I do maintain, however, that my type sheds light on problems that have not yet been clarified. I also maintain that it enables us to forecast, at least approximately, how the type should behave in future situations.

Here I cannot anticipate all the details of the type that I am going to construct. But I can indicate its most characteristic feature. That is what will allow me here at the start to select and organize the materials relevant to my work.

One can establish at least three ideal types in Protestantism:

1. *Right-Doctrine* Protestantism (abbreviated as RDP throughout this book). What is its characteristic feature? The fact that it stresses *agreement with a series of doctrinal affirmations*, which are regarded as *expressions of the truth* and which must be affirmed *without any shadow of doubt*, as the precondition for participation in the ecclesial community.
2. *Sacramental* Protestantism. For this type, profession of right doctrine is of secondary importance as compared with emotional and mystical participation in the liturgy and the sacraments.
3. Protestantism *of the spirit*. Its distinctive stress is neither of the previous two things but rather a subjective experience of intense ecstasy.

It is important to realize that these three types cannot be used as pigeonholes in which we will put the various denominations. Nor can they be combined with Troeltsch's types. The types *transcend* denominations, for we can find embodiments of them in different denominations, Churches, and sects. In another sense, however, they are smaller than denominations; for we can find more than one type present simultaneously in one and the same denomination. In fact, it is precisely the presence of divergent types within one and the same organization that explains the rise of intramural conflicts.

I have drawn my empirical materials from the Presbyterian Church of Brazil. This does not mean that all the members of that Church fit into the type I am describing: i.e., RDP. Nor does it mean that the validity of my conclusions are confined to that denomination. Wherever we find the type, there we will find its characteristic behavior.

This particular denomination is of interest to me for a very simple reason. The fact is that in recent years violent intramural conflicts broke out within that organization. And there is no doubt that in the end type RDP was victorious and surfaced clearly. I am interested in that victorious type, in its spirit. It lay hidden in the denomination. When it was challenged by a different spirit, it revealed itself in a series of concrete political acts that ended up squelching dissident voices.

And so our journey begins. Let me offer a little road map of our terrain. I will begin by considering earlier discussions of the spirit of Protestantism, from which I have derived many suggestions about the ideal type that I wish to construct and clarify here (Chapter One). Then I will tackle our specific object: Right-Doctrine Protestantism and its spirit. First we will examine the emotional experience on which it is based (Chapter Two). Then we will consider the way in which it comes to see and know the world, its theory of knowledge (Chapter Three). We will proceed to examine the structure of its world: its time, its space, and its explanatory models (Chapter Four). Two chapters (Five and Six) will consider the personal and social behavior consonant with the spirit of RDP. We will then see what enemies RDP faces, according to its own outlook (Chapter Seven). Finally, I will offer my own conclusions (Chapter Eight).

Throughout this book the word Protestantism will be used many times. The reader will see that in different contexts its meaning varies. In certain situations it has to do with Protestantism as a world-wide phenomenon. When our empirical materials are being analyzed, however, it has to do specifically with our ideal type.

But please, never forget: an ideal type is a hunch as to something which might be found elsewhere. I feel that the RDP is not a Brazilian phenomenon. It haunts other forms of Protestantism also.

ONE

PROTESTANTISM: MEDIEVAL OR MODERN?

I have not constructed my ideal type (Right-Doctrine Protestantism) from scratch. Before me were the many earlier discussions about the spirit of Protestantism. Not all of them are on the same level, of course. Some are ideological and polemical in nature, while others are of a more critical and scholarly sort. The ideal type which is my object of study here was constructed with the help of those earlier discussions, insofar as I made a critical comparison between those earlier discussions and the empirical materials at my disposal.

We can distinguish two levels in those earlier discussions. On the first level we find an *internal* analysis of Protestantism. Here one simply records and describes the major themes of Protestant discourse, its vision of the world, its understanding of the human being, and its theory of knowledge. These consciously articulated themes are interpreted as constitutive of the spirit of Protestantism. Then the latter is compared with the medieval spirit and the modern spirit in order to point up affinities and oppositions.

On the second level a further step is taken. Besides considering the consciously articulated discourse of Protestantism, one also explores the real functional or dysfunctional relationships established between the Protestant spirit and medieval or modern society. In what way did the Protestant spirit have an impact on society? Did it help to bring about revolutionary transformations, or did it help to preserve the established order?

We need to notice, however, that whatever the spirit and function of Protestantism might have been in the past, nothing authorizes us to use this past as a model for the present. Ideas which, in certain historical moments, functioned as utopias and contributed to the breaking down of a dominant social order, in the subsequent period functioned as ideologies and contributed to the justification and maintenance of the status quo (Mannheim 192–263).

Here I am not looking to the past for an ideal model by which to interpret the present. I simply want to present some of the alternative interpretations we have inherited from the past so that we can proceed to work out our own solution from there.

Protestantism as the Vanguard of Liberty and Modernity

As I mentioned earlier, Protestant discourse exhibited remarkable unity in its polemics against the Catholic Church. Denominational tensions disappeared in the face of a common enemy, giving way to a broad ideological consensus. It is within this polemical discourse that Protestantism answered the question about the nature and function of its spirit. Its identity was defined in terms of opposition to its enemy.

What does Protestantism say about itself? How does it understand itself? What ideas does it point to as the core of its spirit?

Protestantism sees itself as the spirit of liberty, democracy, modernity, and progress. Catholicism, by contrast, is the spirit which fears liberty; as a result, it favors totalitarian solutions and opposes modernity. Protestantism invokes history as a witness in its favor. Back somewhere in the past, now overcome by the light of the gospel, lies the corpse of a dark period which was dominated by superstition, intolerance, ignorance, enslavement of conscience, and a totalitarian Church. It was a sad and somber period, lit up only by the bonfires of the Inquisition. That era still exists in our midst today, however, like a corpse among the living. The Catholic Church is like a fossil from the buried past. If we were to ask history what side it was on, it would reply: "Catholicism is the past from which I come. Protestantism is the future towards which I am travelling."

This, then, is Protestantism's view of itself. Is it a totally naive one? I don't want to answer that question right now. I would simply like to point out that Protestantism, at its moment of birth, did introduce a discourse with a new set of themes; and that this discourse clashed with the prevailing ideological and theological arrangements. One need only read Luther. What is his great obsession? Freedom. "A Christian man is a perfectly free lord of all, subject to none" (Luther: 251). The God spoken of by Luther is the symbol of freedom from all the legal restraints imposed by religion and society. Faith is freedom from the law. One who accepts subjection is one who has not yet understood the gospel.

At this historical distance it is very hard for us to comprehend the concepts that were bandied about in Luther's day, and hence to appreciate the significance of the battle that was joined. Theological language is an enigma for people who regard the operational language of science as the norm. Hence we tend to regard theological discourse as meaningless. We must remember, however, that an epoch can only tackle and resolve its concrete problems by using the conceptual apparatus at its disposal. To be sure, religious language does seem to refer to another world, just as dreams introduce us to a magical world that seems to be devoid of concreteness. But, as Feuerbach reminds us: "Religion is the dream of the human mind. . . . Even in dreams we do not find ourselves in emptiness or in heaven, but on earth, in the realm of reality" (Feuerbach: xxxix). Max Weber was quite right: "Psychologically considered, man in quest of salvation has been primarily preoccupied by attitudes of the here and now'' (Gerth and Mills: 278).

The beyond is a horizon constructed by human beings to give meaning and perspective to their concrete lives in their own social milieu. This helps us to appreciate the revolutionary import of the discourse that was triggered by the Reformation. The Catholic position, ''justification by works,'' was a way of defining behavior in terms of function and adjustment. The human being is a being subordinated to an absolute, transcendent law. Hence the humanity of people—their salvation status, in theological terms—was measured in terms of their ability to reduplicate what the law determined. The human being is what it produces. The Protestant position, ''justification by faith,'' subverted this scheme. The human being is not a being subordinated to a law. He or she is a being before God, and God is essentially ''grace,'' liberty. Here we have a theological version of the modern debate between structure and history.

In the Protestant view the law lost its aura of sacredness. Human beings are free to break it. *Pecca fortiter:* ''sin bravely.'' The law can and should be broken, in the name of love. To rephrase the point in Freudian terms, the ''reality principle'' (law) is to be subverted by the ''pleasure principle'' (grace). As Karl Holl has pointed out, there is a remarkable similarity between Luther's human being who is free from the law and Nietzsche's ''Overman.'' Both break the tablets of the law and enter the world with nothing but their freedom (Holl: 137).

This theme of liberty is what induced Hegel to see the Reformation as one of the decisive turning points in history. It marked a break with the attitude of ''servile deference to authority,'' wherein ''spirit, having renounced its proper nature in its most essential quality, has lost its freedom'' (Hegel b: 348). That is why the Reformation in itself is to be viewed as ''the all enlightening *sun*, following on that blush of dawn which we observed at the termination of the medieval period'' (ibid.). So Hegel concludes: ''This is the essence of the Reformation: man is in his very nature destined to be free'' (Hegel b: 350). With its doctrine of ''the priesthood of all believers,'' the Reformation asserted that subjectivity is in direct relationship with the divine. Hence it affirmed the axiological priority of subjectivity over all institutional crystallizations that stood opposed to it. The human being is divinized, becoming a center of negativity which sets history in motion.

Clearly Hegel saw the Reformation as a forerunner of the spirit of the Enlightenment and the spirit of his own philosophy. It is no accident that he compared it to the ''all enlightening *sun*,'' thereby contrasting it with the darkness of the preceding Middle Ages. The confidence of Enlightenment philosophers was placed in human rationality, which needed only to be freed from the imprisoning chains of past authorities. And this confidence seems to be a secularized version of the doctrine of the priesthood of all believers.

Paul Tillich offers a similar interpretation of the spirit of Protestantism:

The Protestant principle, in name derived from the protest of the "protestants" against decisions of the Catholic majority, contains the divine and human protest against any absolute claim made for a relative reality, even if this claim is made by a Protestant Church. The Protestant principle is the judge of every religious and cultural reality, including the religion and culture which calls itself "Protestant" [Tillich c: 239].

[It] is the guardian against the attempts of the finite and conditioned to usurp the place of the unconditioned in thinking and acting. It is the prophetic judgment against religious pride, ecclesiastical arrogance, and secular self-sufficiency and their destructive consequences [Tillich c: 240].

Thus the Protestant spirit would imply an attitude of permanent vigilance against secular and sacred idols, a refusal to adapt to the status quo, and an iconoclastic rebellion denying obedience to any established order. But why? Because there is a realization that the human situation is basically distorted. It is this basic, essential, insoluble distortion that is embodied in the symbol of "original sin" (Tillich c: 241). It means that there is no situation which conscience can accept tranquilly, merely nodding its yes of approval. Conscience is nay-saying. If alienation from God is the common denominator of all human constructs—institutions, cultures, nations, civilizations—then the only word which can be pronounced by human beings is that of prophetic protest.

As far as I can see, there is no denying the fact that Protestantism originally was a repressed cry for freedom suddenly bursting forth. At the charismatic moment of its appearance it certainly was that. The question is whether Protestantism has preserved its initial vision during the course of its historical evolution.

Protestant ideology answers yes to this question. In so doing, it points to the connections between Protestantism on the one hand and democracy and modernity on the other. One of the major efforts to substantiate this thesis was the work by Karl Holl, *The Cultural Significance of the Reformation*. Holl examines the Reformation and its effects in relationship to many things: religious life, secular life, politics, economics, education, philosophy, literature, and art. His conclusion is that the Reformation signified a radical break with the order of things which had been associated with medieval civilization and Catholicism; that it planted the seeds from which would grow the loftiest creations of our time.

Emilio de Laveleye adopts a similar line in his study of the future of Catholic peoples. He tries to prove that there is a close connection between Protestantism and progress on the one hand, and Catholicism and backwardness on the other. Writes Laveleye: "From history, and from contemporary events in particular, it seems clear that Catholic peoples progress much less quickly than those nations which leave Catholicism behind. By comparison with the latter nations, the former even seem to regress'' (Laveleye: 8). Protestants are always better educated and wealthier.

Max Weber certainly cannot be ranked among the apologists for Protestantism, much less among the apologists for modernity (as we shall see later in this chapter). But in his major work on the subject, *The Protestant Ethic and the Spirit of Capitalism*, he starts off with the following observation:

> A glance at the occupational statistics of any country of mixed religious composition brings to light with remarkable frequency a situation which has several times provoked discussion in the Catholic press and literature . . . namely, the fact that business leaders and owners of capital, as well as the higher grades of skilled labour, and even more the higher technically and commercially trained personnel of modern enterprises, are overwhelmingly Protestant [Weber b: 35].

Weber's analysis does not purport to establish a causal relationship between the spirit of Protestantism and the spirit of capitalism. It claims, rather, to establish the functional relationship of the former to the latter. In other words, the Protestant spirit is structurally similar to the spirit of capitalism; hence it is adapted to the latter and suited to its expansion. So to the extent that the Western world is ruled by the logic of capitalism, we can conclude that Protestantism feels at home in that world whereas Catholicism does not.

The Protestant ideology brings together individual freedom, liberal democracy, and economic progress as expressions of the spirit of Protestantism. In short, the modern world is a fruit of Protestantism.

Protestantism as the Origin of the Monstrous Phenomena of Modern Times

Now it is the turn of the Catholic Church to speak, to say how it interprets the spirit of Protestantism. It agrees with the terms of the Protestant equation. It is true that freedom and progress are fruits of the Reformation. But contrary to the optimism of Protestantism, the Catholic Church turns the whole picture upside down by regarding all these alleged results of the Reformation as so many minuses rather than pluses. Freedom is far from being something positive. It is the seed sowed by Protestantism which led to the disintegration of our civilization; and this is exemplified perfectly in Protestant sectarianism itself.

The spirit of Protestantism is a spirit of revolt against all institutionalized orders. The Reformation sacralized conscience and desacralized the world. As a result conscience finds itself without a home. Civilization no longer enjoys the dimension of sacred depth. The sacred has been replaced by the useful. Since the world is no longer viewed as a mirror of the divine but rather as a product of human activity, it no longer serves as a reference point for the religious needs of the soul. Stripped of its divine aura, desacralized and disenchanted, the world is now simply raw material for human beings to work on. Reverence for the civilized order is replaced by an attitude of haughty rebellion against it.

The great achievement of Protestantism was to sacralize personality. But the reverse side of the same coin was the secularization of the world. The latter can no longer be enjoyed mystically as the divine womb. Instead of being built on the sacred, the world is the fruit of utilitarianism. And with utilitarianism goes the permanent possibility of anomie. In a world where everything is measured in terms of utility, human beings will always feel on the verge of losing themselves because they may lose their usefulness.

Novalis (1772–1801) exemplifies this particular interpretation of the Protestant spirit. The great mistake of Protestantism, he felt, was that it destroyed the unity of Christendom. This was tragic because the latter was the foundation for conceiving the unity of Europe, the prevailing sense of the Invisible, and hence the salvation of Western humanity. With the coming of the Reformation, Christendom ceased to exist.

Commenting on Novalis, Hans Rückert notes that Novalis draws a straight line from the Reformation to the Enlightenment. The latter was the "archenemy of Romanticism," which had assassinated Europe's soul. In the Reformation Novalis also found the source of modern philosophic and scientific thought. The latter eventually turned the eternally creative music of the heavens into the monotonous noise of a monstrous mill perpetually turned by a torrent of circumstances. Thus the Reformation was the start of modern unbelief. It is the key to understanding all the monstrous happenings of modern times (see Rückert).

Protestantism as a Revival of the Medieval Spirit

Catholics and Protestants agree that Protestantism marked the end of the Middle Ages and the start of the modern world. Ernst Troeltsch offers us a totally different version of the Protestant spirit and the historical function of Protestantism. Consider these three statements of his:

> If all these considerations be taken into account, it becomes obvious that Protestantism cannot be supposed to have directly paved the way for the modern world. On the contrary, it appears at first, in spite of all its great new ideas, as a revival and reinforcement of the ideal of authoritatively imposed Church-civilization [Troeltsch a: 85].

> . . . It supplied the incentive to a revival of the Catholic idea, and so, in spite of the contemporary diffusion of the ideas and manners of the Renaissance, Europe had to experience two centuries more of the medieval spirit [Troeltsch a: 86].

The point of primary importance is that, historically and theologically regarded, Protestantism—especially at the outset in Luther's reform of the Church—was, in the first place, simply a modification of Catholicism, in which the Catholic formulation of the problems was retained, while a different answer was given to them [Troeltsch a: 59].

The Protestant Spirit and Bureaucratic Society

There is a fourth approach to interpreting the spirit of Protestantism which I would like to mention here. It is represented by such people as Max Weber and Paul Tillich. Both have been mentioned earlier, but here I would like to spell out their distinctive positions.

Weber agrees that there is great affinity between the spirit of Protestantism and the spirit of modernity. But modernity, represented by the logic of capitalism and by tendencies towards rationalization of behavior and bureaucratization, hardly expresses the ideals of freedom and democracy. Indeed it embodies their exact opposites.

The democratic ideal talks about a political organization that is not imposed vertically from the top down. Its aim is to fashion an order which expresses the social tendencies present at the human grass-roots of society. Thus a democratic society should be an objectification of liberty, an instrument and embodiment of the "reason" immanent in the citizens as individuals.

Is that what we find in contemporary society as it is rationally organized? Weber answers no. Indeed he sees a total opposition existing between freedom and charisma on the one hand and such a rationally organized society. Such a society, committed to progress and economic growth, has a functional need for discipline and organization:

No special proof is necessary to show that military discipline is the ideal model for the modern capitalist factory, as it was for the ancient plantation. In contrast to the plantation, organizational discipline in the factory is founded upon a completely rational basis. With the help of appropriate methods of measurement, the optimum profitability of the individual worker is calculated like that of any material means of production. . . . The final consequences are drawn from the mechanization and discipline of the plant, and the psychophysical apparatus of man is completely adjusted to the demands of the outer world, the tools, the machines—in short, to an individual "function." The individual is shorn of his natural rhythm as determined by the structure of his organism; his psychophysical apparatus is attuned to a new rhythm through a methodical specialization of separately functioning muscles, and an optimal economy of forces is established corresponding to the conditions of work. . . . The ever-widening grasp of discipline irresistibly proceeds with the rationalization of the supply of economic and political demands. This universal phenomenon increasingly restricts the importance of charisma and of individually differentiated conduct [Weber a: 38-39].

Weber is, thus, telling the Protestants: "Either modernity or freedom. They cannot, both, be affirmed at the same time." Note that the text indicates that the functional demands of the system—the very system which is the foundation of progress—do not make any room whatsoever for individually differentiated behavior, be it determined by the needs of the organism or by divergent personal values. In other words, the more the Protestant spirit adjusts to the ethic of discipline and asceticism which is part of the capitalist system of production, the more impossible it will be for it to maintain the ideals of individualism, freedom, and criticism that were initially part of the Reformation. At its beginning Protestantism may have been a conscientious protest against the impositions of a particular system. It may have proclaimed the priority of "grace" over "law." It may have maintained that persons, by virtue of their direct link with God, should be the axiological pole for prophetically denouncing all systems that seek to turn persons into mere functions. But, says Weber, these founding ideas have been aborted by the linkup between Protestantism and progress.

It could be argued that the affluent Protestant countries have been the most democratic ones known to our civilization. Would that annul Weber's argument? I don't think so. This fact suggests, on the contrary, that Protestants, having introjected the functional demands of the system as if they were theological virtues and the specific form of their vocation and responsibility, tend now to behave in a functional, adjusted form, *without there being any need for visible external coercion*. Police coercion becomes unnecessary because each one becomes his or her own censor.

Modernity, defined as the rationalization of behavior for the sake of economic progress, is thus basically repressive. It is a jail. "No one knows who will live in this cage in the future," says Weber in one of the last paragraphs of his classic work on the subject. And he adds, as a denunciation of both the spirit of capitalism and the spirit of Protestantism:

For of the last stage of this cultural development, it might well be truly said: "Specialist without spirit, sensualists without a heart; this nullity imagines that it has attained a level of civilization never before achieved" (Weber b: 182).

Tillich agrees:

Western technical society has produced methods of adjusting persons to its demands in production and consumption which are less brutal, but in the long run, more effective than totalitarian suppression. They depersonalize not by commanding but by providing, namely, what makes individual creativity superfluous (Tillich b: 150).

Freedom is not openly destroyed by force. It is subjugated in a more scientific and durable way by other methods. The result is the same.

Where does Protestantism stand?

We have already shown that, according to Tillich, the "Protestant principle," the vision which shaped Protestantism's founding moments, implies a prophetic denunciation of this order of things. But he adds that the history of Protestantism has been an ongoing betrayal of that very principle.

Historical Protestantism, however, has not escaped the ideologizing of its own principle. . . . The ideology of Lutheranism was in the interest of the patriarchal order, with which Lutheran orthodoxy was associated [just as] the idealistic religion of humanistic Protestantism is in the interest of a victorious bourgeoisie [Tillich c: 246].

The failure of Protestantism shows up today, according to Tillich, in its inability to link up with what he calls the "proletarian situation." He writes:

From many points of view it would seem that Protestantism and the proletarian situation have nothing to do with each other. The facts support this view almost indisputably. Consider, for instance, the intense struggle of nearly a hundred years between the spokesmen of Protestantism and those who have made the proletarian situation the basis of their thinking; the sociological connection of the Protestant churches in central Europe with the *petite bourgeoisie* and feudalism, and in western Europe and America with big business and the successful entrepreneurs; the inner opposition of the proletarian masses to the type of life and ideas characteristic of Protestantism; the political alliance of the proletarian parties with the Catholic party and the opposition of the parties supported by Protestant circles to the political representatives of the working classes. A fundamental difference becomes evidence in all this. The proletarian situation, in so far as it represents the fate of the masses, is impervious to a Protestantism which in its message confronts the individual personality with the necessity of making a religious decision and which leaves him to his own resources in the social and political sphere, viewing the dominating forces of society as being ordered by God [Tillich c: 237].

In other words: Protestant individualism, on the level of consciousness, seems to be a defense of liberty, but in the proletarian situation it can only mean conformity. Inner, individual freedom renders prophetic protest against structures unnecessary and impossible. On the social level, then, individualism functions to mask and justify a situation of repression.

The Four Interpretations of the Protestant Spirit

So, we have at least four interpretative models of the Protestant spirit:

1. The first one, which is practically accepted by all Protestant Churches, and which, for this very reason, I label as the "Protestant ideology," asserts that freedom, democracy, and economic progress are realities which belong to one another and are all, as a cluster, fruits of the Reformation.

2. Model 2, exemplified by traditional Roman Catholic ideology and polemical writings, agrees that Protestantism unleashed freedom and contributed to democracy. It is, therefore, guilty of modernity. But modernity, far from being a step forward, was a step backwards: it is the disintegration of a spiritual synthesis. The spirit of Protestantism, as an expression of rebellious individualism, is thus to be blamed for such a tragedy.

3. Troeltsch rejects as false the presupposition shared by both Catholics and Protestants. Protestantism in no way helped to end the Middle Ages and inaugurate the modern era. Instead it represented a revival of the medieval spirit.

4. There is, finally, the model related to the names of Weber and Tillich. It does see an affinity between the spirit of Protestantism and the spirit of modernity. But it claims that modernity and freedom are incompatible.

It is possible now to advance the main lines of the thesis which will be presented in this book, through the ideal type of Right-Doctrine Protestantism:

1. One cannot deny that the discourse of RDP articulates the themes of freedom of conscience, free inquiry, and democracy at the conscious level.
2. Nor can one deny that at the same level it presents itself as the antithesis to Catholicism, and hence to the medieval spirit.
3. When we explore its nonarticulated level, its "tacit conventions," however, we find structures that are strikingly similar to those of the medieval spirit. So it seems to me that Troeltsch's thesis is correct.
4. Again on the nonarticulated level, and particularly when we examine the ethical discourse of RDP, we find that its spirit stresses the virtues of *conformity to a transcendent law*, thereby tending to produce an attitude of conformity to rational and bureaucratic structures. Protestantism establishes a *civil servant* ethic. Weber and Tillich are correct.

Am I falling into a contradiction here when I claim that the Protestant spirit has affinities with both the medieval spirit and the spirit of modernity? Not at all. On the contrary, this explains a great deal. *It is precisely the sacral vision of the world (typical of the medieval spirit) which, when superimposed on a rationalized, bureaucratic society, leads to a sacralization of the latter.*

That society is thereby elevated to the status of a "value" to which conscience must adapt.

A rationalized, bureaucratic world without a religious mantle to justify it can only be justified by its practical successes. Once sacralized by a religious ideology, however, its functional self-justification takes on a new dimension. Now it is transformed into a divinely ordained order. In other words, when we juxtapose the medieval spirit and the modern spirit in this way, the result is to superimpose another discourse of an ontological nature on the utilitarian discourse which rational, bureaucratic society uses to legitimate itself. The merely functional is elevated to the status of truth.

TWO

CONVERSION:
THE EMOTIONAL MATRIX OF RDP

Conversion as the Starting Point

We now begin our investigation in earnest, focusing on our main object: Right-Doctrine Protestantism and its spirit. Once again I would remind my readers that my empirical materials come from the Presbyterian Church of Brazil, and they should recall my comments in the Introduction to this book (see especially pages 8–9).

To shed light on the road I intend to take, I would like to make a brief reference to Freud. In his *General Introduction to Psychoanalysis* Freud tells his audience what his starting point is to be. He will focus on certain frequent phenomena which are familiar to everyone, and which for that very reason are considered trivial and meaningless: namely, lapses in speaking, writing, listening, reading, and remembering. Freud remarks:

> I am now going to ask you to consider these phenomena. But you will object, with annoyance: "There are so many tremendous puzzles both in the wide world and in the narrower life of the soul, so many mysteries in the field of mental disorder which demand and deserve explanation, that it really seems frivolous to waste labour and interest on these trifles" [Freud c: 453].

Freud offers a reply to this objection, explaining the logic behind his investigation. And to do so, he makes use of a highly suggestive image:

> Or suppose you are a detective engaged in the investigation of a murder, do you actually expect to find that the murderer will leave his photograph with name and address on the scene of the crime? Are you not perforce content with slighter and less certain traces of the person you seek? [Freud c: 454].

This method of investigation will be used tirelessly in his clinical explorations of the depths of the human psyche. What is the underlying assumption? The assumption is that the human phenomenon is a *puzzle* that has to be *deciphered*. What is most obvious is also most deceptive and misleading. So Freud does not take the rationality that we consciously spell out in our discourse as his object and starting point. Instead he concentrates his attention on the slips and involuntary breaks, in their unconscious articulation. The conscious articulation is the alibi of the criminal, the concealing of a crime. The articulated discourse does not reveal, it hides. It does not explain, it dissembles. We must uncover the original emotional trauma that conscious discourse seeks to resolve by forgetting.

I want to adopt a similar logic in my analysis of RDP discourse. Farther on in this book I will attempt to analyze its conscious articulations. But my position is that such rationality becomes meaningful only when we view it as an *a posteriori* elaborated formula, the function of which is to resolve a basic trauma.

There is nothing original about this proposal. I am simply borrowing a suggestion from Rudolf Otto. To understand religion, we must begin with an emotional experience which precedes its rational articulation. Notes Otto: "Both imaginative 'myth,' when developed into a system, and intellectualist scholasticism, when worked out to its completion, are *methods by which the fundamental fact of religious experience is, as it were, simply rolled out so thin and flat as to be finally eliminated altogether*" (Otto: 27; my italics). We cannot even begin with "representations of spirits and similar conceptions," as if they brought us back to the origins of religion: "Representations of spirits and similar conceptions are rather one and all early modes of 'rationalizing' a precedent experience, to which they are subsidiary. They are attempts in some way or other, it little matters how, to guess the riddle it propounds, and their effect is at the same time to weaken and deaden the experience itself" (Otto: 26).[1]

Paul Ricoeur adopts a similar approach: "We must proceed regressively and revert from the 'speculative' expressions to the 'spontaneous' ones" (Ricoeur b: 4). Leaving behind the logical articulations of religion, Ricoeur goes looking for the language which truly expresses "a blind experience, still embedded in the matrix of emotion, fear, anguish" (Ricoeur b: 7). He finds it in confessional language, which "expresses . . . the emotion" and serves as "the light of the emotion" (ibid.). That language will serve as the starting point for his investigation of religion.

We cannot begin with the institutional crystallizations of religion, doctrine, ritual, or organization, as if they truly revealed the foundations of religion. The institutional forms of religion are to the foundational religious experience what conscious discourse is to the trauma that it seeks to resolve. Instead of revealing, they obscure and conceal. I am not denying the possibility of analyzing religion as an institution. Indeed that has been the favorite approach of sociology. Nor am I denying the possibility of describing the rationality of the neurotic person as revealed in his or her logical discourse. What I am saying is that such an analysis, in both cases, is incapable of shedding light on the existential articulations of the logic under study. The analysis remains imprisoned within its own boundaries. It does not apprehend the rationality under study as being simultaneously a concealing-forgetting of some existential problem *and* a recipe for the resolution of that problem.

The language crystallized in Right-Doctrine Protestantism as doctrine, liturgy, and conversation presents itself to us as a structuring of reality. It makes an *inventory* of the real, *names* things, and indicates how they are logically and functionally connected. Everything is rigorously defined: life and death; past, present, and future; the here and the hereafter; body and soul; time and eternity; what is permitted and what is forbidden; who are friends and who are enemies. Language is a map of reality (Polanyi: 81). It reduces the enormous plurality of experience to a limited set of categories and concepts which makes it possible for people to handle that experience in theory and practice.

Later, we shall submit language to an analysis. Right now, however, we must practice the "art of suspicion," adopt the attitude of the psychoanalyst. For the moment we will put parentheses around RDP language. We will not accept its answers, nor analyze its explanations. Right now we are interested in its function. To be specific, we are interested in how it links up with existence, in the relationship between its answer and the question posed. RDP language is an answer, a formula or prescription. We have to know the question that was asked. And to find out, we will accept Ricoeur's suggestion and proceed regressively.

Language is a puzzle. There in front of us are the scattered pieces of the puzzle. Our task is to put them together and reconstruct the puzzle. Now some puzzles can be taken apart and put back together without any regard for the order involved. Any piece can serve as the starting point; we need only to keep adding pieces one by one. In the case of other puzzles, however, we must find out which piece comes first, which one comes next, which next, and so on. In this case the object is not simply the finished product. Part of its definition is the *order* in which it can be constructed. Without the *order* the finished product does not exist.

In psychoanalysis a neurosis is clarified only when it can be reconstructed from an initial piece, the original trauma. The same thing applies to religion. Religious language originates in emotions, so we must identify the emotions upon which it has been constructed in practice. The approach of scientific understanding should reflect the real-life process in the formation of its object.

To show that this is so, I need only point to the fact that RDP language is never accepted in one fell swoop as a whole, complete package containing all its elements already. There is an order to be followed. No one converts to the doctrine of the Trinity, the virgin birth, or the verbal inspiration of Scripture.

Nor does one convert to RDP morality. These doctrines and injunctions are words that do not move the emotions. Would it be possible to reconstruct the structure of RDP language on the basis of such doctrines? I think so, but in that case we would have on our hands a self-sufficient logical structure imprisoned in its own circularity. And our initial problem is to get out of the logical circle and find the point where the language links up with life. For a religious language is accepted only insofar as it responds to an emotional necessity, only insofar as it is *functional* vis-à-vis certain needs and demands of the personality.

Viewed from that standpoint, language is not a homogeneous, continuous whole with free movement in any direction. It has very hot zones, which are directly linked to an existential pole; these zones are linked in turn with other zones ranging from warm and lukewarm to cold and indifferent. They are fields of force around what Erich Fromm has called an "emotional matrix" (Fromm: 59). As William James put it: "All we know is that there are dead feelings, dead ideas, and cold beliefs, and there are hot and live ones" (James: 162). The latter constitute "the hot place in a man's consciousness, the group of ideas to which he devotes himself, and from which he works" (ibid.).

The hot center of discourse reveals the point of connection with the hot center of personality. We must start there if we wish to follow the movement whereby RDP discourse is fashioned. To understand the universe of RDP, we must lay hold of it at its moment of birth.

I suggest that *conversion* is this moment of birth. It is our door into the labyrinth. It is the point where the rationality that will be socially constructed later links up with the emotional needs of the human personality. Conversion is to rationality what the original religious experience is to later intellectual constructs in Rudolf Otto's analysis, and what the language of "confession" is to developed myth and speculation in Ricoeur's approach. Let me clarify what I am trying to say.

Why Do We Change from One Language to Another?

Let us begin with a simple observation: conversion reveals itself in a new way of talking. To undergo conversion is to abandon one discourse and adopt another.

Why do human beings change from one language to another? Why do they migrate from certain linguistic universes to others?

Language is a mediating tool between human beings and their world. We do not contemplate reality face to face. From the moment we are born, things do not come before us in all their nakedness; they come dressed in the names that some community has given them. The community has already *defined* how the world is, and hence it knows *what* the world is. This knowledge of the world is crystallized in language.

Language is not a copy of things and facts. Language is always *interpreta-*

tion.[2] In interpretation objects fuse with emotions, the world and the human being embrace. It is an illusion for us to think that when we talk about the world we are talking about something that exists as an object out there, independent of the speaker. The speaking subject is always present in his or her speech even when he or she attempts to put a parenthesis around the self in talking. To talk about the world is to talk about something that is not a matter of indifference to me. It is something to which I am vitally and emotionally tied, something on which my life and my death depend. So there is no talk that is not *my* talk. Discourse about the object always expresses the presence of a subject. Talk about the world, then, is always interpretation of the world. It is saying what the world means *to me*. The truth of the subject is revealed in the object: "The nucleus of the system, around which the rest of the system revolves, is the individual's valuation of himself. The individual *sees the world from his own viewpoint*, with himself as the center" (Lecky: 153; my italics).

Whether we like it or not, we are the prisoners of an irreducible anthropomorphism. The world about which I speak, the world to which I refer by means of my language, is the world that revolves around my values, a world that *ought* to uphold my values. When I talk about the world, I am being driven by the unconscious dynamics of the ego which is looking for a world in which my values are plausible, a world in which I can truly feel at home, a world in which space and time are friendly to me.

This process is very obvious in the realm of discourse inhabited by art and religion. And there are many indications that the very same process is at work in the construction of scientific language. As Prescott Lecky notes: "Nor should we be surprised if all scientific creations resemble one another in the style of their workmanship, since they are not only symbolic representations of so-called external events, but arrangements to serve our human need for self-consistency" (Lecky: 111).

It is not a matter of simple projection. It is not that I, pure subject, take the aspirations that are welling up within me independently of the world and hurl them out into an alien, external world to which I am related by sheer contiguity. Emotions are not merely internal realities or isolated impulses. They are "structured evidences" of reality, of the "interaction" between organism and environment, for which no other evidence exists except the emotions (Perls, Hefferline, and Goodman: 332).

I exist only as a being-in-the-world. I frequent the world, and the world frequents me. My emotions are evidences of this solidarity. So there are no mere projections, no pure projections. Such could exist only if the subject were a spectator in the world. Projections are expressions of introjections. I throw myself into the world because I previously accepted and welcomed the world. In its most basic form language is "the light of the emotions," the revelation of meaning; it reveals my way of being in relationship with the world. As Jespersen put it, human beings "sang out their feelings long before they were able to speak their thoughts" (Jespersen: 436).

So long as this relationship between human being and world makes sense, I do not call my language into question. I identify its practical functionalness with truth. Recall what Berger and Luckmann wrote: "As long as my knowledge works satisfactorily, I am generally ready to suspend doubt about it" (Berger and Luckmann: 44). That is understandable enough. My interpretation of the world unifies my personality and my world into a meaningful whole. If that interpretation proves satisfactory in organizing my behavior and enabling me to foresee the future behavior of the world, there is nothing to prompt doubts on my part. One's personality feels secure because one feels confirmed in "the ability to foresee and predict environmental happenings, to understand the world one lives in, and thus to be able to anticipate events and prevent the necessity for sudden readjustments" (Lecky: 122).

Frequently, however, interpretative schemes fall apart and collapse. My language ceases to work satisfactorily. It becomes incapable of interpreting the world in a way that will mesh with personal expectations.

What are the causes of such collapse? I am not going to answer that question here, but I would like to suggest a few factors. Sometimes the crises are purely personal. One experiences death or some tragedy: the death of a loved one, an incurable disease, failure in one's career or one's affective life. Many such crises are caused by abrupt social changes: cultural shock, urbanization, migration, economic depression, war, and so forth. In such situations a person's knowledge of the world becomes problematic. I experience the events but I don't know what they mean. They were not foreseen by my interpretative apparatus. I find myself unable to *put names* on things, and my perplexity is embodied in a heartfelt *Why?* Meaningfulness has been lost, and I confront an alien, hostile world that I cannot assimilate.

We must clearly distinguish between a situation of crisis and a situation of pain. The martyr who faces the stake, the prophet who suffers persecution, and the revolutionary who chooses privations and a life on the run—all of these people have incorporated pain and suffering into their meaning-system. To them pain and suffering make sense: "It is therefore not the physical injury which causes the anxiety, but the breakdown of the scheme of understanding and prediction. In a world which is incomprehensible, no one can feel secure" (Lecky: 122).

The collapse of meaning-schemes is the cognitive face of a feeling of impotence. The theoretical impasse is the reverse side of the practical impasse. The world does not make sense. What does that mean exactly? It means I feel *powerless* to force the world to sustain my values. The martyr, the prophet, and the revolutionary can endure pain without their personalities being destroyed because they believe that in some way reality is on their side. Though their values appear to be weak at present, they believe that those values will triumph in the future.

The disintegration of meaningfulness is the dissolution of the unity existing between human being and world. The latter may be the macrocosm of the physical universe or the microcosm of civilization, nature, and society that once joined with me to express my values and serve as the tool for carrying out my intentions. Formerly that world extended the *power* of my values far beyond the limits of my body, indeed to the very boundaries of the universe. Now that world has become an autonomous entity: self-sufficient, alien, alienated, and hostile. The human being no longer feels at home. The world has ceased to be the tool of my intentions. I discover that my program seems doomed to failure. As Freud said about the program of the pleasure principle, which decides the purpose of life: "There is no possibility at all of its being carried through; all the regulations of the universe run counter to it" (Freud a: 23).

Conversion: Restructuring Reality

Conversion is the process of restructuring or reconstructing one's schemes of meaning and value that can follow upon a crisis. I say "can" because there is no guarantee that it will. In the previous section I noted a number of external factors that might be invoked as causes of conversion. In fact, however, they do not explain conversion. They are occasions of conversion rather than its causes.

Why does the collapse of meaning-schemes produce an emotional crisis? It seems that this is bound up with some deeply felt need for unity that is part of the human personality. Notes Peter Berger: "The experience of conversion to a meaning system . . . is liberating and profoundly satisfying. Perhaps this has its roots in a deep human need for order, purpose, and intelligibility" (Berger: 63). Max Weber agrees, pointing out that religious beliefs represent an effort to give meaning to something that is experienced as senseless:

> Behind them always lies a stand towards something in the actual world which is experienced as specifically "senseless." Thus, the demand has been implied: that the world order in its totality is, could, and should somehow be a meaningful "cosmos" [Gerth and Mills: 281].

Here I am using the word "conversion" in a specific, hence limited, sense. It could be used to describe a purely external process whereby a person abandons one religious community and joins another. In itself that external act does not guarantee that consciousness has gone through a process of destructuring and restructuring. From the standpoint of social status or political power it might be advantageous to join a religious group which represents the majority in a given society or its power elite. In this case joining the group does not result from an emotional experience; it is dictated by pragmatic considerations. I am not using conversion in that sense. Here I am referring to a psychosocial process which entails the destructuring of one meaning-scheme and the adoption of another that is structurally different from the former.

It should be pointed out that this phenomenon is not confined to the sphere of religion. It can be observed in the areas of psychology, ideology, and even science. Therapeutic techniques are techniques of conversion. The aim of therapy is always to help the patient fashion a new value-structure. The same holds true for ideologies. I might note in passing that our emotional attitude towards the ideologies we adopt indicates that we are dealing here with hot zones of personality. To embrace an ideology is to discover a meaning-scheme by means of which we link up our personal values with society and history.

So far I think we all would agree. But what about the statement that conversion is also evident in the realm of science? I am simply repeating a point made by Thomas Kuhn in his book *The Structure of Scientific Revolutions*. He stresses that the progress of science is not a continuous, linear process. Science begins with the establishment of a paradigm, a model theoretical structure. There follows a period of stability during which scientists behave *as if* their models were a copy of the real. Then, suddenly, the paradigms prove to be inadequate. New phenomena appear, which cannot be explained by the old paradigms. This crisis is resolved only when the old paradigm is abandoned and a new one is created. Kuhn applies the term "conversion" to the process whereby a scientist abandons one paradigm to embrace another. He is suggesting that what happens in science is very similar to what happens in religion (see Kuhn).

What would make a scientific conversion different from a religious conversion? I don't think it is the logic of the process. The difference lies elsewhere. Science claims to be dealing exclusively with exterior events, so that the scientist as a person is placed in parentheses. Religion, by contrast, is quite clear in pointing out that the human being is a part of the process. In the latter case it is not a matter of organizing the world; it is a matter of organizing the relationship between the human being and the world. It is not simply a matter of knowing the world, but of knowing my own destiny. The meaning of life is at stake, and it is the great issue: "Judging whether life is or is not worth living amounts to answering the fundamental question of philosophy. . . . I therefore conclude that the meaning of life is the most urgent of questions" (Camus: 3–4). In the crisis of conversion what is at stake is the meaning of life. In Tolstoy's terms it is the whole issue of faith: "Faith is the sense of life, that sense by virtue of which man does not destroy himself, but continues to live on" (James: 153).

The new synthesis after conversion indicates that the personality has gone through a metamorphosis. There is a new axiological attitude towards life. A different value has been assimilated into the emotional matrix of consciousness, and this has major consequences: "If a value is assimilated into the organization or expelled from it, the process is not one of addition or subtraction, but rather of general revision and reorganization" (Lecky: 169). Reorganized, the personality sees the world differently. Its messages, which previously were completely dissonant, now seem to be totally harmonious. The earlier emotions of confusion, guilt, and anxiety are replaced by feelings of peace, joy, and power. "The experience of conversion to a meaning system that is capable of ordering the scattered data of one's biography is liberating and profoundly satisfying" (Berger: 63).

The person now tends to divide up his or her life in terms of *before* and *after* conversion. A clear distinction is made between two incommensurable phases of personal experience: the old human being who did not know or see versus the new human being who knows and sees. Gerardus van der Leeuw points to this phenomenon in the Greek mystery religions: "In Greece, also, those adopted by the deity in the mysteries were looked upon as *deuteropotmoi*, 'those to whom a second destiny was given' " (Van der Leeuw: 529). In the Bible human beings who have undergone a radical transformation frequently receive a new name, as if to signify the start of a new identity and destiny. In the New Testament it is a process of rebirth, of the death of the "old" human being and the birth of a "new" human being. Its symbol is baptism. One is immersed in water and dies, then emerges from the water reborn. The Greek term *metanoia*, frequently translated as "repentance," suggests the same sort of process. One must have a "change of heart," breaking away from a particular form of rationality (Greek *nous*) so that another structure of rationality can be formed. Zen Buddhism uses the word *satori* to describe the same process: the attainment of enlightenment, the "opening of a third eye" (Suzuki: 3). The bare facts remain intact, but now they are seen in the framework of a new principle of organization. As a result, the personality recovers its lost harmony with its world.

Still caught up in the emotional ecstasy of this new condition, converts begin to speak in a different way. As yet they cannot logically articulate what has happened to them. Their ideas are not yet clear. Their discourse is expressive, confessional. They are like people who have fallen in love and talk day and night about their loved one, never even imagining that they have to justify or explain their new feelings. And they also feel strong, knowing that reality is on their side. Impotence gives way to a feeling of power. There is nothing to fear: "The believer who has communicated with his god is not merely a man who seeks new truths of which the unbeliever is ignorant; he is a man who is *stronger*" (Durkheim 2: 416).

I hope this has justified my own methodological option: i.e., to begin with conversion. It is there that emotional needs link up with the logic of the language to which the person converts. One converts because the worldview presented by a religion somehow dovetails with one's personal experience of meaninglessness. The doctrinal crystallizations are answers to an existential question, and one cannot understand the answer unless one knows what the question was. So to understand the institutionalized forms of religious language one must start off from the emotional experience which makes it possible for people to accept them. And that starting point is conversion.

Conversion: Naming Emotions

It is an emotional crisis that creates the possibility and necessity of conversion. The crisis involved is the collapse of meaning-systems. Language proves incapable of putting names on things; they lose their meaningfulness. And the collapse of meaningfulness, of the ability to name things, gives rise to anxiety. The painful aspect of anxiety is the very fact that it is not a specific pain that can be pinpointed and labelled. One does not know exactly what it is; it is a blind experience. Anxiety is not something that fills the cosmos; it is an emotion which surfaces when the cosmos has disappeared. It becomes impossible to organize one's behavior, since that requires a world which makes sense. In the case of fear and pain consciousness knows what is threatening it; it knows *in relation to what* its behavior stands. In the case of anxiety, by contrast, consciousness does not confront any object, and so it does not know what to do.

Here, then, is the first task facing conversion. It must *give a name to anxiety*, place one's subjectivity before some object. Once an emotion is named, it can be understood, manipulated, and exorcised. What is the significance of the emotions felt by a human being in crisis? What do they mean? Of what are they evidences? Here we have the first step in constructing a line of rationality around the irrational. Conversion starts when human beings imprisoned in their emotions accept the names given to those emotions by the religious community that addresses them.

Right-Doctrine Protestantism interprets emotions as *revelations of being* in terms of its inner depth and its dimension of eternity. A human being inhabits time and space, is a member of society and a part of history. But these are accidental, transitory relationships, which mask rather than reveal. Emotions are not mere epiphenomena, on the conscious level, of basic sociohistorical phenomena. If that were the case, the puzzle of emotions could be solved by pointing to their sociohistorical causes. They could be cured by psychoanalytic techniques or by radical, revolutionary transformation of the social conditions underlying them. As Marx put it in his *Theses on Feuerbach* (n. 8): "All social life is essentially *practical*. All mysteries which lead theory to mysticism find their rational solution in human practice and in the comprehension of this practice" (Marx: 423). With varying details this is the basis of all sociological interpretations of the phenomenon of religion, and nothing could be further from the spirit of Protestantism under consideration here.

According to that spirit, the human essence is not a product of social relations. I am not the product of biographical traumas in family relationships, nor am I the product of economic and class contradictions in the society where I live. Human beings dwell in time and space, but they are not solidary with them. Their origin and destiny are not to be found there. Protestant anthropology is grounded in an ontology whose horizons transcend time and open out to eternity. It is in agreement with the anthropology that has dominated the Catholic tradition, and that was so well expressed by Augustine in his *Confessions*: "You have created us for yourself, O God, and our heart will not rest until it rests in you."

A cry in time is a reverberation of eternity. Anxiety is a bubble rising from the ocean depths of the soul, depths which touch space and time only on the surface.

The unconverted have not yet realized that their emotions are symptoms of eternity. They are still "carnal." Their consciousness considers only the immediate data of sense experience. Any cures they might effect through science or practice would be mere "distractions" or "opiates," since they would be overlooking the roots of the problem and dulling their ability to see its origins.

Our Protestant who is trying to effect a conversion does not believe that the psychic realm contains its own explanation or intelligibility. It is nothing more than the visible, enigmatic face of an invisible dimension. To decipher the enigma of the visible, one must give names to the invisible, spell it out in a discourse.

The potential convert has nothing but his or her anxiety, together with questions about the meaning of life. Protestantism replies: "Anxiety is a message from eternity. It reveals a rupture with the true foundations of life." A scientific response cannot go beyond a phenomenological description of anxiety, a surface explanation. The religious explanation tells us *why* and points to causes. It offers a diagnosis in terms of polarities: soul and eternity, soul and God.

This is the basis of Protestant anthropology. The human being is not just a being-in-the-world, but rather a being-before-eternity. Anxiety is to be interpreted as a break or rupture in this fundamental relationship. Here is the axis around which the whole universe of meaning will be constructed, the absolute point of origin and the umbilical cord of the universe on which the meaning of life depends. It will serve as the point of reference for all the coordinates of time and space. The rupture of this relationship is the great problem to be solved.

When Miguel de Unamuno compared the Protestant spirit with the spirit of Catholicism, he affirmed that "the element which is specifically religious in Catholicism is immortalization and not justification, as it happens with the Protestants. Justification is basically ethical: religion is made dependent on morals, and not the reverse, as in Catholicism" (Unamuno 67). Nothing is farther removed from truth. Unamuno, I think, made the mistake to take Protestantism for statements made by its philosophers and theologians, of the Modernist tradition. But there is an enormous abyss which separates religion as it is experienced in its founding moments, and religion as it is later rationalized. If Protestantism has a rather strong moral element, it is something which emerges later and not at the beginning of the religious experience. Indeed, it is absent from the crisis of conversion. What is at stake here is ontology and not morality.

The name for the rupture in the basic ontological relationship is *sin*. The original import of sin is ontological, not moral. This is evident from what is asked of the potential convert: not the abandonment of errant moral acts but a change in outlook and *orientation*. The latter is summed up in the notion of *accepting Christ as the sole and sufficient savior*. The formula calls not for *doing* but for *surrendering* to Christ. Indeed moral excellence is often considered an obstacle to conversion. It can camouflage ontological anxiety, making a change in outlook and surrender to Christ more difficult.

Our symbol *sin* is still too abstract, however. It can be analyzed as a *guilty soul facing death* or a *guilty soul facing God*. The two renditions are identical, since death is not viewed as the end but as the moment of transparency and truth. In death being emerges from the cloudiness of its existence in space and time and comes face to face with the *Presence* that had been obscured by existence. Death is the revelation of God as the infinite pole of the soul.

The consciousness of death and the consciousness of guilt go hand in hand in a polar relationship: one cannot subsist without the other.

Suppose, for example, that death is interpreted as the end of existence. I might feel sad or rebellious about its inevitable arrival. But I could not possibly feel afraid that guilt will follow me and take vengeance on me *after death*. If death is the end of existence, then it is also the end of guilt. In that case death puts an end to the whole problematic which religion purports to resolve. There is nothing to be done, and that is tragic. But there is nothing to fear either, and that is liberating.

The same holds true for guilt. By itself guilt is not enough to raise the problem of salvation. If guilt is merely an emotional experience, then it can be solved through therapeutic techniques. It is a transitory thing, devoid of eternal significance. If guilt is merely a passing stage of awareness, and if death is the end of awareness, then death is also the end of guilt. Indeed one could look to suicide as a definitive therapeutic solution for the problem of guilt.

Once we set up the axis—*soul facing eternity*—the whole picture changes drastically. Death becomes the impossibility of dying, and hence the impossibility of doing away with guilt. Protestant preaching puts the word "immortal" before all its references to the soul. Death ceases to be a way out. It becomes the eternalization of guilt.

I would like to quote a passage from *The Sickness Unto Death* about despair, because I believe Kierkegaard caught something essential in the Protestant spirit and expressed it here:

> The torment of despair is precisely this, not to be able to die . . . yet not as though there were hope of life; no, the hopelessness in this case is that even the last hope, death, is not available. When death is the greatest danger, one hopes for life; but when one becomes acquainted with an even more dreadful danger, one hopes for death. So when the danger is so great that death has become one's hope, despair is the disconsolateness of not being able to die [Kierkegaard b: 150–51].

This passage is certainly relevant to the spirit of Protestantism which I am studying here. To exist as a being facing God is to be eternally destined to guilt, and to be unable to die. That is the underlying presupposition in the case of conversion. That is the problem of salvation facing a soul destined to suffer vengeance for its guilt.

The significance of the feeling of guilt is not in the fact that it indicates a de facto breakaway from a morally upright life. If that were the case, guilt would be the result of human actions; it would be a contingent and accidental historical phenomenon. The assertion that the human being is a sinner is not a moral assertion. Human beings do not become sinners in time, as a result of having committed this and that action. It is not my doing that determines my being; it is my being that determines my doing. I don't *become* guilty, I *am* guilty. When it says that the human being is a sinner, and hence guilty, Protestantism is making an anthropological assertion. It is defining the essence of the human being. When converts are being received formally into the Protestant Church and make their profession of faith, they are expected to answer "yes" to this question:

> Do you believe that you were *born in sin*
> and that *by nature* you are incapable of doing good? [my italics]

To be a human being is to be a sinner. To be a sinner is to be destined to eternal damnation. Being lost and damned is part of the very innards of my being, quite apart from any action or decision on my part. The reality of sin is pristine and immediate, not derivative; essential and intrinsic, not historical. The phenomenology of sin, its moral and historical surface, merely reveals a being alienated from the foundations of life. The crisis itself is not historical. It is always there beneath the surface. Psychic, social, historical factors are only so many *occasions* that bring it to the surface.

This explains one of the most basic and important functions of preaching. It must help to bring the basic crisis to the surface by consciousness-raising. The ontological crisis lies buried in the unconscious; it must be brought to the surface of consciousness. Preaching does not provoke or create the crisis; it simply reveals it. It is a maieutic process, forcing the crisis from its hideout. The preacher must go under the seemingly calm, tranquil surface of the human being and drag out the despair that is buried in the depths of the heart.

But how does one do that? By preaching about death and guilt. It is only when faced with the anxiety of death and guilt that the sinner will be able to pose the question: "What must I do to be saved?"

It is not the intensity or horror of sin as a moral act that gives sin its sinister dimension. A little lie is no better than a great crime. Distinctions between them are superficial, human distinctions. The sinister aspect of moral sin is the fact that it reveals the status of the soul before God. If it were the human subject who defined sin, if sin were something related only to human beings, then it would remain human, all too human, to be invested with eternal consequences. But sin is always a stance *before God*, hence an infinite crime that cannot be pardoned or expiated by a human being. An infinitely guilty human being exists because his or her life stands before the Infinite in a misguided way. And to the infiniteness of the guilt corresponds the infiniteness of the vengeance: eternal punishment.

Here we run into something discussed by Ricoeur: the primordial connection between defilement, guilt, and vengeance.

This "synthesis" is anterior to any justification; it is what is presupposed in any punishment conceived as revenge and expiation. . . . We are before a *matrix of terror* [Ricoeur b: 30; my italics].

Eternal punishment is the way in which the guilty conscience experiences God by way of anticipation and expectation. In eternity God will be revealed to the guilty one as endless punishment. God thus assumes a demoniacal face. God is the "Great Eye" which rules out secrets, the implacable sword of wrath, the certainty that the penalty will be carried out. *God guarantees the causal relationship between guilt and vengeance.* Anxiety gets a new name, ceasing to be a merely psychic phenomenon within the human being. It becomes a messenger of eternity and takes on ontological density. It now forms a horizon of terror, becoming an objective problem which conversion is to resolve. If an eternity of infernal darkness were not possible, the message of salvation could not be preached. If anxiety were not interpreted as a revelation of eternity, and if eternity were not interpreted as the impossibility of ending one's state of eternal guilt before God, then the problem of salvation could not arise. Christ would have no function to perform. He would not be the *answer* to some question, for there would be no question.

Preaching salvation, then, presupposes that death is interpreted as an encounter with eternal destiny. It is an ontological crystallization, a solidification of the future. Life is the time of *opportunity*. So long as one is alive, one can alter one's existential *orientation* towards the divine. At death opportunity ceases. What has been, will be:

It cannot be denied that the soul, a moral being, is going to be judged by God. Since judgment is certain . . . another question arises: What constitutes the end of opportunity? There is an end to opportunity, and that end is physical death. Those who have crossed its portals, the Bible tells us, are in a state of retribution . . . [OP, 10/25 June 1957, p. 4].*

What is at stake is whether the punishment is eternal or not [OP, 10/25 September 1957, p. 6].

[It is Jesus] with his authority as Savior and Judge who describes the Dantesque settlement of accounts (Matt. 25)—not of the possibility of

*Citations beginning with abbreviations refer readers to the full bibliography of cited primary sources on p. 211.

life, but of the responsibility of immortal souls. . . . [The wicked] will go to eternal torment, the just to eternal life [OP, 10/25 October 1957, p. 5].

Death as the end of opportunity is one of the central themes preached and sung about in efforts to bring about the conversion of lost souls:

> When the labor of this life ends
> And death appears at your side,
> What is the destiny of your soul to be?
> Life or death, which will you receive? [HE, n. 223][3]

What are the results of indecision?

> Almost persuaded
> To believe in Jesus!
> Almost—will not do.
> Almost—will separate you.
> Almost—will hurl you
> Into perdition [HE, n. 228].

The problem, then, is the eternal perdition that waits, with gaping jaws, for those who do not convert before death. Conversion is an experience in response to another experience: the terror of death. Life—with its certainties and joys, its tasks and its pleasures—must be interpreted as the antechamber to eternal punishment before the soul can feel despair for its condition and pose the problem of salvation to itself.

What Does "Accepting Christ" Mean?

Conversion is marked by the acceptance of Christ as "sole and sufficient savior." The convert is one who has "surrendered to Christ." What does that mean?

The answers given to this question are framed in two very different idioms or languages: the language of the new convert and the language of the community to which he or she has converted. The language of new converts is confessional, emotional. They chant and sing of their new experience. The language of the community, by contrast, embodies a theoretical elaboration of that experience. The convert reveals his or her soul; the community links up those feelings with a comprehensive worldview. The new convert is still under the magic spell of a new object that has exercised its fascination and transformed his or her emotions; the community has already subjected that object to a process of all-embracing reflection. The convert confronts something mysterious and wondrous; the community has already transformed the marvel and mystery into knowledge. Hence the community itself refers to new converts as people who "do not yet know what they believe in." As we shall see in the next chapter, cognition comes at a later stage; it is part of the socialization process whereby converts are initiated into the worldview of the community.

To the Convert

The new convert does not enunciate thoughts. He or she sings out feelings. At the point of conversion, then, the symbol *Christ* signifies the feelings experienced by the soul. To know Christ is to know his benefits. Christ is the symbol of the mysterious power which brought about the miraculous subjective change. How is one to talk about this mysterious power? By *confessing* the metamorphosis that has taken place in one's soul. Before Christ: anxiety, anguish, guilt, lack of meaning in life. After Christ: peace, joy, certainty.

The confessional language of the convert is devoid of ideas about external reality. It has not yet been fashioned into a worldview.

This intellectual vacuum makes us suspicious, *a priori*, of something which can be verified empirically. It is that the *teachings* of Christ are not what is crucial in the experience of conversion. The convert is not one who has abandoned one ethic and philosophy of life to embrace the ethic and philosophy of Jesus. If that were the case, then he or she should have some very clear ideas about the newly embraced ethic and philosophy. However, as indicated above, the conversion experience is characterized by intensity of emotions rather than by clarity of ideas. No one converts to the teachings of Christ—be it the commandment of love, the golden rule, the Sermon on the Mount, the advice not to worry about the future, or the injunction to forgive our enemies. The imperative mood is introduced only later, for the edification of the faithful. Only those already converted *to Christ* can understand the *teachings of Christ*. What counts at the time of conversion is *who Jesus Christ was*, not *what he taught*.

Conversion, as related by the new convert, is an *experience of communion with a person*, not a didactic experience of learning a new body of wisdom. The conversion experience "starts with the absolute need of a higher helper, and ends with the sense that he has helped us" (James: 167). The important thing is not some newly acquired knowledge, but a newly acquired sense of power, as Durkheim suggested. Thus the symbol "Christ" is not a secondary one pointing towards the *philosophy of Christ* as the primary symbol; it is the original symbol pointing directly towards a magical center of power.

At the time of conversion the potential convert is not confronted with Christ the philosopher or Christ the moral teacher. Nor is the convert confronted with the historical Jesus, the human Jesus who "walked among us." It is another Christ that is important here: i.e., the Christ who is the *cosmic center of curative power*, the *savior* Christ who solves the ontological problem of guilt. The cure does not come from a philosophical pedagogy; it comes from *personal, emotional, mystical participation* in the very being of the

Savior. Mysticism precedes morality, being precedes doing. One must reproduce Paul's experience: "The life I live now is not my life, but the life which Christ lives in me" (Gal. 2:20).

I am not proposing a psychological analysis here, and so I cannot explain the mechanisms whereby the emotional act of *surrendering to Christ* effects a metamorphosis in the emotional conditions of consciousness. But I would like to offer a clue for those who might be interested. Here is what Sigmund Freud has to say in his introductory lectures about the cure of a patient in psychoanalysis:

> The outcome in this struggle is not decided by his intellectual insight—it is neither strong enough nor free enough to accomplish such a thing— but solely by his relationship to the physician. Faith repeats the history of its own origin; it is a derivative of love and at first it needed no arguments. . . . Without this support, arguments have no weight with the patient, never do have with most people in life [Freud c: 630].

Perhaps this offers us a clue to what takes place in conversion. Human beings present themselves with their anxiety. Their frames of reference have collapsed, they feel impotent, life has no meaning. Preaching (like therapy) offers a diagnosis. Diagnosis in itself, however, is not enough to offer a cure. But preaching does not stop there. It offers the image of the great physician who can cure, and who wants to. All one has to do is entrust oneself emotionally to this savior-physician.

An objection might be raised here to the analogy. After all, there is a big difference. In the therapeutic situation, the therapist is a concrete person. In preaching, the preacher offers only a symbol, a word. But is the difference so great, really? Consider the power of the therapist. Isn't it due much more to his or her symbolic value than to any manipulative competence? Well, let the matter stand. I am not trying to solve the issue, as I indicated above. I simply wanted to offer one clue that might be fruitful if it were investigated more deeply.

To the Community

The language of the community does not rest content with the sheer emotional expression of the experience of salvation. It tries to *understand* those feelings. To be more precise, it wants to point up the objective reference-points for those feelings. For if the feelings do not correspond to any structuring of the real, how are we to avoid the conclusion that they are nothing more than groundless fantasies and hallucinations?

New converts do not know what they believe in, but the community does. So when someone converts to Christ in an emotional, inarticulate way, he or she is unwittingly converting to a whole series of "tacit conventions" (Wittgenstein b: section 4.002). They are the tacit conventions which are part of the

Church's collective consciousness. What vision of the world is revealed in the Church's tacit conventions?

The various Protestant vocabularies or idioms dealing with sin are particularly instructive here, insofar as Brazilian Protestantism and RDP are concerned. They reveal at least four different angles from which the world can be viewed. It is not a matter of four different worlds, but of four different ways of approaching the same issue of guilt. They are variations on the same theme, and the result is a polyphonic construct of the human condition and the saving function of Christ.

The first type of vocabulary is framed in terms of *penal law*. The world is organized as a legal structure. Sin is *breaking the law*, a *crime*, and that inevitably entails *punishment*. The human being is a culprit, a criminal, on whom eternal pain will be imposed as a punishment. God is law, and the guarantee that the law will be carried out.

The second type of vocabulary is framed in terms of *impurity*. Sin is *dirt*, *stain*, *filth*. The sinner is soiled by it, sunk in muck. For that very reason the sinner cannot be in communion with God, who is light, whiteness, purity. The sinner is destined to remain forever separated from God because of the repulsion existing between the pure and the impure. The very term "repulsion" suggests both a physical force pushing something away and a visceral reaction of nausea against the impure.

The third type of vocabulary alludes to a *medicinal world of health and sickness*. Sin is illness, leprosy, poison. It was introduced into the world by a snake, an animal who stings and poisons. Sinners are people who have cut their ties with the fount of life and hence are mortally ill.

The fourth type of vocabulary is *political and commercial* in nature. Sinners are people who are *enslaved* to a demoniacal power. They have *sold* their souls, lost their liberty, and no longer belong to themselves. Their liberation demands the payment of a *price*, a *ransom*.

In all four types of vocabulary God symbolizes the inexorable nature of the causal connections that hold sway over reality. No one can "pull a fast one." God is law, guaranteeing punishment; purity, guaranteeing repulsion; health, guaranteeing the death of the sick; and the businessman who guarantees that there will be no liberty unless the price is paid.

These vocabularies are basic in constructing the Protestant universe which is being studied here. They reveal a reality ruled by an inflexible causality, one where there can be no gratuitous pardon or cancellation of consequences. Order and terror come together. In my opinion, one can say correctly that *grace, love, and pardon* are not the first words uttered in this universe. They are subordinate symbols, which can be introduced only after inflexible causality, order, and terror have been articulated and given their due priority.

Here, then, we have an ontology which begins not with paradise but with darkness, chaos, and the abyss. The sinner is saved *from* a yawning abyss. That is why the preaching of salvation only makes sense as the negation of a basically sinister reality.

These "tacit conventions" determine the way in which Christ's function as savior is understood. The *office* of Christ as savior must be spelled out in different ways, depending on which vocabulary is being used in preaching. There is no question of eliminating the causal nexus between sin and its consequences. That would imply the abolition of the basic order, indeed of God himself. Christology would demand atheism! If pardon, grace, and love were the basic symbols of the Protestant universe under discussion, then how could one talk about salvation as if human beings were still menaced by the abyss? So the real question is: How is one to speak articulately about grace, pardon, and love in such a way that the inexorable causal order is preserved?

The answer is classic. Christ is not primarily the one who pardons. He cannot abolish the divine order. Christ is the one who *took my place*, who *substituted for me*, accepting the punishment imposed by the divine order. Thus the order itself remained intact. What did Jesus Christ do?

a. He fulfilled the law perfectly yet, *in spite of that*, he suffered the penalty.
b. He was perfectly pure yet, *in spite of that*, he endured divine abandonment on the cross.
c. He was wholly health and life yet, *in spite of that*, he suffered death.
d. He was entirely free yet, *in spite of that*, he was offered up by God as the *price* for purchasing or ransoming us from a situation of bondage. In the drama of Christ's life and death we have a commercial transaction that puts an end to the domination of demoniacal powers over humanity.[4]

The phrase *in spite of that* indicates that in Christ's case no causal relationship existed between his person and the punishment he suffered. It was a matter of *substitution*; Christ put himself in the place of human beings. Once again, as I noted above, the historical life of Jesus and his teachings are not what is important. What is important is the *mystical transaction* that took place in and through Jesus.

The idea of substitution will remain unintelligible unless we enter sympathetically into the world of myth, where all things share in a common sea of being. Reality is a harmonious whole. A vibration in its lowliest part will reverberate through the whole. In this case it is not a physical but an emotional reverberation. The universe has a soul. Intentions and feelings are propagated. It is a body in which each cell exists as part of the whole.

The first Adam sinned; all humans have sinned. The second Adam, Christ, was perfectly just; hence my destiny is mystically linked with his. My dissonances reverberate through the whole universe and are picked up and suffered by Christ, who substituted for me; it is a magical process of *contagion*. But the process works the opposite way as well. Christ's justice, purity, health, and liberty reverberate through the universe and I, by a similar process of contagion, can magically appropriate his reality for myself.

Christ's function is that of a *mediator*. He stands *between* God and human beings, where the lines of inflexible causality intersect. He receives what God has to give humanity, and he offers to God what humanity has to offer him. Hence he offers humanity what God could not offer it: grace, love, and pardon. But notice that grace, love, and pardon do not abolish a universe rigidly structured in terms of cause and effect. Law and order remain as fundamental realities. This scenario will persist at every moment as the universe of Right-Doctrine Protestantism unfolds before our eyes. Law is the first and last word. Grace is a word uttered after it. Grace is the penultimate word because the function of grace is to ensure the triumph of the law.

Nor does it suffice to say who Jesus Christ was and what he did. There is the important question of appropriation. By what mechanisms do the *benefits* of his work, performed *then and there* (*illic et tunc*), become my property *here and now* (*hic et nunc*)? The cosmic drama has already been played out. What we need to know is how human beings, until now immersed in guilt, come to share mystically in another reality.

The Protestant response is that this magical transition takes place through an act of faith. Faith is the emotional act of *accepting Christ in one's heart*. It is not a process of thinking or doing, but a feeling. It is a subjective emotional condition in the face of the symbol, Jesus Christ. And what characterizes this feeling is a surrender, a letting go of one's own destiny. To use Schleiermacher's term, it is a feeling of absolute dependence on Jesus Christ: "The common element in all howsoever diverse expressions of piety, by which these are conjointly distinguished from all other feelings, or, in other words, the self-identical essence of piety is this—the consciousness of being absolutely dependent, or, which is the same thing, of being in relation with God" (Schleiermacher a: 12). We see here a confirmation of William James's assertion: "The act of self-surrender has been and always must be regarded as the vital turning-point of the religious life . . ." (James: 172).

Conclusions

In this chapter I have tried to describe the process of conversion. First I considered it in general terms, then I examined its physiognomy in the Protestant context, with particular reference to Brazilian Protestantism of the RDP sort. The emotional, confessional language of the new convert was distinguished from the logical and metaphysical articulations used by the Church to point up the objective foundation for the convert's subjective experience. I feel it is important to use the representations of the participants in the situation under study here, since it is through their representations that their world is constructed. Now I would like to offer some final observations and draw some conclusions about conversion in the context of Brazilian RDP.

Reinterpreting Rather Than Transforming the World

In conversion a magical transformation takes place, as the emotional change in the convert attests. But how and in what sense? Externally everything seems to be just as before. The poor remain poor, the sick remain sick, and the old remain old. From the viewpoint of the convert, however, those things do not matter. Everything external—the body, society, history—is accidental surface which does not reveal the real. The real is the great cosmic transformation effected in Christ, and it is grasped only through an act of subjective emotion. When that happens, everything is transfigured. The human being comes to feel, and hence see, the world in a new way, as the words of the following hymn make clear:

> It matters little whether I dwell
> High in the mountains or at the seashore,
> In house or cave, comfortable or not.
> It is always heaven
> With Christ in me [HE, n. 328].

The problem is not to transform reality because it has already been transformed, reconciled, and made new in Christ. What we have to do is transform our way of feeling and perceiving it. Thus we could formulate the viewpoint of this sort of Protestantism as a reversal of Marx's eleventh thesis on Feuerbach: "Human beings have tried in various ways to transform the world; the point is not to transform the world but to reinterpret it."

Conversion is the initial step in this process of reinterpretation. When Protestants of this persuasion say that there is an affinity between the spirit of Protestantism and that of democracy, progress, and modernity, they do not mean that the latter goals are the specific ones they propose to tackle. They simply mean that democracy, progress, and modernity are natural, secondary by-products of conversion to Christ.

The Mythological Character of Interpretation

I want to point out that the explanations offered by the Brazilian Protestants under discussion here are mythological in nature. By "mythological" I do not mean "false." I am using the term in the sense which anthropology applies to myths. In other words, there is a radical discontinuity between the categories used to explain things by these Protestants on the one hand, and those that have been adopted by modern science on the other. Science tends to use mechanical and functional explanations that can be translated into the language of mathematics. Its objective is to eliminate the emotions both from the process of cognition and from the object of knowledge itself. The logic of reality is not identical with the logic of our psychic processes. By contrast, mythical explanations contemplate reality in a sympathetic way, seeing an emotional causality in it. There seems to be no way of harmonizing the two different perspectives.

Let's go a step further. I have indicated in this chapter that the aim of preaching, which is designed to produce conversion, is to give names to the emotions that are concretely experienced as various forms of anxiety. Psychological and sociological explanations are ruled out; they are merely symptoms of an ontological condition. Thus anxiety cannot be explained in terms of neurosis, maladjustment, anomie, culture shock, etc. The use of such categories would rob anxiety of its ontological dimension. Again it would seem that the explanatory categories of our Protestantism and those of science are mutually exclusive. But there is a problem which must be solved, and which I shall try to solve in the next chapter: How is it that a large number of scientists can profess the Protestant faith while still engaging in the practice of science?

The Identicalness of the Protestant and Catholic Problematic

In Brazil the effort of the Protestant Church to win converts implies that there is to be a conversion *from* Catholicism *to* Protestantism. The sort of Protestantism under discussion here maintains that there is a radical discontinuity between its worldview and that of the Catholic Church. This presupposition underlies a long history of polemics which is part of the story of Protestantism in Brazil. Protestantism and Catholicism are viewed as two opposite poles, as salvation and perdition respectively.

If my analysis is correct, we must inevitably conclude that this alleged opposition is nonexistent. For the problem of salvation as described above is completely identical with the fundamental problem around which the Catholic faith is structured. We are forced to agree with Troeltsch:

> The point of primary importance is that, historically and theologically regarded, Protestantism—especially at the outset in Luther's reform of the Church—was, in the first place, simply a *modification* of Catholicism, in which *the Catholic formulation of the problems was retained*, while a different answer was given to them [Troeltsch a: 59; my italics].

Catholics and Protestants agree in their anthropology. Both live within the same horizon, inhabit the same universe of meaning.

How, then, can we explain or justify the conflict and polemics? The differences are not to be found in the foundations and structure of their universe. They are to be found in the answers which the two groups give to the same basic problem, both sides agreeing that it is the basic problem. Like two opposing chess players, they can argue and fight only because they are playing the same game, because both sides agree on the basic rules underlying their contest with each other.

Conversion and Suffering

Our analysis has led us to the conclusion that the experience of conversion is a response to a crisis situation. It resolves an emotional impasse.

That is why the Church grows more rapidly in areas where social processes are causing suffering, particularly from anomie and the collapse of meaning-structures. The authors of *Latin American Church Growth* set out to investigate such areas. They suggested that such areas should be given top priority by the Churches, that efforts to build up church life should be concentrated in them. James Goff reviewed the book in question, and I want to quote a section of his review because it is pertinent to the point I want to make here:

> The authors allude to the "theory of growth" which their book deals with (p. 176). It is not easy to say exactly what this theory is. It seems to be that "areas with high potential" should be sought out and explored. In general they are areas where industrial expansion is taking place. More specifically, they are areas where people are suffering—especially migrants from rural areas to urban areas. These people are more "winnable" [i.e., to Christ] than others. In other words, the Church can grow when people are faced with difficulties. The period during which the Evangelical Churches can grow, due to migration, is short. Specific cases of urban growth for Churches in Mexico City, Bogotá, and Belo Horizonte indicate that a rural migrant takes a decade or two to adjust to the new situation. The migrant is responsive during that period of adjustment. We must act quickly if we want to act effectively.[5]

You see, I am not saying anything that is news to Protestants. There is no conversion without crisis, no conversion without suffering. Conversion is a process whereby one assimilates suffering to a new meaning-structure and thus makes it meaningful.

This fact raises a question of a theological nature. By that I mean that we face a problem which can and should be pondered from within the context and framework of faith itself. Indeed it might seem to be a senseless question to anyone standing outside the circle of faith.

Isn't it curious that Christ cannot be preached to people who feel secure and happy, to people who feel that life is worth living, to people who are not going through a crisis? Isn't it odd that Christ can only be proclaimed and made meaningful in morbid situations where people are infected with existential anxiety, guilt feelings, and terror of death? What really is the task of the evangelist? His or her task is to give theological names to a crisis that could well be psychosocial in origin. The evangelist seeks to activate a crisis which might not have been sensed before, so that then, and only then, he or she can proclaim that "Christ is the answer."

Now if that is the case, we are forced to conclude that the world makes room for Christ only when it feels ill, when it has come down with some sickness. Is there some theological reason why dread of death and guilt are the privileged sacraments of salvation? To put it another way, the experience of conversion presupposes that the *meeting-point* between God and the world is suffering and anguish—the world's state of pain and sickness. *When there is health and happiness, language about God loses its meaningfulness.* Isn't there a sadomasochistic vision of reality buried underneath such presuppositions?

Suffering is transformed into a blessing, because it provides an opportunity for the sinner to encounter Christ. The greater the suffering, the greater the opportunities for evangelization! Doesn't that suggest that the Church is being put in the curious position of praying for more human suffering so that human hearts will be more receptive to its message? That was a question which Dietrich Bonhoeffer posed to the Church. As far as I can tell, it was never even given consideration. What do the apologists for the Christian faith, the bearers of the "good news," really do?

> They demonstrate to secure, content, happy mankind that it is really unhappy and desperate, and merely unwilling to realize that it is in severe straits it knows nothing at all about, from which only they can rescue it. Wherever there is health, strength, security, simplicity, they spy luscious fruit to gnaw at or to lay their pernicious eggs in. They make it their object first of all to drive men to inward despair, and then it is all theirs [Bonhoeffer: 196].[6]

This relationship between suffering and conversion has one consequence that I want to bring out.

Conversion is a *solution* to a painful problem. One starts from conversion to structure a world whose function is to *prevent* the reappearance of the initial experience of anxiety. The aim is the exorcism of terror. Now if the conversion has proved adequate in exorcising this terror, consciousness will be firmly glued to that conversion-experience and its attendant cognitive worldview. That is why arguments won't work at this level. You may offer all sorts of evidence—logical, scientific, or whatever—to call the convert's basic experience into question. It will be immediately and flatly rejected by the convert. Only the reasons of the heart can function here. The experience of conversion was enough to solve the existential problem, therefore it must be true. Even the slightest suggestion of doubt poses a threat: i.e., that consciousness may fall back into its original state of anxiety.

This mechanism is not specific to Protestantism, RDP, or religion. *Resistance* to criticism of our meaning-structures is a constant in human behavior. Freud tells us that it is part and parcel of the behavior of the psychoanalytic patient, even when he or she is spending time and money on a cure. The patient resists the cure. Why? Because the cure calls for a transformation in his or her neurotic ways of structuring reality, and that is precisely what the patient cannot permit. The neurosis may indeed cause many problems for the patient. But it persists because in some way it is *functional and suitable* in resolving some emotional problem. Underlying the neurosis is a painful experience that must be forgotten, that must not be allowed to return to consciousness. All efforts to shake the mechanisms which the ego has established to achieve this purpose will be met by fierce resistance. In short, *constructions of reality which are a response to a painful experience tend to put up fierce resistance to anything that may threaten them with collapse.*

I should point out that this same mechanism has also been noticed by people using the behaviorist approach. Borger and Seaborne describe a simple experiment which will illustrate the point. Mouse A is in a cage with a lever which produces a shock when pressed. Mouse B is in another cage where the pressing of a lever gives food. Once mouse A learns the connection between the lever and the shock, it will not press the lever any more. Its behavior is characterized by *avoidance* of the painful experience. Mouse B behaves quite differently. Whenever it is hungry, it will press the lever. Now suppose we switch their situations, so that mouse B gets a shock when it presses the lever while mouse A gets food. What will happen? Mouse B will press its lever and discover that something has changed. After repeating the experience a few times, it will have learned something new; it will have reorganized its experience. What happens with mouse A? Nothing. Its fear, based on its initial experience, prompts it to continue to avoid the lever. Fear has crystallized and solidified its initial experience. It is unable to reorganize itself. Because of its fear it is unable to discover that the pressing of the lever now produces food instead of a shock:

> The interesting and important feature of the situation is that once avoidance behavior has become established, it tends to continue for comparatively long periods, apparently without reinforcement. . . . The interesting feature of avoidance behavior would seem to be that it insulates the learner from exposure to highly relevant aspects of the environment [Borger and Seaborne: 42].

Conversion is a response to a painful experience. Hence the incipient organization of experience involved in conversion tends to construct mechanisms that will prevent any restructuring of that experience. Otherwise there is always the danger that the initial painful experience will return. At the level of religious discourse, then, the new organization of experience is interpreted to be *absolute*. It is absolutely true, absolutely final, absolutely beyond doubt. One of the proofs of conversion is the *certainty* that surrounds it. The convert "is certain of his or her salvation." Not to have certainty, to doubt, is to confess that the crisis has not yet been resolved.

The actual experience of salvation demands that the universe be known in an absolute and final way. There is no room for doubt and critical questioning. Here, then, we have the bedrock emotional foundations for the dogmatism that will characterize the universe constructed by Right-Doctrine Protestantism.

THREE

A PROTESTANT CONSTRUCTION OF REALITY

Emotion and Rationality

New converts talk very differently from those who underwent conversion a long time ago. The former are on the threshold of a universe, but they have not yet gone inside. The latter dwell in that universe and know it in a familiar way. New converts talk about almost nothing but their inner emotional change. They still don't know the rules which structure the world they are going to enter. The old-timers have already learned the rules. They have been initiated into the world of RDP, and they know how it is constructed.

Two distinct and discontinuous discourses. That of the new converts is emotional, expressive, confessional; it reveals what goes on in their souls. The discourse of the old-timers expresses knowledge, articulates a world-view, reveals a structured rationality. What is the relationship between the two discourses? How do we get from the emotion of the new convert to the rationality of the old-timer?

At first glance everything might seem to suggest that we are dealing with two incommensurable worlds. Emotion would seem to be identified with the irrational, and rationality would seem, of necessity, to be unemotional. In his *Anthropologie* (1798), Kant clearly seemed to espouse the view that emotions are irrational and false, if not dangerous. Once reason entered the picture, the voice of emotion would shut up:

> Passions are cancers for pure practical reason. . . . It is folly . . . that strictly contradicts reason even in its formal principle. Therefore the passions are not only . . . *unfortunate* moods that are pregnant with many evils, but also, without exception, wicked . . . not only *pragmatically* pernicious but also *morally* reprehensible [Kaufmann a: 34–35].

There is a very different interpretation of the relationship between the emotions and reason. Nietzsche expressed it briefly and pointedly, as he was wont to do, in *Thus Spoke Zarathustra:*

47

The body is a great reason, a plurality with one sense, a war and a peace, a herd and a shepherd. An instrument of your body is also your little reason, my brother, which you call "spirit"—a little instrument and toy of your great reason [Kaufmann b: 146].

The opposition disappears. Beyond any apparent conflict lies a functional, instrumental relationship. The articulations of logic are products of vital needs. We find ourselves close to Freud's view: "Do you suppose that human thought has no practical motives, that it is simply the expression of a disinterested curiosity? That is surely very improbable" (Freud b: 22). Reasoning is rationalization. It is a construction process whereby we dress our dreams and wishes in the garments of logical plausibility. As Dewey noted:

If we are willing to take the word dreams with a certain liberality, it is hardly too much to say that man, save in his occasional times of actual work and struggle, lives in a world of dreams, rather than of facts, and a world of dreams that is organized about desires whose success or frustration form its stuff [Dewey: 7].

This is the center from which knowledge arises: "Knowledge is not something separate and self-sufficing, but is involved in the process by which life is sustained and evolved" (Dewey: 87). We are back at Anselm's old formula: *fides quaerens intellectum*, "faith seeking understanding." Wherever we find faith, there we will find a search for intelligibility. By the same token, wherever we find reasoning, there we will find an emotional experience on which such rationality is grounded.

The relationship between emotion and reason cannot be viewed as one of opposition. Is the validity of such a statement to be confined to the realm of so-called common sense? Louis Wirth answers that "without valuations we have no interest, or sense of relevance or of significance, and, consequently no object" (Myrdal: 51). I must agree with Werner Stark when he writes: "Value-free thinking may be an ideal, but it is certainly nowhere a reality" (Stark: 71). All rationality, be it religious or scientific, is grounded in prerational, emotional experiences. We are led back to Durkheim's conclusion: "As we have progressed, we have established the fact that the fundamental categories of thought, and consequently of science, are of religious origin" (Durkheim a: 418).

The Ambivalence of Rationality

I have suggested that rationality is a function of the emotions, that the relationship between the emotional discourse of the new convert and the cognitive discourse of the religious community cannot be one of opposition. That does not mean, however, that the community's rational discourse is the convert's emotional discourse articulated with clarity. Recall what Rudolf

Otto said: religious rationality *is not* an expression of a fundamental experience, but rather a masking of that experience. The primordial experience contains an element of menace that has to be forgotten. So my conclusion is: the function of religious rationality is to *resolve* a problem posed by experience and lived out emotionally, and the solution requires that the basic, initial experience be obscured and forgotten.

This mechanism is not restricted exclusively to religion. It is a characteristic of language itself, which both reveals and hides. Along with what is spoken clearly we have the white spaces and the silences that attest to what is not supposed to be uttered. Language simultaneously lets me see and blinds me. Why?

Rationality is a process of assimilation. It takes the multiplicity of data coming from outside and tries to "make it similar" to itself. After all, what do we mean when we say that we *understand* something? We mean that we have succeeded in subjecting it to the logical criteria governing the reasoning process at our disposal. Each piece of information is like a brick that must be fitted properly into the architectonic project of reason.

There is no guarantee that everything can be assimilated, but reason has totalizing and totalitarian pretensions. Its basic creed is that the real is rational, that all the potential objects of cognition can be assimilated to it. Indeed it is the assumption that an object can be assimilated to reason that gives the object its status as a reality. Anything that cannot be assimilated is reduced to the status of irrelevant, meaningless material. For if reason took into consideration such refractory material, then the structures of reason itself would be shown to be inadequate, partial, and unilateral, and they would lose their epistemological status.

So rationality creates a zone of clarity and knowledge, a zone where it can explain and comprehend. But at the same time there is fashioned a zone of obscurity and ignorance. Notice that the latter zone is not to be viewed as the sum total of objects *as yet unknown*—as if to suggest that reason had not yet had the time to take them into consideration. No, this zone is the complex of objects which *ought not be known* because knowledge of them is dangerous; it could subvert the already established rationality. So we are talking about a necessary, deliberate, intentional ignorance, an ignorance demanded by the very same rationality which requires and makes possible knowledge in other areas. From an emotional standpoint it is frequently more functional not to know than to know. So all rationality requires the elimination of data that cannot be assimilated, that would tend to undermine the world constructed by it. Ignorance has its place:

> Ignorance, like knowledge, is purposefully directed. An emotional load of valuation conflicts presses for rationalization, creating blindness at some spots, stimulating an urge for knowledge at others [Myrdal: 29].

What sinister aspect in the emotional experience of conversion is RDP rationality trying to exorcise? I am going to give my basic response right here, so that my readers will have some idea of where I am going. *In the basic experience of conversion there is a combination of faith and doubt. Doubt is the terror that has to be forgotten. This is accomplished by establishing a line of rationality which makes claims to absolute knowledge. When that is done, faith is transformed into dogma.*

Faith and Doubt

In the previous chapter I suggested that the conversion experience is devoid of knowledge. Only the community is aware of the "tacit conventions" which constitute the theoretical horizon of the convert's experience.

What do the new converts know? They say that they have surrendered their heart to Christ. But who is Christ? They cannot describe him. Christ is the symbol of the feelings of peace and joy that now possess them. The immediate data of their experience are their feelings. At this point feelings constitute the essence of their religious experience, so I agree with Schleiermacher's insistence that the essence of religion is a simple *feeling*, not some form of thinking or doing (Schleiermacher b: 26–118). The new converts are not aware of a divine object outside them, but they are aware of the divine character of their own feelings. These divine feelings are the object of their experience. At this point religion is almost no theology and almost all anthropology.

What do I mean when I say that feelings are the object of religion in the initial, foundational experience? I am simply paraphrasing Kierkegaard's famous dictum: "Truth is subjectivity" (Kierkegaard a: 169). And what does that mean? Kierkegaard answers us with a parable:

If one who lives in the midst of Christendom goes up to the house of God, the house of the true God, with the true conception of God in his knowledge, and prays, but prays in a false spirit; and one who lives in an idolatrous community prays with the entire passion of the infinite, although his eyes rest upon the image of an idol; where is there most truth? The one prays in truth to God though he worships an idol; the other prays falsely to the true God, and hence worships in fact an idol [Kierkegaard a: 179–80].

What matters is not the infiniteness of the object, but the infiniteness of the passion. If the passion is not infinite, no matter what the object may be, then the human being will not feel the divine. But if the passion is infinite, then the human being will feel the divine even if the representation of its object is not infinite:

It is the passion of the infinite that is the decisive factor and not its content, for its content is precisely itself. In this manner subjectivity and the subjective "how" constitute the truth [Kierkegaard a: 181].

Faith is not knowledge of something. Suppose someone challenged Kierkegaard's view with the following question: Does that mean that in faith consciousness is not directed to any object, is not intentional consciousness? Kierkegaard would say that the problem is that there exists no empirically given object which corresponds to the infiniteness of subjective passion. Faith, as an infinite passion, cannot be explained as the effect of any historical cause because then the effect would be greater than the cause: "Is an historical point of departure possible for an eternal consciousness; how can such a point of departure have any other than a mere historical interest . . .?" (Kierkegaard a: 18).

History offers me nothing but objective uncertainties, whereas in faith consciousness finds itself with an infinite passion. Faith, then, cannot be explained *as a result of* anything. It must be described as sheer gratuitousness, as something existing *in spite of*. In the experience of faith, a human being is not dominated by an object because there are no mediations between the finiteness of objects and the infiniteness of the passion. This faith, in the words of Paul Tillich, "has no special content; it is simply faith, undirected, absolute" [Tillich a: 176]. It is "ultimate concern."

So we can see the paradoxical situation of new converts. What guarantees of the validity of their experience do they have? Only the emotions which dominate them. If they emerge from their emotional ecstasy for a moment to think about their experience, they find that their subjective certainty is not grounded on any tangible objective evidence. The new convert can say: "I feel saved." He or she thus confesses personal emotions. But he or she has no logical way to deduce reality from those emotions. The convert cannot conclude: "Therefore, I am saved."

Radically considered, the experience of faith is revealed to be the twin sister of doubt. Please note: I am not suggesting at all that faith is lacking something, that it is incomplete because the shadow of doubt lies over it. I am saying something very different—namely, that faith and doubt go together. Doubt is one of the dimensions of faith because there is an impassable gap between the intensity of the subjective passion and the perduring uncertainty of the objective experience:

When one man investigates objectively the problem of immortality, and another embraces an uncertainty with the passion of the infinite: where is there more truth, and who has the greater certainty? . . . Let us consider Socrates. Nowadays everyone dabbles in a few proofs; some have several such proofs, others fewer. But Socrates! He puts the question objectively in a problematic manner: *if* there is an immortality. He must therefore be accounted a doubter in comparison with one of our modern thinkers with the three proofs? By no means. On this "if" he risks his entire life [Kierkegaard a: 180].

There is a real incompatibility between objective certainty and the passion of faith: "In the case of a mathematical proposition the objectivity is given, but for this reason the truth of such a proposition is also an indifferent truth" (Kierkegaard a: 182). Camus returns to a discussion of the same question in *The Myth of Sisyphus:*

> I have never seen anyone die for the ontological argument. Galileo, who held a scientific truth of great importance, abjured it with the greatest ease as soon as it endangered his life. In a certain sense, he did right. That truth was not worth the stake. Whether the earth or the sun revolves around the other is a matter of professional indifference. . . . On the other hand, I see many people die because they judge that life is not worth living. I see others paradoxically getting killed for the ideas or illusions that give them a reason for living [Camus: 3–4].

Everything objectively true remains in the realm of the finite, and "what is finite to the understanding is nothing to the heart" (Feuerbach: 6).

Socrates should be regarded as someone who doubts. How else could we account for the *if* which he places before immortality? This *if* is a sign of the objective uncertainty. Immortality cannot be grasped as an object of knowledge. And yet uncertainty and doubt are embraced in a passionate risk.

> Thus the subject merely has, objectively, the uncertainty. . . . The truth is precisely the venture which chooses an objective uncertainty with the passion of the infinite. . . Without risk there is no faith. Faith is precisely the contradiction between the infinite passion of the individual's inwardness and the objective uncertainty [Kierkegaard 182].

As Ricoeur suggests, it is necessary that we move beyond the circle of endless hermeneutic approximations, which place us on the level of simple comparisons. And this is done by means of a *wager* (Ricoeur 355). The assertion of faith, therefore, is not "I know that" but rather "I wager that".

When pondered radically, the faith-experience lays down a prohibition. It prohibits its infinite passion from being crystallized verbally as an object of knowledge. Language can only denote the objects of experience univocally.

Doubt and the Ban of Dogma

And all the objects of experience share in objective uncertainty, which is incommensurable with the infinite passion of subjectivity. Thus the loftiest symbol created by religion, God, cannot refer to an object of knowledge, to something which can be assimilated by reason. As Tersteegen observed: "A God comprehended is no God" (Otto: 25).

The language of faith is a language of symbols, not a language of signs. Signs point directly and univocally to the objects to which they refer; the communication is direct. Symbols never communicate directly because what is to be communicated by them transcends rationality which is normative within the limits of the experience. "Objective thinking," notes Kierkegaard, "is wholly indifferent to subjectivity, and hence also to inwardness and appropriation; its mode of communication is therefore direct" (Kierkegaard a: 70). Where subjectivity and appropriation are of central importance, there the process of communication is doubly reflected, indeed a work of art:

> Ordinary communication, like objective thinking in general, has no secrets; only a doubly reflected subjective thinking has them. That is to say, the entire essential content of subjective thought is essentially secret, because it cannot be directly communicated. This is the meaning of the secrecy [Kierkegaard a: 73].

How are we to crystallize truth in language? How are we to reduce subjective experience to words? Does this mean that the subjective passion is condemned to silence, to muteness? By no means. It speaks. Its words spring up from its experience. It is a confession. But the experience lies beyond its verbal expression. We can try to describe the beauty of one of Mozart's sonatas by means of words. This description emerges out of an experience of beauty. But nobody would be foolish enough to think that those who understood the description have also grasped, at the same time, the esthetic experience which is confessed. Confession expresses and reveals an experience. But those who confess know the infinite gap which there is between their feeling and their talking. Faith, thus, forbids the crystallization of an absolute language. Since the experience of faith cannot be expressed directly, all forms of language are inadequate. In other words: faith rules out dogma.

The Temptation of Absolute Knowledge

It seems to me that this conclusion is valid for every level of human cognition. If knowledge is built upon emotion, if it is the rationalization of a *subject's way of relating to an object*, then even scientific knowledge cannot be absolute. As Popper put it:

> *We do not know: we can only guess.* And our guesses are guided by the unscientific, the metaphysical (though biologically explicable) faith in laws, in regularities which we can uncover-discover [Popper: 278].

Yet the transformation of guess into certainty, of risk into absolute knowledge, of faith into dogma, is one of the constants of human experience. Why? In theory it is not difficult to acknowledge the relativism of all our constructions. For one to understand this fact it suffices to go through history and all the divergent cultures which have existed. Practically, however, things are different. We need *one* stable structure to live in. We could not organize our behavior if we did not assume that our guesses are the truth. A stable world is an emotional, psychic need we have, and this emotional need is at the root of our tendency to dogmatism.

But what happens in the transition from faith to dogma? The world solidifies, we ourselves solidify, and experience crystallizes. The foundations are laid for authoritarian behavior. Authoritarianism is the result of an emotional obsession that requires that risks be transformed into absolute knowledge. In a state of risk, reality remains beyond our control. In a state of absolute knowledge, we affirm that we have achieved intellectual dominance over the real.

It is worth noting that the biblical myth of the fall deals precisely with this issue. The scriptural accounts indicate that the essence of the temptation is the desire to transcend the limits of existence. Those limits confine us within the provisional circle of uncertainties, and they become palpable in the permanent possibility of dying. The serpent says:

> Of course you will not die. God knows that as soon as you eat it, your eyes will be opened, and you will be like God, knowing good and evil [Gen. 3:4–5].

Here is Ricoeur's comment on the scene:

> A "desire" has sprung up, the desire for infinity; but that infinity is not the infinity of reason and happiness . . . it is the infinity of desire itself. It is the desire of desire, taking possession of knowing, of willing, of doing, and of being. . . . The soul of the serpent's question is the "evil infinite," which simultaneously perverts the meaning of the limit by which freedom was oriented and the meaning of the finiteness of the freedom thus oriented by the limit [Ricoeur b: 253].

What is being sought? A knowledge which renders faith unnecessary, a knowledge in which there is no doubt or risk. In the case of faith, truth is appropriated at the risk of uncertainty. Hence absolutes are prohibited. The temptation offers another course: the magical elimination of doubt by absolutizing a segment of the finite. The human being's mode of existence vis-à-vis life ceases to be an expression of *gratuitousness*; it becomes the consequence of an absolute foundation. In a posture of faith, passion is affirmed as the foundational experience. Knowledge follows as a precarious vision and doubt, and that situation is a permanent one. When one succumbs to the temptation, however, absolute knowledge is laid down as the point of departure; existence is built on that. The tension is eliminated, which is gratifying from a psychological point of view. But the cost is the solidification of the real, the hardening of experience, dogmatism, and authoritarianism.

Knowledge thus achieved is transformed into an *idol*. Idols are products of human creativity which eventually become the masters of their creators. Sociology describes this process as *reification* and *alienation*. Human beings produce something, their product becomes autonomous, and then they submit to this product as if it were independent of them and superior to them. The product assumes the function of a god, an absolute. The quest for absolute knowledge, impelled by an obsession with certainty, inevitably tends to produce idols.

In my opinion, this is the essence of dogmatism: it denies the provisional character of knowledge, the permanent lack of fit between language and reality. As Hegel put it in *The Phenomenology of Spirit* (n. 40):

> *Dogmatism* as a way of thinking, whether in ordinary knowing or in the study of philosophy, is nothing else but the opinion that the True consists in a proposition which is a fixed result, or which is immediately known [Hegel a: 23].

When I claim to have the truth, what happens? I have the truth; my thinking duplicates the real. In the future the real will not be able to reveal itself as different from the way I see it now. My vision of the real in the form of absolute knowledge demands that all possible experiences confirm it. My absolute knowledge *prohibits* the real from surprising me, from revealing itself differently. Experience is not the criterion of my thinking; my thinking is the criterion of any and all possible experiences. My language is not subordinate to an unforeseeable, mysterious reality; reality must subordinate itself to my language.

Faith Seeking Absolute Knowledge

I have suggested that religious rationality is essentially ambiguous. It is built upon a basic emotional experience, yet one of its functions is to obscure the terror contained in that experience. Our problem is to find out how this process takes place in RDP. What does the latter do with faith insofar as it entails doubt and risk? Does RDP elaborate its universe as a precarious vision or as absolute knowledge? Is it open to experience, or does it subordinate experience to its own certitudes?

It is very important for Protestants to be *certain* of salvation.[7] Candidates for baptism are frequently asked: "Are you *certain* of your salvation?" The question is not an accidental one. It reveals the fundamental motif of RDP rationality, the aim of which is to establish certitudes. RDP rationality can be described as *faith seeking certainty*. It is a faith that is terrified by the doubt which attends it. Driven to desperation by its status as guesswork, this faith devotes itself to the exorcism of all uncertainty.

Protestants are not simply people who have "accepted Christ in their hearts." It is not possible to verify the feelings which live within the soul. Feelings are prisoners of subjectivity. Confessional language expresses these feelings, and indeed it is their only evidence. But there is no guarantee that this confessional language is true; it is always possible to lie. The Church, then, cannot accept the confession of new converts as proof of conversion. Moreover, confessional language is not theological; it is merely anthropological. It points to the soul, but it articulates neither the soul's knowledge nor knowledge of objective reality. New converts as yet "do not know what they believe in."

By contrast, the community does know what the convert believes in without knowing. So right after the conversion experience, there comes a process of initiating the new convert into the correct way of talking. The aim is not expression but impression, not extrojection but introjection. The convert's consciousness can maintain its feelings, but it must realize that those feelings are devoid of cognitive status. It must now learn to express correctly the knowledge that goes with its feelings. The ability to do that signals that the new convert is ready to join the Church, that he or she has introjected the crystallized knowledge of the community. This knowledge is the visible sign of invisible grace.

The new believer is unable to perceive that there is a hidden and absolute knowledge in his experience. For him, feelings are more than enough. "I feel that I have been saved"—what other authority is needed? One has the evidences of the heart. These evidences, however, bring always within themselves an element of risk and uncertainty. The PRD, in its concern for truth, cannot, therefore, take these emotions as the foundation of faith. The experience of conversion, thus, must lose its condition of origin, and must be incorporated into an absolute, final, propositional, dogmatic knowledge.

The Bible: The Words of God

The RDP theory of knowledge begins with a definition of what the Bible is. This is a crucial question. Just for the sake of clarity I will offer an alternative answer, different from the one of RDP.

And how is this result achieved?

In our case, one proceeds by denying to the original emotional experience any cognitive significance. And this is obtained by means of a reversal: the new convert "learns" that his or her experience, far from being the origin of knowledge, is rather based on an absolute knowledge which antecedes it. And this is done by means of the doctrine of the divine origin and character of the Scriptures. Instead of ascending from earth to heaven, our Protestant world descends from heaven to the earth.

One could view the Bible as a book of confessions. Back in the distant past certain men and women had an experience of the divine. It was a vivid, ineffable experience. The intensity of their infinite subjective passion—be it guilt, love, or hope—gave rise to words, to a book of testimony and witness. The words point to a vivid experience in life which can only be *hinted at*; but they are not identical with that experience. Hence the Bible is a book of symbols, not a book of signs. The bare facticity of events, persons, places, and dates is not what matters; the facts in themselves are meaningless. What matters is the subjective *how* that is expressed in the words, that wells up from the realm of lived experience which gave birth to the text, but which the text itself cannot contain.

According to this view, then, the Scriptures do not contain a set of propositions that are true in and of themselves, that can be affirmed as one might affirm a theorem of mathematics. Their mode of communication is indirect. A person who stops with the text cannot get to where the text itself is pointing. In reading the text one must be guided by a very specific intention: not to codify truths, but to re-enact "in sympathetic imagination" (Ricoeur b: 9) the feelings which lie beneath the words but are buried too deep to find expression in them.

In that case, however, the text is not the authority. The authority which constitutes the text is the living experience from which the text springs. That experience was truth at the moment the text came into being. Experience precedes talk. The text is a footnote to existence. Who speaks in the text? Human beings. About what? About their experience with God. But if experience rather than the text is the authority, why do I turn to the text? Isn't my own experience enough? I turn to the text because the experiences confessed in it are closely related to my own experiences; the two horizons are interwoven. The confessions of those human beings in the distant past become my own voice; they help me to understand my own life. Personal biography is illuminated by history.

This possible view of the Bible may help us to better understand and appreciate RDP's answer to the question: What is the Bible? According to RDP, the Bible is not confession or testimony or the voice of human beings. The Bible is the Word of God. It would be more correct to say that it is "the words of God," since *all* the things contained in the Bible are the words of God himself. The text is not a revelation of some human experience that has to be recaptured. It does not point to any vital experience. The text contains words which welled out of eternity and were written down in time. God spoke in a complete and final way. Does God still speak today? Yes, but his speech today does not add to, or subtract from, what he said once and for all in the distant past. God's talking today is the repetition of a recording made thousands of years ago. All sorts of recombinations are possible, of course. What is not possible is that his talking today might contradict, add to, or subtract from, what he said in the past.

This view dislodges the conversion experience from its place as the originating experience, subordinating it to the authority of a normative, absolute discourse.

Once one accepts the definition of the Bible as the Word of God, life comes to be governed by a fixed text. The text becomes the norm governing my perception, willing, thinking, and action. What I feel and think is subordinated to what is written down. The heart is forced to renounce confidence in itself, to submit to a verbal norm that is external, alien, and imposed by the community. The proper sequence is not lived experience and then knowledge, but rather absolute knowledge and then experience. Consider the Westminster Confession of Faith, which is said to present the correct system of doctrines taught in the Bible. It begins with a chapter entitled "Of the Holy Scripture." That is the absolute starting point from which everything else follows. Conversion will be treated only in Chapter X. Here is the very first article in the Westminster Confession of Faith:

> Although the light of nature and the works of creation and providence do so far manifest the goodness, wisdom, and power of God as to leave men inexcusable, yet they are not sufficient to give that knowledge of God and of his will which is necessary unto salvation; therefore it pleased the Lord, at sundry times, and in divers manners, to reveal himself, and to declare that his will unto his Church; and afterwards, for the better preserving and propagating of the truth, and for the more sure establishment and comfort of the Church against the corruption of the flesh, and the malice of Satan and of the world, to commit the same wholly unto writing: which maketh the Holy Scripture to be most necessary, those former ways of God's revealing his will unto his people being now ceased [LC, n. 6.001].

It is not always safe or correct to cite an official theological declaration as evidence when one is trying to analyze how a community really thinks. Theology often expresses the thinking of the elite and has little connection with the religious categories of the average believer. But the attitude toward the Bible is a significant exception to this principle. Perhaps there is no point on which the thinking of the average believer more faithfully duplicates the official theological view. We would do well, then, to analyze the passage cited above.

The core of the text, around which the whole argument is structured, is "that knowledge of God and of his will which is necessary unto salvation." Salvation is the result of knowledge. And notice that the function of experience is a purely negative one. Nature and the works of creation and providence are accessible to all human beings, and they do "manifest" the goodness, wisdom, and power of God. They have a revelatory function. But the knowledge derived from them cannot save human beings; it merely serves to condemn them. The function of such natural knowledge is to render human beings "inexcusable." Instead of leading them to heaven, it hurls them into perdition. No human being can appear before the divine tribunal and allege ignorance. Thus natural knowledge safeguards divine justice but it does not protect the human beings who acquire it. That is the reason why God decided to reveal himself, to declare his will.

Above I pointed out how the Bible might be interpreted as a book of confession and witness in which human beings tried to express their experience of the divine in words. The communication in that case would be mediated, indirect, and symbolic. In this case, however, it is God himself who declares his will. There is a direct, univocal relationship between a word and its meaning; signs have replaced symbols. And it is God himself who saw to it that it all was written down, thereby establishing a direct relationship between the written word and the will of God. The Bible is established as an absolute finite.

Knowing God means knowing the written word of the text. Scripture is now indispensable because the "former ways of God's revealing his will" have ceased. Before the scriptural canon was established, it was possible for human beings to invoke, personal experience with God; that is what the prophets did. But God has ceased to speak directly, so no one can appeal to experience as something revelatory. *All human experience is stripped of every vestige of authority and made subject to an absolute text.*

The Shorter Catechism spells out even more clearly what is meant by knowledge necessary for salvation:

> *Q. 2.* What rule hath God given to direct us how we may glorify and enjoy him?
> *A.* The Word of God which is contained in the Scriptures of the Old and New Testaments is the only rule to direct us how we may glorify and enjoy him [LC, n. 7.002].

Notice the big difference between viewing the text as an expression of feelings and lived experience on the one hand, and as a series of *rules* on the other. Rules for what? Rules of faith, rules in which I must believe. Faith is no longer viewed as an infinite passion that cannot be reduced to words; it has been turned into knowledge. Faith is now intellectual assent to a revealed proposition. It is also a rule of practice: behavior is subjected to a series of formulas which differentiate between what is commanded and what is prohibited.

The Elimination of Mediations

In order to establish the Bible as the authority and the absolutely certain starting point that resolves all trace of doubt, it is of crucial importance to eliminate all human mediations. If the Bible is a book of confessions and testimonies, if it contains the words of human beings about a primordial experience that lies beyond the text, how can we have any certainty? If the Bible is the product of a people and the embodiment of a culture, how can we avoid the relativism that characterizes all cultural productions? The Bible would then be a document deriving from Jewish religion and Christian piety, but how could we affirm that it is the truth? If the Bible is part of the web of history, wouldn't we be forced to admit that history, not the Scriptures, is the foundational experience? But history loses itself in the past, is accessible to us only through the countless interpretative mediations of those who wrote it and reflected on it afresh. Once again we would be confronted with a permanent state of doubt, and the truth would remain undetermined forever.

The sort of Protestantism under study here uses the doctrine of inspiration to abolish all human mediations in one fell swoop. It is God himself who determined "to commit the same wholly unto writing":

> Under the name of Holy Scripture, or the Word of God written, are now contained all the books of the Old and New Testaments . . . All which are given by inspiration of God, to be the rule of faith and life [LC, n. 6.002].

> The authority of the Holy Scripture, for which it ought to be believed and obeyed, dependeth not upon the testimony of any man or church, but wholly upon God (who is truth itself), the author thereof [LC, n. 6.004].

> [These books] being immediately inspired by God, and by his singular care and providence kept pure in all ages, and therefore authentical [LC, n. 6.008].

Suppose we were to ask a believer: Do you believe in the Bible because you believe in Jesus Christ, or do you believe in Jesus Christ because you believe in the Bible? If the order of experience were observed, the believer would have to answer: "I believe in Jesus Christ. That is my primordial experience which generates all the others. So I believe in the Bible because it is the text which speaks to me of Jesus Christ."

That is not the way it goes, however, with the Protestantism we are examining here. Every approach which begins with personal experience is blocked off. One starts with a dogmatic *a priori*: the Bible was written under divine inspiration. But one cannot rest content with saying it *was* written that way because that still leaves room for human mediations. After all, the text might have been corrupted and then there would be room for some doubt. So one must affirm that the text was also *kept pure* in all ages. Thus the whole text we have before us today contains the very words of God. The Bible is the voice of God.

A member of the Church asked the ecclesiastical authorities if one could regard the Letter to the Hebrews as anonymous. The question reveals an historical preoccupation: Who is the person behind the text? The answer given is very revealing. It shows that historical mediations are irrelevant in the eyes of RDP, since the authors are not really the authors:

> The fact is that there is no anonymous writing in the Bible, none without an author's name, because in the last analysis the whole Bible is the work of God himself [BP, 1 and July 15, 1963, p. 5].

The Scriptures are the *a priori of all knowledge;* for that very reason they can never be treated as an *object of knowledge.* The Bible is a miracle, a singular exception, the one and only document that came straight out of eternity and is not bound up with life. Its author does not dwell in space and time, so what he says has nothing to do with emotional and social condition-ings. The text is the absolute truth. This Protestant theory of inspiration renders hermeneutics superfluous and impossible.

The starting point for hermeneutics is the solidarity of the text with life. The meaning of the text is the life experience which it expresses. The text is not autonomous; it does not contain its own intelligibility. One must try to feel again, in one's imagination, the emotional state of the author, his inten-tions and aspirations. This is possible because we share one and the same life-situation, even though the author and I are separated by a vast expanse of space and time: "Historical understanding always presupposes a relation of the interpreter to the subject matter that is (directly or indirectly) expressed in the texts" (Bultmann: 293). If our existential experiences were qualitatively different, no comprehension would be possible; we would inhabit worlds that did not touch each other at all. But superficial differences are built upon similar life-structures, and that makes understanding possible.

The doctrine of inspiration demands that this solidarity be denied so that the absolute character of the text can be preserved. I cannot delve into this text as I might delve into some object of knowledge, asking questions about its origin, its emotional foundations, or its sociocultural and historical condi-tionings. The text is a primary datum, an absolute starting point; we are forbidden to go beyond it. The RDP theory of knowledge is based on a text enjoying absolute authority. It cannot be handled by any scholarly or scien-tific category. It constitutes an exception, and for that very reason it is the font of all true generalizations. The text of Scripture is the absolute center of the sacred—not the experience of conversion and its attendant feelings and emotions. The latter were only the initial moment, marking the turn of con-sciousness towards the font of all truth.

Absolute Authority

It is a mistake to believe that, as we are involved in knowing, we proceed free from any kind of authority. In their daily research scientists organize their experiments on the basis of some model which, according to their judg-ment, is invested with authority. Kenneth Burke refers to the so-called "god-terms," that is, points of departure which scientists have to accept as a presupposition for their whole scientific work. And they do this on the basis of faith. Popper points to the same thing. And Kuhn mentions the scientific dogmas which those involved in research have to accept, without questioning. Behind any kind of research there exists an act of faith—the belief in laws and regularities—and this belief is the ultimate authority which controls the whole investigation. A science which does not make use of a theoretical authority is unthinkable. It is true that many scientists do not perceive this. They believe that their method begins with "observation and experiment and then proceeds to theory'' (Popper 279). If this were the case science would not depend on authority. It would simply collect facts and arrive at conclusions. The history of science, however, tells another story. Scientists invest their loyalties in certain models, as a starting act of faith and hope—in Kuhn's suggestive wording—and it is from this beginning that they attempt to interpret their data. Models are ''god-terms,'' ''first-causes,'' to be believed exactly because they are, at the same time, ''both fundamental and inaccessible to experience'' (Rieff: 34). Every thought-process demands a starting point. And every starting point implies that authority is given to it. As Kierkegaard put it, ''such a beginning is not the consequence of an immanent movement of thought, but is effected through a resolution of the will, essentially in the strength of faith'' (Kierkegaard a: 169).

What characterizes science is not that it thinks without recourse to an authority but rather that, according to the rules of its game, authority is always under the judgment of intelligibility and understanding. A theoretical model is and continues to be accepted to the extent that it helps us to understand experience, making it intelligible. Understanding and intelligibility are the tests to which authority is permanently submitted. When they are obscured, the authority on which they depended falls down. It ceases to be authority.

It is obvious that within such a scheme it is impossible to ever have a final certainty. Our truths are always precarious and provisional. Guesses. Popper comes again to my mind: ''The old scientific ideal of *epistēmē*—of absolutely certain, demonstrable knowledge—has proved to be an idol. The demand for scientific objectivity makes it inevitable that every scientific statement must remain *tentative for ever*'' (Popper: 280). The old scientific ideal of Cartesianism, of a body of knowledge *grounded* on declarations beyond the shadow of a doubt, has been abandoned as impossible. Scientific knowledge and doubt go hand in hand. Indeed it is doubt—the perduring possibility that my theoretical authority will be contradicted by facts—that makes science open to successive corrections.

RDP, however, is a faith seeking certainties. It cannot allow authority to be subordinated to intelligibility because that would introduce an ''uncertainty principle'' into the postulates of faith, something which the Protestant spirit cannot accept. In its discussion of the Bible, therefore, we will never see RDP trying to explain or justify biblical authority *in terms of* the understanding or comprehension of existence that it offers. The authority is affirmed as the starting point, and all conclusions are derived from that. If real-life experience is not clarified by the authority, forget about real life. If life is not rendered more intelligible by the reading of Scripture, forget about the ideal of intelligibility. If the facts oppose the text, abolish the facts.

This question shows up clearly whenever there is a question of dealing scientifically with the texts. The latter approach is an effort to shed light on the authority by appealing to the mediation of experience. The RDP mentality rules out any such approach. It insists that the authority must be upheld even if that means eliminating all the pieces of evidence. Consider the following:

> Perhaps the question, "Who wrote the Book of Genesis?" could be better phrased this way: "Who wrote the Pentateuch?" For the answer to the two questions will probably be the same, no matter what our opinion about their authorship might be. The response of the historical Christian Church to that question is definite: "Moses wrote them." If Moses did not write the Pentateuch, then the apostles (e.g., Paul and John) made a mistake when they said that he did. If they erred on this matter, how can we believe them when they deal with truths concerning heaven and the future life? If Moses did not write the Pentateuch, then Jesus lied or erred when he said Moses did. If Jesus did not know this, though he said he did know, how can we believe him when he talks about the things of heaven? [BP, October 1959, p. 1].

This line of argument can be reduced to a simple syllogism:

> Major premise: Everything in the Bible is true.
> Minor premise: The Bible says that Moses is the author of the Pentateuch.
> Conclusion: Therefore Moses is the author of the Pentateuch.

This is a deductive way of writing history. One takes for granted that the text is ahistorical and absolute. It cannot, for this very reason, be submitted to the criteria of historical comprehension. The text is thus taken as authority and the conclusions are derived therefrom. Pieces of evidence to the contrary are obviously rejected. Why? Because they are insufficient, or hasty, or weak? No. Because the text, being absolute and free from errors, imposes itself "*a priori*," vis-à-vis the facts.

In the opening sentences of the cited passage, the respondent suggests that the question of the authorship of Genesis is equivalent to asking about the authorship of the Pentateuch. Or, more precisely, that the latter question is more correct than the former. This is a curious statement since there is nothing in the texts in question that would compel us *a priori* to assume a single author. Indeed the historical evidence points in the opposite direction. Why, then, does the respondent approach the issue in such terms? The answer is simple. The New Testament refers to the Pentateuch as a whole, frequently using nothing but the word *Moses* for it. If the Bible is inerrant, because it was inspired by God, then logically Moses has to be the author of the Pentateuch.

Perhaps we can see the argument even more clearly if we turn it around. If the inspiration of Scripture is to be maintained, then it cannot contain a single error. The important thing, and the aim of the whole argument, is to maintain the authority of the Bible in terms of inspiration and inerrancy. Only then can the dimension of doubt and risk be eliminated from faith; only thus can faith be transformed into absolute knowledge. But if we admit that there is a single error in the text, how can we continue to believe in inspiration? One error would inject an element of doubt into the whole text, so it must be avoided at all cost. Otherwise the whole RDP theory of knowledge based on inspiration comes tumbling down, along with the RDP universe. If Moses is not the author of the Pentateuch, then there are mistakes in Scripture. And if there are factual errors about historical events, then there can be no certainty about spiritual realities. Spiritual credibility depends on historical credibility. Kierkegaard was correct when he said: "Anyone who posits inspiration, as a believer does, must consistently consider every critical deliberation, whether for or against, as a misdirection, a temptation for the spirit" (Kierkegaard a: 27).

The Destruction of Symbols and Myths

There is no logical need, however, for historical veracity and spiritual veracity to be mutually interdependent. Poets let their imagination soar and write about things that are not there. Are they employing language in the camp of falsehood because it cannot be verified empirically? And what about dreams? Considered in terms of their correspondence to real facts, dreams are nothing more than fantasies that often end up as hallucinations. But psychoanalysis has shown us that their seeming absurdity is a form of confession, a way of telling the truth.

Let me go back to a question I discussed earlier. Insofar as signs are concerned, the precondition for their meaningfulness is their reference to empirical content. That criterion is not operative in the realm of symbols. The essence of a symbol lies in the fact that its real signification is distinct from its obvious signification. So when RDP makes spiritual truth depend on the historical truth of the text, it is putting signs and symbols on the same level. To be more precise, it is reducing all symbols to signs. The language of spiritual things is the very same language covering material things. Our mode of signifying an historical fact is the very same mode we use to signify the sacred. To every sign there corresponds a fact, in a direct, univocal way.

What we are dealing with here is a positivist theory of language. Truth is "adaequatio rei et intellectus," the adequation of things and the intellect. This implies that myths and symbols are taken as lies and there is, for them, no room in the Scriptures. For me it was a surprise to discover that Norman O. Brown arrived at a similar conclusion, not from the study of an obscure group of Protestants in Brazil, but from the study of Protestantism as a world phenomenon.

The orthodox Protestant faith is Protestant fundamentalism; if meaning is restricted to the conscious intention of the author, then divine inspiration means that the holy spirit is literally the author; the holy scripture is literally inspired. The inspiration of scripture is reduced to the infallibility of scripture, literally understood [Norman O. Brown, *Love's Body* (New York: Random House, 1966), p. 195].

Q. What can we say about the text narrating the first temptation?
A. It is a narrative of real, historical facts. It is not symbolism, myth, legend, or metaphor of any sort [OP, June 25, 1952, p. 3].

Q. Where was the Garden of Eden?
A. Obviously the park, forest, or garden of delights that God put in Eden . . . was a literal garden existing on earth. . . . It must have been in the Near East, on the central plateau of Asia [OP, January 10, 1955, p. 3].

Thanks to the findings of anthropology and psychoanalysis, we realize today that a myth is not an account of historical facts. To be sure, it is a narrative drama involving characters in a certain time and place, so it gives the impression that its aim is to describe and explain primordial events and origins. A positivist philosophy of language accepts the seeming intention of myth as real; so it proceeds to label myth as mere fiction or fable without any truth. If the intention of the creation myth were scientific, if it did aim to offer a factual account of the events surrounding the origin of the universe and the world, then we would have to abandon it as naive science; we would have to challenge it in the name of rigorous, critical-minded modern science.

Brazilian RDP adopts a positivist approach to the creation account in the Book of Genesis, but it reaches a very different conclusion. Yes, the aim of the creation account is to offer a factual report of the origins of the world. Therefore, on the basis of the doctrine of divine inspiration, the conclusions of modern science must be rejected:

Q. I am a college sophomore. My professor accepts the view that *homo* originated as the product of natural evolution. Does the Bible support this view?
A. The Bible disagrees completely with this thesis or theory. The so-called theory of evolution, espoused by Darwin, Huxley, and others, is today a dead issue that has been scientifically discredited [OP, January 10, 1957, p. 3].

The theory of evolution was invented to completely rule out the idea of God's existence. . . . It is, first and foremost, an attack on the inspiration of the Scriptures [BP, February 1959, p. 1].

It is somewhat ironic that such a conflict should exist between science and this form of Protestantism. Ironic but significant. It is a perpetuation of Galileo Galilei's situation vis-à-vis the Holy Office of the Roman Catholic

Church. His crime: he presented evidence based on his own observations that contradicted an authoritative theological cosmology. He was forced to retract and repent. Today, in the eyes of RDP, the theory of human evolution seems to attack the doctrine of scriptural inspiration. To advocate that theory is to sow doubt and challenge scriptural authority. This is the most serious of crimes: the crime of thinking differently, of being heterodox and heretical.

The Text as an Atemporal Structure

Because of its view of divine inspiration, RDP is forced to treat the biblical text as if it were ahistorical. We know that all human texts are rooted in earthly reality and bodily life, in struggles and hopes, in social and political events and circumstances. They speak of the worlds from which they arose and to which they are bound in fellowship. But the Bible, says RDP, has its roots in eternity. It came into existence because God decided to record his will in a book, and his will is absolute, eternal, immutable, and indifferent to the accidents of history. The succession of chapters in the Bible is an accidental succession. It does not reveal any before or after, any going-on in time. Why? Because the will of God in its entirety is immediately present to the consciousness of the divine legislator. All the verses of the Bible are equidistant from eternity. None can have temporal, epistemological, or axiological priority over another. All reading of the Bible takes place on the same level. If one passage is not clear, one need only consult another that deals with the same subject. No matter where the latter passage is in the Bible, it will provide the needed clarification.

The Bible is inspired from cover to cover, since it is the one, eternal will of God reduced to language. The biblical text, then, is to be viewed as one unique structure. The effort of exegetes to establish distinct traditions and theologies in Scripture must be considered dangerous and heretical—an attack on the doctrine of inspiration. If God was the one who dictated everything in the Bible, how can one talk about different traditions or theologies? A preestablished harmony pervades the text, and one of the tasks of an orthodox exegete is to resolve seeming discrepancies and reveal the unbroken unity of the whole work.

One person asked about certain discrepancies that could be found in the Synoptic Gospels when they were dealing with the same facts or events. This is the response given by a church theologian:

> There is no discrepancy at all between Matthew, Mark, and Luke in the case in question. When the unified accounts are brought together, the facts normally are self-explanatory. . . . And the Word of God proves to be precisely what it is—the Book of God [OP, April 1956, p. 2].

What is invoked to prove that the Bible is the word of God? Not the excellence of its teaching or the profundity of its spiritual wisdom but rather the *formal* concordance, the structural harmony, of the various accounts. Because if the accounts did not agree and harmonize, how could one defend the inspiration of the Bible?

Note that the criterion of logical unity is more important than moral criteria. Suppose, for example, that the Bible presents us with a shocking, brutal deed. Can I use that to question the inspiration of the text? Not at all, because then I would be assuming that my wisdom is superior to God's wisdom. That would be an act of spiritual pride. In the next chapter I will show how the doctrine of divine providence is used to transmute all human contradictions into divine harmonies. Some seeming moral contradiction does not disqualify the sacred texts. The point here is that a logical contradiction is much more serious in the eyes of RDP. Such a contradiction would prove fatal to the Bible, since it would show that the texts are not products of one divine intellect. And that would topple the doctrine of verbal inspiration.

One simple way to resolve the moral problems in the Bible would be to attribute them to the mistaken moral and ideological judgments of the authors. How, for example, are we to reconcile God's commands in the Old Testament to massacre entire peoples, including children, with the New Testament command to love one's enemies and forgive wrongs? It would be easy enough to say that the Old Testament writer mistakenly interpreted the order of a military chieftain as a divine command. But that approach would reintroduce the element of doubt. The Bible in its entirety would not be the Word of God. The text would have been corrupted insofar as authors attributed to God words that were not his. At best the Bible would merely *contain* the word of God. But, by what criteria can the word of God be separated from the word of men and women?

The problem is solved by recourse to the idea of "progressive revelation" (OP, November 25, 1951, p. 1). God, the Lord of the complete, immutable truth, makes concessions to the hardheartedness of human beings. He takes into consideration their intellectual and moral infantilism. He formulated a gradual, progressive pedagogy which takes off from where human beings are. He clothed his eternal truth in transitory forms. Only the form is transitory, opening up gradually to God's full revelation. So we can find a phenomenology of the spirit in the Bible, a progressive process which starts from vulgar rudeness and ends up with purity. But it is not the Divine Spirit that goes through this process, developing along the way. It is the human spirit which gradually progresses in its apprehension of the truth. The truth itself is eternal, so it cannot undergo development.

The Abolition of History

I have indicated that Protestantism constructs its theory of knowledge around the notion of an absolute and final truth. Now I would suggest that such a notion of truth prevents the object *history* from ever taking shape. Absolute knowledge presupposes the immutability and eternity of essences.

Only then can knowledge be final and definitive. The idea of history, by contrast, is built around the notion of process, of old syntheses collapsing and new syntheses taking shape. Truth is a promise, not a possession; it is something created and constructed, not something found in ready-made, finished form. Those who no longer have any doubts are already contemplating pure, eternal essences beyond history. Already freed from transient time, they have entered the definitive realm. Discordant thinking is error, heresy.

It is not necessary to analyze—it is enough to suggest—the consequences of such a posture for individual and sociopolitical behavior. People who already possess the truth are bound to be intolerant. To be sure, they may be tolerant in a polite and sensitive way with those who think differently. But such tolerance has nothing to do with the other kind of tolerance which recognizes that our knowledge is precarious, that right now we can only see through a glass darkly (Paul). I am talking about the tolerance that is open to some new truth that may transcend or even contradict what we thought we already knew.

Here I want to cite a text which I think is significant and indicative. It reveals the intolerant spirit which I have just described. It also reveals the disturbing presence of a different, more tolerant, spirit within the church community. The latter spirit, still doubting and searching, would later have to be silenced by the community in the name of truth:

> We are beginning to see a spreading dissatisfaction with the theological luminaries of the past and the theology which shaped the mentality of our elders, the late "old guard." Today it is the names of other, modern "scholars" that are quoted. No one wants to run the risk of being passé, out of date. Hence preachers and writers embellish and inflate their work with the names of new "theologians." To justify this obvious evolution under way from what they judge to be old and stale to what they consider modern and appetizing, they have fabricated the slogan: "Ecclesia Reformata est Semper Reformanda [a Reformed Church is always in the process of being reformed].". . . Nothing is to stand still in the area of doctrine. The truth believed and taught today is not absolute. Tomorrow it will cease to be the truth. Something else, something different, will take its place. Let us be on the alert! It is error that is fickle and variable because it is not based on facts, not planted on the rock that is Christ [BP, August 1962, p. 3].

Compare this text with the following comment of Pope Paul VI: Modern mentality, subversive of the truths of faith, "tells you that truth is not immutable, not definitive, not certain" (Audience of April 3, 1968). But this the Church cannot accept. Its thinking is the "philosophia perennis"—the "perennial philosophy," which is made up of the formulas in which the Church sealed and certified its dogma so that the latter might be "handed down through the centuries, carefully preserved and ever identical" (Audience of April 3, 1968).

Identical also are the protests against those who wish to reform the church. "They have fabricated the slogan 'Ecclesia Reformata est Semper Reformanda,' " says the Protestant. The Pope echoes: "There has been, and continues to be, talk about the 'structures' of the Church. But this is nothing more than an impersonal, external transformation of the building. The first and most important transformation that the Council intended . . . was . . . moral, personal and inward renewal . . ." (January 15, 1969).

If an institution has been granted the whole truth, then that institution has been uprooted from history. It no longer shares in the doubts and uncertainties of history. So how can one talk about reform? Institutional rigidity is a by product of absolute knowledge.

Wherever absolute knowledge is found, there we also find a prohibition against anything new. How can one talk about something new in a discourse that is grounded on the *a priori* of a complete and final revelation of the truth in the remote past? The "new" is a category of history; truth dwells in eternity. History changes; truth is immutable. "To the Scripture nothing at any time is to be added, whether by new revelations of the Spirit or traditions of men" [LC, n. 6.0006].

Truth was handed down in the past. A prohibition lies upon the present and the future: no changes and no additions! Experience has no cognitive function. It cannot discover or invent anything. Such is the epistemological consequence of this ontology. There is no room for new geneses, new syntheses, new beginnings. There is no place for a process of qualitative change, for the surprising or the unexpected.

An epistemology always reveals some underlying vision of reality. A finished epistemology always goes with a closed universe. Revelation is an act in which the truth presents itself in all its eternal identicalness and all its eternal transcendence over time and space. *Becoming* is not a mode of being for the truth. Logically, then, human beings cannot create anything new, cannot construct new truths. Truth is discovered, not constructed.

And the *locus* of the truth is a text, so knowing means *reading*. But never *writing*! As writers, we assert ourselves as creators of meanings. As readers, we submit to meanings already created. Perhaps that is why Brazilian Protestantism of this type seems able to create philologists and exegetes, but unable to produce any real literature.[8]

Certainty and the End of Interpretation (Free Inquiry)

This theory of knowledge imposes a clear-cut and unmistakable mission that is to be carried out by RDP discourse:

> To expound the clearcut truth of the biblical faith,
>   without vacillations
>   or concessions

Stressing the fundamental doctrines of Calvinism,
  in the terms of the symbols of faith
  we profess to accept,
So that, lord of the truth,
  every spirit that knows what it believes in
  will know how to render an account of the faith it professes
  and perceive the corrupting error
  [BP, second half of December 1963, p. 2; my italics].

The above text has been printed deliberately in this form so that its basic architecture will show up a bit more clearly. The focal point is the italicized *So that*: the spirit must be lord and master of the truth. This points up one of the most basic traits of the RDP spirit: its intellectualism.

In every age mystics have maintained that the truth is infinitely broader than the narrow limits of our intellectual grasp of it. What is more, they have said that there is a discontinuity between the structures of reason and the divine. Hence it is impossible for us to use signs in speaking about God; we must use symbols. And what do symbols reveal? That we do not possess the truth but rather are possessed by it. That we speak out of the truth but cannot speak the truth.

So we might pose this question: What does it mean to be "lord of truth"? What presupposition underlies such a statement? The presupposition is that the truth has been captured by a universe of discourse. The biblical faith is a clear-cut truth; no shadow of doubt lies over it. Sign and signification coincide completely. God became word, in a sense very different from that meant in the Prologue of John's Gospel. To be more precise, God became *words*.

However, we know that words never reveal their meaning in a full, clear-cut way. Language hides as well as reveals. Unless I am mistaken, the language of mathematics is the only system of signs that is absolutely clear, univocal, and unambiguous; it does contain everything that it wishes to signify. Language, therefore, is clear-cut and devoid of latent meanings only to the extent that its structure and function approximates that of mathematical language. Only then can one speak without vacillations or concessions, because only then is everything precise and clear-cut.

People who vacillate or hesitate are people who do not possess certainties. People who make concessions are people who have a relativist view of truth. That is not the case with Protestants.

Protestants boast that it was Protestantism which gave the right of "free inquiry" into the Sacred Scriptures to the faithful: "Reading the Word of God with critical-minded freedom is the privilege of Protestants especially. Free inquiry into the Scriptures is the blessed fruit of the Reformation" (OP, June 25, 1955, p. 1). God speaks directly to the heart, through the text. So every believer has the right to freely examine the Holy Bible.

However, there was a serious problem calling for a solution: the hermeneutic situation. The physical proximity of the individual to the text in no way guarantees the proximity of the reading mind to the meaning of the text. The word *suggests* a meaning, but it does not contain it. The meaning is not a datum handed to me; it is something I dig out of the text through a process of interpretation. The text responds to questions which I pose to it. And my questions are conditioned: by my biographical experiences and my neuroses; by my culture and social condition; by my age and economic situation. If the structures of reason were universally identical, if they were not conditioned by life-circumstances, we could at least imagine a uniform reading by all. But that is not the case. As Bultmann indicated, an objective exegesis of the text is not possible. Various mediating factors come between the reader and the Bible, introducing an "uncertainty principle." This makes room for doubt, and it rules out an attitude "without vacillations or concessions."

How are we to solve the problem of the oneness of truth over against the diversity of interpretations? It seems that the Catholic Church was right, after all: free inquiry tends to produce divisions and schisms. It became obvious that the interpretation, as a consequence, cannot be at the mercy of the individual. It must be established by a *magisterium*. But Protestantism could not accept this solution. On the one hand it had to be different from the Roman Catholic Church. On the other hand it could not accept the indeterminism and doubt which emerge out of the clash of conflicting interpretations. This violates the oneness of truth. The Protestant solution was not a magisterium but an authoritative text called a *confession*. The *magisterium* of the Catholic Church and the *confessions* of the Protestant Churches perform exactly the same function: they establish a uniform reading or interpretation of the text. Confessions are documents which, it is said, "contain the system of doctrines taught in the Holy Scriptures."

What is the correct reading of the text? Wherein lies the clear-cut truth of the biblical faith? What exactly is the truth of which the believer is to be lord and master? It is that which is codified in "the symbols of faith we profess to accept." In short, it is what can be fitted into the text of a confession, like a piece in a puzzle.

A curious conclusion, after all. In fact, there is no free inquiry because that would reintroduce doubt and indefiniteness; and the latter are incompatible with the absolute knowledge which RDP wishes to maintain. The only right accorded the believer is the right of physical closeness to the text. Each individual can read the Scriptures directly. The mechanical act of reading is granted, but not the right of individual interpretation. The correct interpretation has already been crystallized in an authoritative document.

What, then, separates Protestants from Catholics? Nothing, absolutely nothing. Protestantism rejected those institutions which were set up by Catholicism as mechanisms for the control of consciousness. But its passion for certainties compelled it to create a "functional alternative." At first sight the solution may appear to be different. But the function of the confessions is exactly the same as that of the magisterium.

The Intellectual Task: To Repeat and Deduce

Given this point of departure, we must now investigate another question: What methods should be used to guarantee that the development of knowledge remain true?

Let us recall an observation we have just made. The intellectual task of creating new meanings is completed. The doctrine of inspiration privileges the past—not just any past, but the past delimited by the text—as the time of truth. In this past, all truth became words, and a confessional document has already organized them into a coherent system of doctrines. Accordingly the search for truth has ceased. The truth of present and future has already been revealed in the past. Thus present and future are devoid of meaning. They contain nothing new. Nothing exists in them which might surprise or innovate.

Then what intellectual task is incumbent upon us? In the present and in the future, what methods can we lay hands on in order to speak the truth? To repeat and deduce.

Knowing the truth means repeating the truth. Of course, this tends to produce an emotional state of boredom, since all possibility of surprise is ruled out. If the past is the absolute norm, we can be sure it will be the same today, tomorrow, and the day after tomorrow. On the other hand the tranquillizing effect of repetition is ample compensation for the boredom. Desmond Morris relates the lulling, hypnotic effect of binary rhythms to the binary beating of the mother's heart when the baby is in the womb. This effect is engraved on our biological memory, along with the sense of security and tranquility we felt in the womb. Repetition becomes a symbol of security. According to Morris, all routines which go on uninterruptedly have the same lulling effect (Morris: 117). They reassure us that everything is under control. Everything is as it was before. We do not face the unknown with feelings of anxiety welling up inside us and our cognitive structures in danger of collapse. Hence we do not face the painful, unexpected task of reorganizing our cognitive apparatus. It may be a boring world without novelty, but it is also a secure, tranquil world.

Repeating for the Protestants means saying that the "old message" is still valid. It also means that I am valid: I don't have to do any rethinking. Sermons that pose questions and leave them unanswered always tend to create feelings of anxiety in Protestants of this type. Not giving an answer is a tacit admission that one does not accept the old answers, and that gives rise to doubts. The recipe for a well-done sermon is its dogmatic, final tone, its reaffirmation of certitudes. One person had this to say about a preacher who had many questions and few answers: "I don't like the sermons of that minister because he says things that *I am not used to hearing.*" The important thing is to say what people are used to hearing. The things already implanted in their memory become the criterion for separating what is false from what is true.

If you want even more tangible evidence of this pattern of repetition, you need only examine the Sunday School curriculum. The objective of Sunday School is to educate Protestants in their faith. Sunday after Sunday they come to class to study. What is noteworthy, however, is the cyclic pattern of the lessons. They proceed from some starting point to some end point, but that does not lead on to any new horizons. One simply begins over at the old starting point. It is a cycle of eternal return. Knowing means taking the same trip over and over again, repeating over and over again.

Only history is infinite in its manifestations. Only in history can the past not be repeated. Only history can produce new and novel things. It is no accident that the word "novelty" has a pejorative sense in the universe of Brazilian RDP. The preachers of new things, of "novelties," are people who have broken away from the pattern of repetition and the safety of absolute knowledge; they have headed down the road of doubt.

Although my remarks here refer specifically to Brazilian Protestantism, we must remember that this pattern has been repeated systematically in other forms of Protestantism. Perhaps the theologian who advocated this position with the greatest elegance—and yes, beauty—was Karl Barth. He wrote: "The problem of the Word of God consists in the fact that to this particular man today, through the proclamation of this other particular man by means of this particular Bible text, this particular manifestation of God is imparted; that a particular *illic et tunc* becomes a particular *hic et nunc*" (Barth: 170).

Repetition breeds *comfort*. Believers are always looking for comfort when they go to church on Sunday. Repetition comforts them because it affirms the immutability of truth. Insofar as the truth spoken at this moment is the truth they are used to hearing, they enjoy the certainty that they are indeed lords and masters of the truth.

It is no accident, then, that Brazilian Protestantism has not produced theologians. There can only be vocations for possible tasks. When everything has already been done, how can one feel called to it? A young theology student went to see one of his professors to inform him of his plans to go to Europe and study theology. The reply was: "Young fellow, why study theology? There is nothing new in it. Theology can only be a repetition of what you have already studied here. Instead of studying theology, why don't you study pastoral psychology?"

Does that mean there is no sort of theology study in Brazilian Protestantism? Not at all. I am simply saying that the RDP theory of knowledge does not allow for theology as a critical, exploratory, creative enterprise; for that would presuppose that the thinking crystallized in the past is not absolute. The task is not to create new knowledge but to justify the old knowledge. Theology means *learning the deductive processes* whereby the text has been transformed into a system of doctrines. It is a formal discipline, since the important thing is to master the logical process underlying cognition.

Believers know the truths. They know what they believe in. Often, however, they do not know the deductive process of logical transformations to which the text was subjected in order to work out a given doctrine fully. Theologians are people who know how to perform the logical mediations between text and doctrine. When a believer asks a theologian about the why and wherefore of some doctrine, the latter usually responds in a set pattern. Starting with one or more biblical texts, the theologian processes them through a particular logic and finally ends up with the doctrine in question. The thing that is of fundamental importance—and hence the ultimate criterion of orthodoxy—is that the doctrine contain nothing new. It can only explicate a truth *already* contained in the past. One can talk about the "history of doctrines" only in the sense that the logic of the process is akin to that which links fruit to seed in a continuous, uninterrupted process. Everything was there in the beginning, though perhaps unseen; it is simply revealed and enunciated.

Once again we see that there is an affinity between this Protestant theory of knowledge and the Roman Catholic. "As the tree is the development of the seed, so the history of the Church is the process which deepens and amplifies the seminal elements of gospel origin, conducting them to perfect realization without altering them, modifying them, or corrupting them." Such a statement could have been made by any orthodox Protestant. But it was spoken by Pope Paul VI, in May 1969.

My personal criticism is not directed against the wager that was made in some specific past. It is directed against the presupposition that confession and theology are not the products of a particular hermeneutics, that they are not expressions of *one* relative, provisional perspective which might be wiped out by some new interpretation. That one has chosen some horizon as a point of departure is not the problem. The problem lies in the fact that one has absolutized a perspective of this horizon that is not exhausted in my book.

The certainty that one possesses absolute knowledge harbors two attitudes which might seem contradictory but which, in fact, are complementary. The first is *intellectual pride*. *We* possess the truth, *others* are in the dark. We have a monopoly on knowledge, so we can speak "without vacillations or concessions." This explains the radically anti-ecumenical outlook which has characterized the Protestantism that we are studying. Ecumenism is an attitude which presupposes a large dose of intellectual humility. I do not possess the whole truth. There are other ways of viewing the same historical horizon. One has to listen. But real listening is more than the simple politeness of well-bred people. I must have the humility to admit that my talk does not say everything and that it is open to correction. We share in one and the same truth, which is not exhausted by our talk. Our truth, then, is not the truth of absolute knowledge but the truth of faith; there is risk involved because faith cannot be separated from doubt. Absolute truth and truth's oneness are not a knowledge we *possess* but an eschatological horizon toward which we are moving: "For we have been saved, though only in hope. Now to see is no longer to hope: why should a man endure and wait for what he already sees?

But if we hope for what we do not yet see, then, in waiting for it, we show our endurance'' (Rom. 8:24). Absolute knowledge affirms itself as contemplation, not interpretation. But we do not even contemplate the truth: we don't see, we only wait. We must listen, which means that intellectual pride has to be abandoned.

The second attitude that inhabits absolute knowledge and which appears to be the opposite of intellectual pride is *scorn* for intellectual activity. Only people who don't yet have homes build homes. Students who are struggling with a problem reveal that they do not yet have their answer. Activity is always a symptom of poverty, of some lack. One has not yet gotten possession. Those who claim to have absolute knowledge are saying that the activity which is part of cognition is no longer necessary. Once knowledge has been attained, all the required preliminary activity ceases. The only task remaining is to *proclaim* the truth. Pride of possession entails scorn for the struggle that betrays deprivation.

At the climax of the centennial celebration of the Presbyterian Church of Brazil in 1959, a Church spokesperson declared in a sermon: "Brazilian ministers are not like Karl Barth, wasting his time doing theology by the fireplace amid clouds of smoke from his pipe. Our ministers are men of action." A very revealing statement. On the one side, Barth, seated, idle, in thought. Note the identification of intellectual work with idleness. Indeed, once presupposed that the intellectual task has been concluded, to do theology is the same as seeking to discover the demonstration of a theorem long since demonstrated. On the other side, the active minister, who does not waste his time in intellectual games. He already knows. Therefore he has no more need of tasks that are preliminary to knowing. On this account he acts: he proclaims the truth of which he is the possessor.

The Indicative Mood Versus the Imperative Mood

The theory of biblical inspiration and inerrancy might well lead us to conclude that Protestant exegesis must be literal. But there is a whole series of texts which are not interpreted literally, and we must investigate why. Here are a few sample texts:

If your right eye is your undoing, tear it out and fling it away. . . . And if your right hand is your undoing, cut it off and fling it away [Matt. 5:29–30].

If a man wants to sue you for your shirt, let him have your coat as well [Matt. 5:40].

Do not store up for yourselves treasures on earth, where it grows rusty and motheaten, and thieves break in to steal it [Matt. 6:19].

If you wish to go the whole way, go, sell your possessions, and give to the poor, and then you will have riches in heaven [Matt. 19:21].

Protestants affirm that these texts—which exemplify a set of texts—were divinely inspired just as other texts were. Indeed in this case they are the very words of Jesus. At the same time, however, these Protestants assert that these texts cannot be taken literally. Believers are not obliged to castrate themselves when they commit adultery, to give away their possessions to those who ask for them, or to the poor. Indeed many of them are rich and prosperous, and once they get rich, nothing obligates them to sell all their possessions and give them to the poor.

There is another set of texts, however, which must be interpreted literally: the universe was created in six days; the serpent really spoke; Adam and Eve were real people who ate a real fruit; Balaam's ass spoke; Joshua made the sun stop in the sky; Jonah was swallowed by a big fish and remained three days in its belly; and the virgin birth of Jesus is a historical fact. Once again these few examples stand for a whole set of texts.

How do we explain the two varying types of interpretation since the whole biblical text is of divine inspiration? What is the rule which the RDP believer unconsciously uses when he or she says one kind of text is to be interpreted literally while the other is not?

Looking at the above texts, we know that the latter ones are texts which refer to matters of fact. *Their verbal mood is in the indicative mood.* They simply describe how things happened. We could say that those texts are not descriptions of facts but myths. But since myth is ruled out as a possible category, the indicative mood of a verb can only indicate real happenings.

The first set of texts cited above, however, have their verbs *in the imperative mood.* They don't describe facts; they enunciate moral commands.

Here we have the rule of interpretation underlying this sort of exegetical practice: *texts in the indicative mood must be interpreted literally; texts in the imperative mood do not have to be interpreted literally.* In the first case, letter and spirit are identical. In the second case, they are not: "the letter kills, but the spirit gives life." The imperative mood can be explained in terms of context and the customs of the time; it is relativized. The texts in the indicative mood, however, can never be relativized by appealing to the state of science at the time. That is why Bultmann's effort at demythologization is systematically rejected as a dangerous heresy.

The obvious privilege of *knowledge* over *morality*, of *wisdom* over *goodness*, of *doctrine* over *life*, is noted.

No one is excluded from the Church for not literally interpreting and obeying some moral imperative: e.g., the command to sell one's goods and give the proceeds to the poor. I don't know of any instance where ethics has provoked a crisis in the Brazilian Church. But it is fatal to challenge the literal veracity of texts in the indicative mood, of texts which tell us how things were. Denial of the literal truth of the accounts of creation, the fall, or the virgin birth are proofs of heresy, and that the person involved no longer inhabits the Protestant universe.

That is why one who denies the "scientific" knowledge of the texts is more dangerous than someone who denies the literal validity of moral imperatives. An orthodox minister was listening to the sermon of another minister who was not so orthodox. The latter mentioned Albert Schweitzer as an example of a Christian. The minister listening got up and walked out. A life of heroic gospel morality, without the correct confession of faith, is insignificant from the standpoint of Protestant logic. Doing good is less important than thinking correctly. Those whose thinking is heretical are feared far more than those whose morals are lax.

How are we to explain the flexibility evident in the interpretation of imperative texts vis-à-vis the inflexibility evident in the interpretation of indicative texts? I don't dare try to offer a satisfactory answer to that question. I will leave the fact for my readers to draw their own conclusions. I would simply point out that possessing the truth seems to be more crucial than living the truth. Moral sins can be pardoned, but intellectual sins cannot. The "crime of thinking," referred to in *1984* by George Orwell, cannot be forgiven.

Faith and Science

I have already indicated that Protestantism makes no distinction between the language of signs and the language of symbols, reducing the latter to the former. This means that the RDP world is one-dimensional. It does not imagine that there are different levels of meaning.

The consequence is that the knowledge of faith and the knowledge of science exist on the same plane, so they cannot contradict one another. The language of revelation and the language of science have the very same function: to tell how things are. Indeed, when RDP gives priority to the indicative mood over the imperative mood, isn't it telling us that the language of faith *is* science?

> The Bible and science cannot contradict one another, since both are of divine origin. When we see them in conflict, either the interpretation of the scientist or the hermeneutics of the theologian is mistaken [BP, December 1961, p. 14].

Does that mean we can imagine some situation where theology would be corrected by science? What criteria are we to use to decide whether the scientist or the theologian made the mistake? Well, the ultimate criteria for such a judgment are not scientific. If that were the case, then the authority of the text would be subject to the authority of science; but that is expressly ruled out. The ultimate criterion of truth is the scriptural text as it is systematically presented in the Church's confession.

The admission that a theologian might be in error does not mean that there are cases where theology should bow to science. I know of no single instance in which Brazilian Protestants have reconsidered their theory of knowledge in the light of scientific or scholarly evidence. Absolute knowledge cannot make concessions, not even to science. One finds, rather, an opportunist or apologetic use of science. As one seminary professor put it: "When science agrees with revelation, we should accept it: When it disagrees with revelation, we should reject it." After all, revelation *already has* the knowledge that science is *still looking for.*

This attitude is well exemplified in the discussions which took place in the middle fifties over Werner Keller's book, *The Bible as History: A Confirmation of the Book of Books.* One commentator noted that the book presented archaeological data which "demonstrates the historical truth of the Sacred Books." That point is very important, as we have seen, if the Bible is to be credible when it talks about spiritual things. Keller, however, could not accept supernatural events, such as Balaam's ass talking or Jonah surviving three days in the belly of a big fish. Therefore his book had to be "read with discrimination, *making good use of* its stock of proofs for the truth of the Bible, *but without relegating to the realm of legend and fairy tale* those things for which the picks and shovels of archaeologists had *not yet* found historical confirmation" (my italics). There follows a passage which typifies the RDP method of verification. The inerrancy of the biblical text is assumed. So one need only cite the biblical passage dealing with the fact in question, and the fact is proved:

> As for the case of Balaam, we find it confirmed by Peter (2 Peter 2:15-16), who was on intimate terms with the Master (see Matt. 12:40). . . . In short, the Christian does not need the support of archaeology to give credit to the Bible. That God speaks to us there is enough: "Thus says the Lord," *and the question is closed* [BP, September 1958, p. 12; my italics].

What does the author of this passage mean by *making good use of* Keller's book? The clear implication is that the science of archaeology is not to be taken seriously as a whole. One adopts a selective approach, seeking materials that can be used as proofs and rejecting materials that cannot. But doesn't the same scientific method underlie both kinds of material? How does one justify the acceptance of one kind of material and the rejection of the other kind? That would be legitimate only if one found some flaw in the method employed. But that whole problem is not even raised.

Ready-made results are sought to be used as proofs. Science is valid when it confirms the text. And when it does not? When science says no, absolute knowledge behaves as if it had said nothing. There is, therefore, a good and bad science, a true and a false science. How to distinguish the two? This is not done with methods proper to science. The criterion for determining this is science's harmony or disharmony with the biblical text as interpreted by the church confession. A science that is in disagreement is so because it *has not yet* found the necessary proofs. But absolute knowledge knows that such proofs might some day be unearthed. One seminary professor put it this way when he was discussing the biblical accounts of creation and the fall of humanity: "In fact, these texts are not scientific because they were not the result of direct observation. But if science had photographed what really took place, we would find that it happened exactly that way."

Readers may wonder if I am trying to suggest that Protestants cannot be scientists. I am not. If Max Weber was correct, there are many affinities between the practice of science and the spirit of Protestantism. Cognition of the world is part and parcel of the process of rationalizing and winning domination over the world; through that whole process Christians fulfill their vocation and verify their predestination. Insofar as the specific case at issue here is concerned, what I am suggesting is that science is affirmed as a *technique* but rejected as an *overall vision of reality*. And how is that possible? By making a distinction between primary causes and secondary causes:

> Although in relation to the foreknowledge and decree of God, the first cause, all things come to pass immutably and infallibly, yet, by the same providence, he ordereth them to fall out according to the nature of second causes, either necessarily, freely, or contingently [LC, n. 6.025].

As this statement in the Westminster Confession of Faith suggests, reality is split into two levels: the invisible and the visible; primary causes and secondary causes; a deep level hidden to the senses and knowable only by revelation, and a surface level which can be known by the senses and human reason.

Science is the organization of phenomena, of the things that come to human awareness. The categories of the understanding are valid for that level, but only there. Reality, the thing-in-itself, lies beyond that level; only revelation can speak of it. Science cannot construct a metaphysics. It cannot penetrate to the essence of phenomena, to the source of real causality. As Kant suggested in his preface to the second edition of the *Critique of Pure Reason*, science is denied metaphysical competence in order to make room for faith.

So it is possible for one and the same person to be both believer and scientist. He or she may be expert in using the techniques of science on the data of experience, while still possessing absolute knowledge which lies beyond science and its categories. Revelation does not take the place of science. Revealed knowledge has to do with the problem of salvation. Science is still needed to manipulate the visible world. Knowledge of the visible world, by the same token, is not competent to make pronouncements about the invisible realm. There revelation rules. Absolute knowledge and science dovetail nicely, but the unifying principle comes from knowledge by faith, not from experience.

Once again we find that this spirit of Protestantism is not so different from the spirit of traditional Catholicism as it might appear at first glance. Superficial differences conceal an extraordinary degree of agreement insofar as the unconscious structures of thought are concerned. Here is a Catholic example from Brazil (in *Pastoral Letter and Catechism of Opportune Truths Which Are Opposed to Contemporary Errors*, by Bishop Antonio de Castro Mayer):

> Philosophy and the sciences have their own proper object and their autonomous method. Nevertheless, since Divine Revelation is infallible whereas human reason is fallible, the scientist and the philosopher ought to regard the teachings of the Church, the authentic interpreter of Revelation, as the criterion of certainty and the least negative guide in their studies and investigations. . . . There is no possibility of collision between reason and faith. When such incompatibility seems to exist, it is due to the fact that either the teaching of faith is not formulated with objective precision or, more likely, that reason has misfired in its investigations. . . . Faced with an infallible teaching of the Church, the philosopher or scientist must always reject the conclusions of their disciplines when those conclusions clash with Church teaching. This is the traditional teaching of the Church, reiterated by the Holy Father in this passage of *Humani Generis*: "It is necessary to be very cautious in the area of sheer (scientific) hypotheses, though they may have some scientific foundation, which touch upon doctrine contained in Holy Scripture or tradition. If such hypotheses go against revealed doctrine either directly or indirectly, then they can in no way be accepted" [see Mayer].

I cannot see a single point of basic disagreement between this Catholic position and the Protestant position discussed above.

Discourse Substituted for Life

If my analysis so far is correct, we cannot escape the conclusion that the adherent to RDP dwells in a world of discourse. This Protestant world is a discourse. Since its knowledge is revealed, absolute, infallible, beyond all doubt, anything in life that might raise questions or pose criticism is declared false *a priori*. Life is ruled out as the starting point; it is constricted and repressed by absolute knowledge.

We are before a problem: how to explain the fact that individuals and communities accept the repression of life and submit themselves to a knowledge that does not allow for the expression of life? For, in a system in which absolute knowledge is revealed—from the top down—an *expression* of that which is human cannot be accepted as revealing truth. Some conclusions from depth psychology and psychotherapy might throw light on the problem. Freud showed that one of the techniques used by the psyche to solve its conflicts with reality is to substitute words for reality. Words become "substitute-gratifications," *replacing* direct contact with things and persons when one *fears* contact with reality; words descend as a protective curtain between the talker on the one hand and everything else on the other. Even the talker's own body may lie on the other side of the protective curtain, beyond contact (Brown: 150–51; Perls, Hefferline, and Goodman: 324, 105).

If from the very start we possess a verbal definition of the meaning of our experiences, we are freed from the anxiety of confronting and feeling them directly. So we do not really experience our experiences. Instead we experience a way of thinking about experience. And why would we do this? Because we are afraid of life. Life, after all, is filled with uncertainty, change, and unpredictability. It raises problems, destroys absolutes, and forces us to reorganize our perceptions. Language, by contrast, offers us stable definitions and ready-made recipes. That is why people might feel more secure dwelling in a world of words rather than their own real lives. Religious people are not the only ones who allow themselves to be bewitched by language. It happens in everyday life, in the world of science and scholarship, and in the realm of ideologies.

The point here is that it does happen in the area of religion too. In RDP we see a process whereby language is absolutized, underlying emotional levels are left unconscious, and a line of reasoning and rationalization is consciously affirmed by means of the doctrine of biblical inspiration. Does such an obsession with absolute truth embody some neurotic component in the make-up of individuals and groups?

Absolute Knowledge and Sectarianism

It is a cliché to interpret the existence of numerous Protestant denominations and sects as the result of free inquiry and liberty. Catholic unity, by contrast, is explained in terms of a centralized, monolithic hierarchical structure which has ruled out free inquiry into the Scriptures.

My analysis suggests an inversion of this interpretation. What condition is imposed on the Roman Catholic who wishes to be part of the ecclesial community? An intellectual act of assent to doctrine? Basically, no. Doctrine is secondary when the issue at stake is participation in the "mystical body of Christ." The truly basic thing is mystical, emotional participation in the sacramental mystery. Sacrament takes priority over doctrine. The sacraments are channels of grace, doctrines are not. That is why deviations from orthodoxy are not enough to provoke ruptures. Roman Catholics with diametrically opposed theological ideas can still share in the same sacraments.

That is not the case with Protestantism. The criterion for participation in the ecclesial community is the confession of right doctrine as defined by the official confession of faith. Since doctrine is broadly defined, any intellectual deviation is bound to provoke a rupture. In other words, there is more room for dissidents and "heretics" in the Catholic Church than there is in Protestantism. It is much harder to define a heretic in the former context.

Thus the Protestant vocation to denominations and sects cannot really be interpreted as an expression of freedom. Just the opposite is true. Precisely insofar as Protestants inhabit a language and that language is rigorously defined, any deviant talk is bound to provoke a crisis and subsequent breakaways. Dissenters must leave voluntarily or be expelled because the RDP universe is intellectually tight and compact, with no free space for doubt, indefiniteness, or questioning. Divergent interpretations of the Gospels must be regarded as acts of rebellion. It is not intellectual freedom that creates schisms, but rather the lack of it.

Absolute Knowledge and Absolute Power

We frequently forget a very simple fact, which Wittgenstein called to our attention:

> Let us not forget that a word does not have a meaning given to it, as it were, by a power independent of us, so that there could be a kind of scientific investigation into what the word really means. A word has the meaning someone has given to it [Wittgenstein a: 28].

What is the meaning of a word or a text? What is the correct reading of Scripture? In the Protestant universe everything is arranged to obscure the fact that meanings and interpretations are produced by a reader who *asserts* them. For all practical purposes, the meanings and interpretations defined as orthodox have, as it were, been defined by God himself rather than by human beings like ourselves. That is why knowledge is absolute: it pertains to divine knowledge and to human knowledge. In fact, however, certain human beings had to assert that such was the meaning and that it was God's. Then how were they able to impose their definitions as the true, orthodox ones while at the same time defining all other interpretations as false and heterodox?

> "When I use a word," Humpty Dumpty said, in rather a scornful tone, "it means just what I choose it to mean—neither more nor less."
>
> "The question is," said Alice, "whether you *can* make words mean so many different things."
>
> "The question is," said Humpty Dumpty, "which is to be master— that's all" [Carroll: 247].

The meaning of a text is not resolved within the text itself. What matters is who has the last word. And what decides who has the last word? Not the text but power.

The orthodox are those who had the political power to impose their definitions. Thus orthodoxy always embodies the ideas of the stronger. By the same token heresy points to the ideas of those who were weaker, who did not have the political power to impose their definitions on the ecclesiastical community. In the last analysis, the definition of truth is a question of power.

Protestants assert that their ultimate authority is the text of Sacred Scripture. In the face of many possible readings of the text, it was necessary to make a decision about the correct reading. This was done by formulating a text, a confession, and making it official. This act was political because heretical interpretations were heretical only from the standpoint of those who had the power to impose their own interpretation. As the heretics saw the matter, their reading was the correct, orthodox one; it was the opposing orthodox reading that was false and heretical.

The authority of Scripture was thus transferred to another text, with authority to decide about the correct reading. But this did not solve the problem. Even the official confession was open to various interpretations. There had to be some authority here and now to speak the final word on both the scriptural texts and the official confession. Thus the final word on revealed truth is not the voice of that truth itself but the voice which, by virtue of its political power, can silence dissidents and declare the issue settled and closed.

Wherever some knowledge is defined as orthodox and absolute, there we find an arbitrary and authoritarian exercise of power. The certainty of truth is the smiling face of intolerance. The fact is that the notion of absolute knowledge can neither logically nor practically be reconciled with the tolerance implicit in a conception of provisional knowledge, open to doubts.[9]

FOUR

THE WORLD INHABITED BY RIGHT-DOCTRINE PROTESTANTS

Masters and Apprentices: Socialization in the World of RDP

It is now time for us to accompany the new converts as they step into the world inhabited by Right-Doctrine Protestants. The expressive, emotional language of the converts must now be replaced by a language which articulates a certain knowledge of reality.

The situation of the new converts is akin to that of children going to school for the first time. They know nothing. Knowledge will be mediated to them by a person who *has* knowledge. The learning experience is not a spontaneous one. Knowledge is given by someone whom society has defined as a bearer of knowledge. The learning process is a process of apprenticeship. The social interaction between the two parties involved is not an interaction between equals. Master and apprentice, teacher and learner, are not on the same level. One is subordinate to the other; hence *power* is involved in the equation. The teachers are those who have the power to impose their definitions of reality; the learners are those who do not have the power to maintain their own definitions of reality. The teachers are strong; the learners are weak.

New converts are not expected to construct their new universe from their own insides out. It is not to be their own spontaneous elucidation of personal experiences. Conversion is acceptable as an emotional experience, but the community defines the new converts as those who *do not know* what they believe in. The world which will be presented to new converts does not lie hidden and buried in their own unconscious. This particular learning process will not bear any resemblance to the approach of Socrates, who tried to act as a midwife and draw out into awareness the knowledge which lay buried inside his listeners.

"All interpretation of the world," notes Alfred Schutz, "is based on a stock of previous experiences of it, our own and those handed to us by parents or teachers; those experiences in the form of 'knowledge at hand'

84

function as a scheme of reference" (Schutz: 7). In our case here, RDP asserts that it has a monopoly on the needed stock of knowledge. So it defines the apprenticeship situation in terms of initial polarity: one party possesses knowledge, the other party does not. Underlying the learning process from the very start is a tacit agreement about the *social distribution of knowledge*.

Even before new converts learn anything about the world, they are taught to view themselves as people who know nothing. *Their own* knowledge is placed between parentheses and called into doubt. It is not permissible for them to appeal to what they think they know in order to criticize the knowledge that the church community wishes to transmit to them. Why? Because their knowledge is a heritage from their earlier period of darkness and damnation. Their minds are reduced to blank pages. They have nothing to say; their job is to listen. As apprentices and learners, they must submit silently to the church institution. They now know that the institution has a monopoly on absolute knowledge, hence a monopoly on the right to talk.

In the RDP world, then, the learning process begins with a lesson in a particular kind of social relationship: the teachers speak, the learners keep quiet; the teachers teach, the learners repeat. If the learners do not know what they believe, they are not qualified to speak. It is true that the converts are free to sing their emotions. But the discourse of knowledge is still impossible. This is why the proper mode of speech for the learners is *repetition*, as catechisms clearly illustrate. Catechisms are primers for apprentice-learners. They contain questions and ready-made answers. When do learners know their catechism? When they can recite by heart the printed answers in it. The learning of the church community is defined in terms of that knowledge, and the test of learning is the ability to memorize and repeat the catechism questions and answers. In this way the collective conscience of the community is imprinted as truth on the mind and conscience of the individual member. What about free inquiry? What about letting converts break their own ground? That is nowhere to be found.

The knowledge of the church community is the *a priori* in constructing the new convert's world. It is a preexisting stock of knowledge which needs only to be handed out. Rather than flowing from the personal experiences of the new converts, it is the precondition for their experiences. Lying beyond all relativism, it is necessary and universal. Its logic and limits are those of any and all possible objects of experience.

Obviously neither the convert nor the community takes notice of the social foundations of this knowledge; otherwise it would cease to be absolute and become relative. For all practical purposes the knowledge of the community is a copy of the real, not a social construction of the real.[10] This knowledge is absolute and impersonal, not social:

> In fact, logical thinking is always impersonal thinking, and is also thought *sub specie aeternitatis*—as though for all time. Impersonality and stability are the two characteristics of truth [Durkheim a: 484].

What does learning the truth mean here? It means making sure that the individual thinking of the new convert dovetails with the consciousness of the church community. The spontaneity of individual consciousness must be corrected and guided. Socialization in the world of RDP does not escape the mechanisms operative in every socialization process. Some sort of *coercion* must be exercised on the individual to make sure that his or her own individual consciousness submits to that of the community.

At the end of the initiation process one comes to a "public profession of faith." The new convert is not asked for his or her opinion about certain things. The question is: "Do you believe that . . . ?" The rest of the sentence is some orthodox formula held by the community. And to this series of questions the candidate is to answer: "Yes" (MC, pp. 16–22). A negative answer or a hint of doubt would disqualify the candidate immediately. Henceforth individual conscience is to be silent; the candidate can express only what the community *already* knows.

The correct confession of faith is the knowledge that properly goes with the conversion experience. *The evidential proof of salvation is the convert's affirmation of the knowledge which is upheld collectively by the church community.* Weber's conclusion, that economic success is the proof of salvation, does not hold here. Economic success is a *blessing* which God *can* grant his elect. But economic hardship might also be a divine test of faith. After an analysis of Protestant groups in Chile, Christian Lalive d'Epinay has concluded that Weber's point does not apply there either. In the case of the Chilean groups, however, moral virtue seems to be the proof of salvation. While moral rectitude is important in the case of Brazilian RDP, it is not decisive. Catholics, spiritualists, and atheists may live lives of great moral beauty and grandeur. Moral nobility by itself is not proof of salvation, however. Moral sinfulness can be pardoned. But intellectual error is fatal for the soul's salvation. To be saved, the individuals must adjust their consciousness completely to that of the community. The collective consciousness is a sacred absolute. The evidence of individuals' salvation is their spoken *repetition* of the community's knowledge.

The Organization of Space and Time

Dualism: The Two Possible Roads

Protestantism has traditionally accepted and produced art in a selective way. Over against the power of its music, so well exemplified by Bach, we find an enormous void in the realm of the plastic arts. One need only enter a Protestant church to see that. There are no pictorial representations of the divine, and the churches look more like classrooms or lecture halls. The central focus is the pulpit, where one stands and talks. Protestantism gives priority to spoken discourse over contemplation.

That is not by accident; it has theological underpinnings. In contrast to

Catholics, who tend to stress the contemplative and visual dimensions of religious experience, Protestants have viewed the prohibition against graven images in the second commandment as a solid motive for artistic asceticism. Depicting the divine is idolatry because the divine cannot be visually represented. And since it could not be depicted by visual form, color, and movement, Protestantism could only point to it with language. That is why language is the chief means by which Protestants live their religion. They preach, they sing, and they listen.

In the case of the Brazilian RDP, there is a significant exception to this traditional rule. It is a picture which is sold in Protestant bookstores, and which can be found hanging in Protestant churches and homes. It might have either of two titles: the Two Roads, or, The Wide Road and the Narrow Road. It was not made in Brazil; it was imported.

The point of this picture is not to depict the divine. To be sure, the divine is there in it, but depicted in the most ascetic form possible. There is a triangle symbolizing the Trinity, and inside the triangle a large eye symbolizing divine omniscience. That is not the center of the picture, however, the inner source of its dynamism and movement. God is not an actor. God is a great eye— faceless, armless, bodiless—floating in the blue firmament. God does nothing but contemplate the scene silently. The real actors are human beings, and their destiny is the theme of the picture.

There are two roads. On the left side of the picture is the wide road. At its start we see the figure of Bacchus and Venus. Wine and love-making symbolize pleasure, the priority of instinct, the voice of the body. They are the door to perdition. Actually we see a wide street rather than a road. The setting is urban. The dress of the strollers indicates that they are well-off. Desire for pleasures and wealth go hand in hand. If we try to discern their attitude, we get the feeling that they are unaware of the fact they are travelling down a road. They are unconcerned about the destiny that awaits them. They move from one side of the street to the other, from one pleasure to another, thinking only of the present moment. They seek only what the "world" has to offer: food and drink, dancing, entertainment, gambling, sex. In a more up-to-date version of this same picture one will also find smoking depicted. Meanwhile these people seem to be totally unaware of where they are heading, of their destiny, which is the only important thing. For at the end of their road lies an abyss of hellfire, into which they will sink forever.

The scene on the right side of the picture is completely different. The entrance is narrow, and a preacher stands outside. The journey starts with knowledge. Once on the road we find a rural, bucolic world with trees, meadows, and streams. A fountain of water, the water of life, gushes from beneath a large crucifix. We see no places of entertainment, only tents and churches. There was no church on the wide road. Perhaps this was an artist's scruple, but actually everyone knows that the Roman Catholic Church is the Church of the wide road. (cf. Westminster Confession of Faith, 1647 ed. [LC n. 6.130, note]). The dualist contrast between the wide road and the narrow

road is equivalent to the dualistic contrast between the Catholic Church and
the Protestant Church. Otherwise there would be no need to convert Catholics. They would be brothers and sisters travelling the same journey. At the
end of the narrow road lies the "heavenly city," the eternity of blessedness
that awaits "believers."

This theme is one of the most frequently recurring ones in the Protestant
hymns. We often find it expressed with a different but parallel set of images.
Life is a stormy sea, and there is always danger of shipwreck. My life is
boarding a ship and setting sail, hoping to arrive at a safe harbor off in the
distance:

> Pilot my ship, Christ,
> Over the stormy sea,
> Which, angry and evil,
> Seeks to shipwreck it and me.
> Come, Lord Jesus, come
> to pilot my ship [*Seja Lou vado*, n. 208].

> Fear nothing! Christ himself
> Takes the helm to steer.
> The boat will not drift aimlessly
> Over the deep sea
> To the harbor,
> Where we will find rest [HE, n. 351].

> Along this coast death reigns.
> We cannot anchor here.
> On the other side lies a new life
> That we are going to seek.
> Hoist the sail!
> We're on our way [HE, n. 351].

> O kindly Savior,
> Be my protector!
> Dark waves of affliction
> And strong winds are near.
> From this panic and terror
> Come save me, O Good Lord,
> And bring my boat to port
> Without shipwreck [HE, n. 365].

Here the duality of roads assumes the form of duality between alternatives:
to shipwreck, or to arrive at the harbor. Here we have the basic structuring of
the Protestant world, a map of two—and only two—possible roads to take.
Now maps mean one thing to geography students, and something very dif-

ferent to travellers who are lost. To the former, a map is simply a symbolic representation of space. They may draw and study maps without drawing up any travel plans. But a map becomes something far more crucial for people who have set out for some destination and lost their way. Picking the wrong road may be fatal. The map can point the lost travellers in the *right direction*, show them *the right way*. The world of RDP, then, is a map for the lost, showing them the right way.

Dualism, the notion that there are only two possible roads, is a fundamental category in the organization of the Protestant universe. To those who do not see with the eyes of faith, it might seem that there are not just two possible paths. To them it might seem that there are many different choices and destinations. For the Protestant, however, this seeming multiplicity dissolves into a basic dualism. Time and space as a whole are subordinated to this basic, original division. No portion of space and time is neutral, secular, profane—in the sense that it is not affected by these two basic fields of force. Etymologically *profane* means that which lies outside the limits of the temple, of the sacred (*pro*—"outside"; *fanum*—"temple"). But for the Protestant, that which lies outside the temple does not lie outside the sacred. Every human being is a priest; so wherever we find a human being, there we find the sacred.

Remember that Protestantism initially abolished monasteries and a privileged or special priestly class. Why? Because Protestanism transformed the world into a temple, and all believers into priests. In that sense life as a whole was garbed in the mantle of the sacred. In that sense the statement that religion is characterized by a division of the world into the sacred and the profane does not hold for Protestantism. Even things which a sociological perspective would place outside the bounds of religion—e.g., professions, politics, economics, leisure, and science—are included within the Protestant's religious mapping of all reality in terms of two possible roads.

To be sure, not everything religious is divine. There is a religious realm that is demoniacal. The wide road is grounded on a religious definition, but in this case religion represents a rebellion against the divine. By the same token, what we call profane or secular is not a realm indifferent to salvation. Rather, it is both an *obstacle* and a *means* on the road to heaven. As obstacle, it is *the world* and *temptation*. As means, it is one's *calling* or *vocation*.

Human Beings as Pilgrims

Protestant organization of reality as a dualistic map also implies a definition of the human being. What are human beings? Human beings are lost travellers, "alien[s] in a strange land" (HE, p. 427), pilgrims and wayfarers. This world is not their homeland or destination.

What does it mean to be on the road? It means refusing to accept this present space as one's destination. Each stop on the road points ahead to the next stop, but all of them are temporary resting places. They must be left behind if one is to reach one's destination. I am travelling in this space and time now and must leave it to get to another space and time; the road must be rejected as a permanent home. Being on the road means living in terms of *not yet*. It means experiencing the here and now as manifestations of poverty, privation, and incompleteness. Every oasis on the road is a temptation, for that is where people build idols.

The world is not the believer's home or destination. There is no solidarity between the believer and the world. It is a relationship of uncomfortable closeness between strangers. The world is a means, not an end. Believing in Christ means seeing oneself as a pilgrim on the way to heaven, as one who passes through space and time without loving them, as a traveller whose journey will end only at death.

Here we have another dualism which typifies the Protestant world. Besides the dualism of the two possible roads, we find a division between *the temporary* and *the definitive*, time and eternity, earthly life and eternal life. The wayfaring believer is moving from the realm of the temporary to the realm of definitive reality.

From a human standpoint travellers have two options: the wide road or the narrow road. But they cannot choose to be travellers or not. Being a pilgrim is part of one's very essence. One cannot escape the fact that human life, bounded by birth and death, is a temporary course. One's destiny and destination, the definitive realm, lies beyond life itself. Life is a *praeparatio mortis*, so one must be "prepared to die." Knowing how to live really means knowing how to die. Death is not the end but the moment of truth. It is the birth of eternity, the point where one's journey through life is crystallized. Questions about the meaning of life ultimately are answered in terms of the meaning of death.

"What does life offer me in the way of chances for happiness?" There is no way that this question could be uppermost in the Protestant soul. It suggests an interest in life for life's own sake, in life as an end. The first and foremost question is: "How can I live in such a way that death will unfold into a blessed eternity?" In the face of what is definitive, what is temporary loses all meaning of its own: "Earthly life is an opportunity for greater conquests and represents a struggle to reach heaven" (OP, March 1949, p. 2).

Standards of happiness or unhappiness based on pleasure collapse. What I feel as a result of my relationship with the world tells me nothing about the direction in which I am travelling. Pain or pleasure, poverty or affluence, sickness or health: none of these things tell me anything about my real condition. What counts is the teleological orientation of my life, its relationship to the ultimate end which lies beyond death. It is the end that gives meaning to the means. Even suffering, poverty, and sickness can be experienced as blessings, so long as the believer is convinced that they are the means to his or her eternal happiness. Hope in the final end effects a magical transformation of the means, so that tragedy is turned into triumph. Pain is not pain; misfortune is not misfortune.

The Eulogy of Death

Since they interpret reality in the above terms, Protestants necessarily eulogize death. Death is the dissolution of the superficial and the revelation of the essential. Life, as the realm of surface appearances, puts false masks on the real. The visible is false. Death destroys the illusion. The invisible is the true. Death reveals the truth of the invisible, which has been obscured by the lying curtain of appearances. To that extent believers can repeat the prayer of Francis of Assisi: "It is in dying that we are born to eternal life."

Notice that I am not talking about a eulogy of death in general.[11] Only in the death of believers is there buried an eternity of blessedness. The death of believers is not really death. They are "promoted to glory," and now dwell or sleep "in the Lord"; they are "raised to the eternal tabernacles." The temporary experience of *testing* gives way to the definitive experience of *reward*:

> Right after death the souls of believers are perfected in holiness and enter immediately into glory . . . saved, redeemed. . . . The wicked go to their place right after death for eternal punishment [BP, February 1961, p. 6].

So we have another dualism: the believer versus the wicked person. Who is the believer? In Protestant language it is the Protestant. The wicked are all those who do not belong to that category. The death of the believer leads to eternal salvation, that of the wicked to eternal damnation. In the passage quoted above, there is one little phrase that might not be noticed by readers unfamiliar with the subtler insinuations of this language. Note that the believer "enters *immediately* into glory." The allusion is clear. It is a slap at the Catholic doctrine of purgatory and the spiritualist doctrine of reincarnation.

For human beings, then, the real begins with death. It is the moment of liberation and fulfillment for the good. The eulogy of death is one of the most typical features of the manner in which Protestants live their world. It is sung in hymns and proclaimed in day-to-day life.

An old woman had lost her daughter long ago, while the latter was still a child. This is what she had to say about the child's death:

> It was good that she died so young, so pure. The world is so full of temptations and sufferings.

A woman missionary offered this word of consolation to a mother whose baby daughter had just died:

> Don't cry. Heaven, too, needs little angels.

When a close friend was being buried, a minister had this to say to a teacher who was deeply shaken and who asked him what meaning there might be to dying:

> What a glorious thing! I am anxious and ready to get going.

Death is the means by which God takes possession of human beings. God cannot possess them completely while they are still alive. To be alive is to be absent from God. When God really wants to take possession of his children, he does so by means of death. An old pastor had this to say to his grandchildren when their father died in the bloom of youth:

> God wanted to give himself a big present. The present was your father.
> So God had to call him from this life.

Life is thus defined over against death as an inferior level of reality and so it does not merit our affection.

Eternal Punishment

The Protestant universe is grounded on the two eternal destinies open to human beings. If those two poles were taken away, the RDP map would lose its meaningfulness as a guide for those who are trying to flee eternal damnation and win eternal happiness.

That is why Protestantism has zealously affirmed the existence of *eternal punishment*. Some Brazilian Protestants, including well-educated and truly pious people, have been forced to leave the Church because they raised doubts about the correct translation of the Greek term *aiōnios*. They wondered if it had to be translated as "eternal," because such a doctrine seemed to go contrary to God's love. Protestants realized that this doctrine was one of the pillars of their whole structure; if it were removed, the whole structure would topple. If there is a chance for the universal salvation of all in eternity—the notion of *apokatastasis*—if the punishment of the wicked is not eternal, then the Church's reason for being disappears. There is no sense in undergoing conversion or engaging in missionary work. The dualism of the two possible roads disappears, since there is only one ultimate destiny for all.

This issue became a crucial one for Brazilian Protestants in the early fifties. At first there was jubilation when Father Humberto Rohden converted to Protestantism. His literary work drew admiration because of the way he dealt with evangelical themes. The initial enchantment soon wore off, however, because Rohden began to show monistic and pantheistic tendencies in his thinking. In a monistic world there could be no dualism; in a pantheistic world there was no room for evil, the devil, sin, or eternal damnation. Both point towards the ultimate reconciliation of all opposites. In many sectors of the Church Rohden's thought seemed to offer a new possibility in comprehending the gospel message. But others saw great danger in it, and a large number of articles were written to combat his views. If the dualities are abolished between believers and the impious, between the two roads and the two destinies, what remains? One road only that leads to a sole destiny of blessedness. One of the most typical representatives of our Brazilian Church dealt with the matter in an article entitled "Letter to the Devil," which I feel sure was aimed against Rohden's views even though his name was not mentioned explicitly. That the addressee is the Devil is significant. It implies that the whole issue has cosmic implications. The author of the article is talking about a young woman who had decided to become a missionary:

> She preached enthusiastically for some time. Then, it so happened that she attended some philosophy classes and read a book published and sold under Protestant auspices. In the book and in her philosophy classes she learned, so she reports, that we all are going to be reintegrated into God. There is no damnation. She logically drew this conclusion: "If all are going to be reincorporated into God and there is no damnation, then there is no need to preach the gospel message or the death of Jesus." . . . But you [i.e., the Devil] know very well what is said in the clear-cut message of the Word of God and in the teaching of Jesus Christ: there is damnation and punishment for the wicked. *Hence* the obligation to preach the gospel message unceasingly [OP, June 10, 1953, p. 16; my italics].

In other words, the Church's reason for being depends on the duality of destinies.

Conclusions

We are now in a position to identify the poles and cardinal points of the Protestant universe, its way of organizing time and space. At the apex is eternity, the magnetic pole which inexorably attracts and engulfs time. Human beings float in the waves of time and, wittingly or unwittingly, they too are attracted and absorbed by eternity.

But eternity is not uniform. It is split into two poles which repel each other. At one pole we find light and salvation; at the other we find darkness and damnation. So we have heaven and hell, a sublime height and an abysmal depth.

If we ask Protestants about the origin of the universe, they will repeat the creation accounts to be found in the Book of Genesis. When we analyze their universe, however, we find that its historical origin (according to them) is not the basic explanatory category. It is the basic structure of their universe, not its genesis, that makes the whole thing intelligible. In short, it is eternity and its conflicting polarity which determines the organization of time and space. Time and space are visible projections of a cosmic conflict that is invisible but ultimate. The future is not viewed in terms of the present, nor is eternity viewed from the standpoint of time. Instead the whole construct of an eternal future provides the *a priori* forms by which one perceives time and space.

Salvation and damnation emit their rays, making two roads. But as they move out from eternity and form space and time, we see a process of inversion and masking. The dark light becomes luminous whereas the bright light turns into a shadowy zone. Phenomena are not revelations but masks over the essential. Human beings are deceived insofar as they live by the "wisdom of the flesh" alone. Only the eyes of faith can see the real light amid the darkness. Only the eyes of faith can contemplate the thing-in-itself.

There is a dividing line which starts from eternity and penetrates space, separating right from left, salvation from damnation. And there is another dividing line which runs perpendicularly through the first, separating time from eternity, the provisional from the definitive; it is death. Time is divided into two phases: before death and after death. Before death is the time of superficial appearances, when essential things are invisible. After death is the time when appearances dissolve and essences are revealed. The believer is one who contemplates reality *sub specie aeternitatis* even while he or she is still living in the time before death.

Most important of all, however, is the fact that the time before death is the time for making a crucial decision. After death time is crystallized and solidified. Eternity can pronounce "forever" on what was only provisional in time. There are no more decisions to be made. The journey has become destiny.

This structuring of space and time is obviously not the result of human activity, be it theoretical or practical. The Protestant universe possesses the solidity of things, the immutability of nature, the inevitability of mountains and seas. Indeed its rigidity and immutability is far more real and enduring than theirs.

What can one do with such a universe, since it cannot be transformed? One can *understand* it. Once its fatality is understood as such, one need only adjust oneself to it. Believers can echo the sentiments of Spinoza: "Not to laugh at, not to lament, nor to detest, but to understand" (Cassirer b: 70). The question of salvation becomes a matter of *comprehension*. That is why the mark of salvation is not action but absolute knowledge, why Protestants give priority to the indicative mood over the imperative mood. The indicative describes things as they are. One must adjust to the dynamics of the real insofar as that leads to salvation.

The Categories of Understanding

We must now move forward in our analysis. So far we have been considering the *a priori* elements governing the Protestant organization of time and space. But reality is not just an aggregate of temporal and spatial forms, of corporal shapes and movements. It presents itself to us as a system unified by connections. This unification of events derives from the questions we ask about them. We ask about causes and about ends. We ask ethical questions, wondering how human will and activity link up in the whole complex of efficient and final causes.

The first part of our investigation led us to its "forms of sensibility." Now we must consider its "categories of understanding."

The Efficient Cause: Divine Providence

Why? There is only one direct, unequivocal answer to cover every situation: "It is the will of God." It is a shorthand version of the doctrine of divine providence. In some way we cannot comprehend, all things and events are effects of one primary, transcendent cause. Above and beyond the universe, it guides all processes—physical, biological, historical, and individual—to the inevitable destiny that a sovereign will has appointed for them. As the Westminster Confession of Faith puts it: ". . . in relation to the foreknowledge and decree of God, the first cause, all things come to pass immutably and infallibly" (LC, n. 6.025). Nothing that is not supposed to happen, happens; nothing that is supposed to happen, fails to happen. Reality is defined by a rigorous, omnipresent causality. There is no room for accident or chance.

Our previous analysis of the Protestant organization of space and time revealed a world driven by dualism: left versus right, the wide road versus the narrow road, the wicked unbelievers versus the good believers, damnation versus salvation. The doctrine of providence, by contrast, ushers us into a monistic universe where there is only one cause, the will of God; that one cause is invoked to explain everything. How can RDP simultaneously uphold structural dualism and causal monism? That is done by appealing to the doctrine of twofold predestination. In his wisdom and goodness God has effectively predestined some human beings for salvation, and the rest for damnation. No one predestined for salvation is lost; no one predestined for damnation is saved. All the dualisms cited above are effects of one single cause: God's decree.

Divine providence is the supreme category for explaining things in the repertoire of Protestant reasoning. It is invoked as the first cause of all events, no matter what they may be. In everything that takes place the eyes of faith see the unfolding of God's immutable decree. If a baby dies, it was God's will. If one makes a good deal, that too was the will of God. One person who had bought a piece of property on very good terms described it as "a present from heaven." A church elder had this to say about the ins and outs involved in his purchase of a home:

> I had already closed the deal with this character. Then at the last minute he slipped away from me. I was angry that he broke his word, but I didn't realize that the hand of God was behind it all. He prevented me from making a good deal so that I could make an even better one. It so happened that another guy had bad money trouble and had to raise money quickly. He was forced to sell his house for peanuts, and I bought it. So the whole thing was due to the hand of God.

We might well question the divine ethic which causes financial disaster for one person so that another can profit from it. How do you explain God's partiality? Isn't the same divine causality used to explain the death of an undernourished poor baby and the healthy, contented smile of a rich baby?

One of the most eminent leaders of the Presbyterian Church of Brazil, a professor who taught many generations of ministers, thus described the mysteries of divine providence:

> Large numbers of women and children perished when the roof of the Rink movie theater collapsed, stunning the city and the whole nation. Near my home, a pretty baby girl under the age of three accidentally slipped out of her grandma's hands on the sidewalk and fell under an oncoming streetcar. There was no time to rescue her, or even for the driver to see her. But it happened under the gaze of her mother, who watched with stricken heart from a window as the awful tragedy took place. One cannot describe the general consternation of neighbors and friends, who were all deeply affected by the mysteries of divine providence. But believers in the Bible, and in the God of the Bible, bow down before the powerful hand of God, trust that he does what is good and just, and believe in the sovereignty of God in all that happens. This is not stoic indifference but a privilege to suffer which only the true believer knows [OP, April 10, 1952, p. 6].

Notice, first of all, that the appeal to divine providence renders an analytic understanding of the problem unnecessary. The movie house collapsed. Why? Perhaps the construction work was defective. Perhaps the building was old, or the wood had rotted. And why did the little girl die? Perhaps her grandmother wasn't paying attention. Perhaps the little girl didn't see the streetcar coming. Perhaps the conductor didn't have time to put on the brakes. All these explanations deal with secondary causes. But secondary causes are not real causes at all. They are the result of a primary cause, divine providence, which is invisible, irresistible, mysterious, and unanalyzable. There is really no point to any analytical explanation of the tragic event.

In the text quoted above, tragedy is directly associated with the *mysteries* of divine providence. That confronts us with a serious problem still to be solved. It is hard to see anything divine in senseless deaths. Indeed that sort of tragedy seems to be demoniacal. How exactly can we relate divine causality to cruel and inhuman results in a cause-effect way? How can we explain the apparent discontinuity between God's intention and benevolence? Is it perchance that the ethical standards which hold for human beings do not hold for God? A father who pushed his baby daughter under a streetcar would be considered a monster. Doesn't the same hold true for God?

All such questions and considerations are ruled out when the actor is God. A paradox: either God is not the cause of evil and hence is not omnipotent, or else God is the cause of evil and hence is not love. Believers cannot consider such paradoxes. They must "bow down before the powerful hand of God." Ethics is suspended in God's case. Ethics apply to people, but not to God.

The expression "the mysteries of providence" embodies precisely the perplexity and fright in the face of the absurd. But because of the doctrine of divine providence, the absurdity must be regarded as something "good and just."

I noted earlier that experience possesses no cognitive function for believers. In the doctrine of divine providence that assumption is carried to its furthest limits. Not even our moral sense can be invoked to criticize doctrine. The mysterious and benevolent shadow of divine providence falls over every human experience, including famine, poverty, pain, injustice, Biafra, Viet Nam, Buchenwald, Hiroshima, and Nagasaki.

The doctrine of divine providence effects a magnificent metamorphosis. It sacralizes the tragic, transforming it into a theophany. How is this miracle performed? The answer is simple. The tragic is a category of experience. It has to do with the realm of surface appearances, of falsity. What is immediately felt and lived is devoid of meaning.

That is why it is impossible to invoke an ethic of life-values or social justice to criticize Providence. The meaning of an event is not in the way we experience it but in the good intention of God who always does what is good. Providence guarantees that the end result will be good and just. Tragedy is the means needed to attain glory. Ethics is suspended in the name of a "happy end." Our suffering matters little if it is the means by which God leads us to an eternity of happiness:

> *Q.* 1 Thessalonians 5:18 tells us to "give thanks in all circumstances." Does this mean we should give thanks for accidents, disasters, and the mistakes we make?
> *A.* Yes, that is exactly what the holy teaching of the passage tells us. The point is that, no matter what circumstances divine providence may place us in, be they good or bad, we should continue to display the spirit of faith, submission to God's positive or permissive will, and gratitude and trust in our Father who, in everything, "works for good with those who love him" (Rom. 8:28) [OP, March 10/25, 1954, p. 3].

From the standpoint of eternity all suffering is transformed into a cosmic symphony. My own personal dissonances become part of a glorious universal harmony.

Permit me at this point to introduce two outside speakers into this discussion. They have nothing to do with the brand of Protestantism under discussion, but they do raise questions which Protestants might well consider. The first is Hegel, while still a young man. He notes that Christians have

> piled up such a heap of reasons for comfort in misfortune . . . that we might be sorry in the end that we cannot lose a father or a mother once a week [Kaufmann a: 58].

Under the mordant irony there is a warning that the doctrine of divine providence just might end up making us totally insensitive to life. The young Hegel contrasts Christians with the honest, courageous ancient Greeks. For the latter "misfortune was misfortune, and pain was pain."

The second outside speaker is a character in *The Brothers Karamazov*. Ivan Karamazov is arguing against divine providence with his brother, Alyosha:

> This poor child of five was subjected to every possible torture by those cultivated parents. They beat her, kicked her for no reason till her body was one bruise. Then, they went to greater refinements of cruelty—shut her up all night in the cold and frost in a privy, because she didn't ask to be taken up at night. . . . They smeared her face and filled her mouth with excrement. It was her mother, her mother who did this. And that mother could sleep, hearing the poor child's groans! Can you understand why a little creature, who can't even understand what's done to her, should beat her little aching heart with her tiny fist in the dark and the cold, and weep her meek unresentful tears to dear, kind God to protect her? . . . Why, the whole world of knowledge is not worth that child's prayer to "dear, kind God"! I say nothing of the sufferings of grown-up people, they have eaten the apple, damn them, and the devil take them all! But these little ones. . . . what am I to do about them? That's a question I can't answer. . . . If all must suffer to pay for eternal harmony, what have children to do with it? Tell me, please. It's beyond all comprehension why they should suffer and why they should pay for the harmony. . . . I understand, of course, what an upheaval of the universe it will be, when everything in heaven and earth blends in one hymn of praise and everything that lives and has lived cries aloud: "Thou art just, O Lord, for thy ways are revealed." When the mother embraces the fiend who threw her child to the dogs, and all three cry aloud with tears, "Thou art just, O Lord!" then, of course, the crown of knowledge will be reached and all will be made clear. But what troubles me is that I can't accept that harmony. . . . While there is still time, I want to protect myself, and so I renounce the higher harmony altogether. . . . I don't want harmony. From love for humanity I don't want it. [Dostoyevsky: 223–26].

Ivan has presented his argument. Providence is the doctrine of universal harmony. Reasons exist for all suffering. From eternity, God, as the supreme conductor, conducts his symphony. There's no fortuitous, accidental, or unnecessary suffering. Imagine one, only one, unnecessary groan. How is it possible to guarantee that other groans are unnecessary as well? The symphony is interrupted, invaded by dissonances that do not harmonize with it. The guarantee of a "happy ending" is destroyed.

Hegel and Dostoyevsky suggest that such a doctrine can make us insensitive to tragic events. But why would human beings close their eyes to such events? Because such events are an attack on the cosmos that we so carefully construct for ourselves. We have a need for order and meaning. The doctrine of divine providence is one of those symbolic universes "which proclaim that *all* reality is humanly meaningful and call upon the *entire* cosmos to signify the validity of human existence" (Berger and Luckmann: 104). It proclaims that reality is indeed a *cosmos*, and it lays down the *nomos* or standard governing the right order of existence.

Now we can appreciate the emotional function of this doctrine. One must exorcise the specter of disorder and chaos. One must also exorcise those spirits which call into question the *nomos*, bringing doubt, disorganization, and anomie in their wake. Tragedy must be interpreted as theophany, as the revelation of God's mysterious but loving designs.

A distinction should be made here between two different situations. We can readily appreciate why some poor mother, at the sight of her dead child, might be led to say: "It's God's will." In this brief expression are combined her feelings of impotence in the face of the irreparable and her hope that her love and tears have some meaning. It is a protest against the irrational, uttered out of the depths of sorrow; and it uses the doctrine of divine providence to make this protest. But when this same doctrine is used by people who are not suffering, then talk about divine providence ceases to be a profession of hope and becomes a cold, logical justification of absurdity. Since I don't suffer, I can, rationally and coldly, offer to the suffering the arguments to explain the need for their disgrace. Providence then becomes a justification of reality as fatal necessity; it absolutizes things as they are. *Facts are transformed into values.* This rules out ethical talk as to whether something should or should not be.

On May 2, 1960, Caryl Chessmann was executed in a California gas chamber. A wave of perplexity swept over public opinion. What was going on in Western civilization? Were we retreating into barbarism? How could the courts, in a country which claimed to be Christian and Protestant, calmly, coldly, and scientifically take away a human life?

That very same month an editorial defending the death penalty was published in the official organ of the Presbyterian Church of Brazil. Entitled "The Death Penalty and Our Doctrinal Standards," the thesis of the editorial was that Presbyterian doctrine supported the death penalty. It sought to induce all believers to adopt a uniform position vis-à-vis the issue, in line with official doctrine. Here is an excerpt:

> No one should be surprised. We should have one single view on this momentous question, like the good Presbyterians we ought to be. We need only consult what the Westminster Confession of Faith has to say about the Civil Magistrate: "God, the Supreme Lord and King of all the world, hath ordained civil magistrates to be under him over the people, for his own glory and the public good; and, to this end, hath armed

them with the power of the sword, for the defense and encouragement of them that are good and for the punishment of evildoers" (LC, n. 6.119). And here is the answer to Question 135 in the Longer Catechism: "The duties required by the sixth commandment are all the legitimate care and efforts needed to preserve our lives and the lives of others . . . through *just defence* against violence." And here is the answer to Question 136: "The sins prohibited by the sixth commandment are . . . taking our own lives or those of others, *except in the case of public justice, legitimate war, or necessary defense.*" Such is the thinking of the Westminster theologians, and it should be our faith as well [BP, May 1960, p. 3; my italics].

In September of that same year there was a reply letter printed in the same magazine. Written by a university professor from a different Protestant denomination, it challenged the earlier editorial:

The Westminster theologians were under the influence of the milieu in which they lived (England), where the death penalty and other medieval barbarities were in use. There is no reason why Brazilian theologians should cultivate those same influences.

The professor then went on to offer a series of reasons against the death penalty:

1. In Brazil we are accustomed to seeing the rich and the powerful easily escape mere imprisonment . . . So we would only see the execution of the poor and downtrodden. . . .
2. [The death penalty] is irreparable, and human justice is imperfect. . . .
3. It is against the New Testament teaching about conversion and regeneration. If we had had the death penalty in Brazil, a certain Baptist colporteur and a certain Presbyterian elder would long ago have gotten the worst of it because they committed many murders and received many prison sentences before their encounter with Christ. . . .
4. There is a more effective penalty: i.e., a prison sentence for a specified period of time. . . .
5. It is difficult to say exactly which criminal deserves the death penalty, especially in a society without social justice, such as ours [BP, September 1960, p. 8].

The line of argument seems logical enough. But, alas, it is totally illogical from the standpoint of those to whom it is addressed. Their line of reasoning is completely different. Let's take a look at the professor's reasoning.

First, his argument assumes that theology is conditioned by sociohistorical situations. He concludes that there is no reason to perpetuate mistakes of the past. But absolute knowledge cannot accept sociohistorical conditionings, since that would destroy it.

Second, he appeals to concrete experience. The courts are partial to the rich. Mistaken executions are irreparable. It is difficult to pinpoint the real criminal in an unjust society. Who is really guilty: the person driven by starvation to kill, or the person who causes such starvation by paying unfair wages? These arguments are on the level of secondary causes, but they have no explanatory power.

I have gone into these long citations and comments on the ideological function of the doctrine of divine providence for a reason. I wanted to provide the proper context for another article that I am going to cite. It is crucial, in my opinion. It was not written by just anyone. It was written by the secretary-editor of the journal, who may well have written the original editorial. It is a response to the professor's letter against the death penalty. I quote it at length because it is necessary:

One of the topics discussed on the editorial page of our May issue was the death penalty, a much-debated topic today. Attentive readers will have noticed that what was expressed in the editorial was not the private opinion of the editor of the editorial page but the authentic doctrine of our Church regarding the matter: i.e., the doctrine of our standards, the Westminster Confession of Faith and the Catechisms. . . .

[Respondents] attack the theologians who prepared the aforementioned creeds, alleging that on the matter of the death penalty they were "under the influence of the milieu." This comes down to saying that they did not express the doctrine they were claiming to extract from the Bible, but rather the belief of the people of that age; that they bowed to the ideas around at the time. . . . They do not seem to realize that this is an insult to the memory of those pious men whom we were taught to revere. . . . Others cite cases of crooks in prison, serving sentences for which they might have received the death penalty, who have undergone conversion, become new creatures in Christ, and are now bearing beautiful witness to the regenerating power of the gospel. They ask: If those criminals . . . had suffered the death penalty before their conversion, wouldn't their judges have impeded the work of the Holy Spirit . . . and wouldn't they themselves now be in hell?

It is immediately obvious that those who argue in such terms are not conscientious Presbyterians. They do not believe in Predestination, the consoling doctrine that "for his own glory, God has immutably pre-destined whatsoever comes to pass, especially with reference to angels and human beings." . . . The aforementioned argument is typically

Arminian: those convicted murderers needed to have their lives spared, in the absence of the death penalty, so that they might still have an opportunity to practice faith in Christ, receive salvation, and render service to the Kingdom of God. The initiative in undergoing conversion was theirs. God was awaiting the decision they would make. If death had intervened before their decision, they all would be damned.

We Presbyterians think differently. The initiative in the salvation of anyone and everyone has always been God's, and that is how it will always be. From eternity all those who have already been saved, and those who are still to be saved, were elected immutably and infallibly for life. Not one of them has been, or ever will be, lost. God predestined them for eternal life and, at the right time, he effectively summons them. Nothing can possibly abort or interfere with the divine decree governing the salvation of his chosen ones. . . . So we are not shocked or surprised by the ideas of an unrepentant criminal being executed, without Christ, for fear that if he were to go on living he might, perhaps, one day resolve to convert to Christ. God's work in the salvation of sinners cannot float in such uncertainty. . . . So we know for sure that if murderers escape the death penalty and convert . . . indeed the very nonexistence of the death penalty . . . entered into the eternal, wise plans of God [BP, November 1960, p. 4].

Let us examine the logical structure of this argument:

1. Doctrine is not historically conditioned. It is absolute knowledge. What was said in the past is the voice of eternity. It holds true forever.
2. Absolute knowledge affirms predestination, "the consoling doctrine that God 'has immutably predestined whatsoever comes to pass. . . .' "
3. To allege that the death penalty can interfere with the possibility of salvation is to make God's decree relative and subordinate to human actions: "God's work in the salvation of sinners cannot float in such uncertainty."
4. "So we are not shocked or surprised by the idea of an unrepentant criminal being executed." The doctrine of predestination guarantees that, if they are executed, it is because God so determined. *The occurrence of the event or fact guarantees that it is the will of God.*
5. Thus goodness or kindness cannot be invoked in opposition to facticity, what actually happens. What is, is what ought to be. Ethical discourse comes down to justifying what is.

The Inquisition was more compassionate. Women accused of witchcraft were often subjected to the water-trial. Hands and feet tightly bound, they were thrown into a well filled with water. People knew that water and the devil were mutually repellent because water was the symbol of baptism. So witches did not drown. If the poor victim survived drowning, her guilt was clearly established; so she was strangled to death. If she died by drowning, her innocence was established and she was in heaven at that very moment. In our present case, however, the very fact that a criminal is executed before conversion proves clearly that he was not divinely elected for salvation. Death at the hands of the law is evidence of his eternal damnation. And if God has no mercy on such a creature, why should human beings?

At this point some readers might suspect that I am being enormously unjust to Protestants. They might ask: Are there really many Protestants who think that way? After all, Alves's conclusions may not be based on a solid or significant sample. Isn't this an isolated case, an aberration?

I am not saying that all Protestants think that way. Indeed few of them have stopped to think about this question at all. I am not interested in making a statistical inquiry into the opinions of Brazilian Protestants. What interests me here is the logic that guides their way of thinking. And what I am saying is that this particular defense of the death penalty is nothing less than a specific instance of the logic that everything is the will of God, a logic to be found on the lips of every believer. Starting with the conclusions of the argument, one can proceed logically to trace them back to the basic propositions from which they are derived by deduction. And the basic, underlying propositions center around the doctrine of divine providence.

The argument cited above is strictly orthodox, and it did not provoke any strong reaction from church sessions or councils. If the argument had been heterodox, if it had violated the collective conscience, then the councils and theologians of the Church would have immediately leapt up to denounce it as heresy. Indeed when questions about social justice and ecumenism came up a little later, the Church reacted promptly and vigorously. In this case, however, there was total silence. It clearly suggests that this extreme case harmonizes perfectly with the logic of predestination or providence.

Here again we find the dualism noted before. The doctrine of divine providence equates facts and values. What is, is what ought to be. Why? Because it has been decreed by God. That is why the attitude of the orthodox believer should be one of "submission to God's positive or permissive will, and gratitude and trust in our Father who, in everything, 'works for good.' " When human consciousness refuses to accept facts, it is an emotional assertion that facts as such do not have moral status. Facts are denied in the name of values which arise out of human desires. Reality must be transformed. Insofar as the doctrine of providence turns facts into values, it forbids consciousness to rebel against them. It thus rules out the critical-minded use of human emotions. The indicative mood is made the imperative mood as well, and we cannot employ the imperative to challenge and transform the indicative statement of fact.

Logic is not confined to any limited sphere; it covers all time and space. It is possible to withdraw all objects and events from logic, reducing the latter to a completely formal and empty scheme. But it is not possible to withdraw this overriding logic from objects and events, because it governs their theoretical construction. The logic of divine providence goes beyond individual events and embraces the political order as well:

> God, the Supreme Lord and King of all the world, hath ordained civil magistrates to be under him over the people [LC, n. 6.119].

If we examine the above statement closely, we will find that it leads us to some sinister conclusions. Note that the text does not say that civil magistrates *ought* to be under God; it says that they *are*. Any hint of uncertainty would be dangerous, for it would suggest that in certain instances civil magistrates are not truly subject to God. That would destroy the doctrine of divine providence, because magistrates might be doing the things that were not decreed by God. Magistrates *are* under God's sway. Hence what they do as magistrates is the will of God. Here we have the sacralization of the powers that be. How can we possibly criticize or oppose them?

Note what this does to the democratic ideal. Democracy is rooted in the wise lessons of history, in the realization that power corrupts and absolute power corrupts absolutely. That leads to a system of checks and balances whereby each branch of government can exercise some control over the other branches and be controlled by them in turn. Democracy is possible only when we assume that the exercise of power is dominated by selfish interests; that power, left to its own devices, always tends towards totalitarianism. But if the civil authorities *are* under God, how can we set up a system of checks and balances? Applied consistently to the realm of politics, the doctrine of divine providence leads to a theocracy in theory and absolutism in practice. The democratic ideal rose out of the ashes of Plato's ideal of the philosopher-king, of a ruler who would combine power and wisdom in his own person. We must make do with a pragmatic arrangement which leaves aside the question of truth and settles for a balance of conflicting interests. But the doctrine of providence equates what is with what ought to be, thus sacralizing the established powers. What room is left for the pragmatism of the democratic ideal when such a doctrine goes hand in hand with the assumption that a minority possesses absolute knowledge?

If people are absolutely sure of the truth, then logically they should suppress error, even by force if necessary. In that respect Calvin was consistent: witches continued to be burned at the stake in Geneva. Consider the following items, dated 1545 and 1553 respectively:

> Calvin leads a campaign against witchcraft in Geneva; 31 persons are executed as witches.

> Michael Servetus, Spanish-born physician and discoverer of the pulmonary circulation, is burned alive as a heretic in Geneva [Szasz: 296; also see Bainton].

Tolerance is possible only when people assume, first, that what is in fact is not necessarily what ought to be, and second, that no one holds a monopoly on truth. No community, be it religious or political, can adopt an attitude of tolerance toward error and desires for reform if it assumes that it possesses absolute knowledge and knows that what is in fact must be.

I believe, therefore, that Troeltsch was right in affirming that "democracy, in its strict sense, is altogether foreign to the spirit of Calvinism." For "the aristocratic idea of predestination" leads toward thinking of the state as a "modified form of aristocracy" [Troeltsch a: 116, 113].

The Final Cause: Divine Providence as Power

When we come to the question of the aim and end of events, their *telos*, we realize that our question has been pretty much answered already. Efficient cause and final cause cannot be separated; they constitute one single reality. The efficient cause is the power of intention, and the final cause is the intention of power. Both come together in the doctrine of divine providence. If we wanted to put it in purely formal or abstract terms, we could say that the doctrine of divine providence is a theory of the universe in which efficient causes are subordinated to final causes as means to ends. Behind everything that happens in the world lies an ever-present intention. Events are arrows which God shoots toward his target. We see the arrow in flight, but we do not know where it came from or what target it will hit. We can be sure, however, that the arm which bent the bow belongs to the intention which chose the prey.

On the cognitive level, then, the doctrine of providence solves the practical problem lurking behind politics: i.e., the divorce between intention and efficacy, between love and power. Underneath surface appearances there is a divine politics at work; and it brings together the two seemingly divorced aspects. Here is the foundation for an attitude which combines fatalism and optimism. Those who have given themselves to Christ *know* that life is a problem which they are not to solve—since it has *already* been solved:

> Your hands guide my destiny.
> For me they bled on the infamous cross.
> Your hands guide my destiny.
> Chance will play no role with me!
>
> The great Father is just and benevolent,
> And will not afflict me without reason.
> In darkness or in light, all is as you will,
> And all is good, if it be your will [HE, n. 350].

There are no problems calling for human effort and exertion. Problems cannot be based on the superficial look of facts and events. We must look for the hidden design of God. What is the real problem? It is our inability to see that all problems have *already* been solved. So it matters little *that* we suffer. What counts is *how* we take suffering. Seen *sub specie aeternitatis*, facts and events cease to be problems and become sacraments of the divine intention. There is no need to transform anything. All we have to do is understand.

So we must learn how to *hear* what God is telling us in and through what happens. Events are the visible face of God's intention, but that face does not tell us anything by its visibility. Only those who have learned how to listen can hear the voice of events. In themselves events are the effects of certain causes, functions of certain structures. What they say to us is banal and insignificant because it has nothing to do with the ultimate aim of existence: the soul's salvation.

The doctrine of divine providence tells us that facts speak, that every phenomenon points to some essential thing. But we do not get from one to the other automatically. Only the eyes of faith possess the hermeneutic key that will enable us to read and interpret the true meaning of events.

Galileo had a similar insight. He discovered that nature was speaking to us. We did not understand the message because we were not speaking nature's language. And what language is this? The language of geometry, of triangles and squares, circles and spheres, cones and pyramids. Geometry became the hermeneutic key to the understanding of the voice of nature. Believers, on the other hand, know that the facts speak, not about mathematical relations, but about the heart. *The soul is the meaning of the world:*

> *God uses the language of facts.* In the miracles of Jesus he did not offer people the mere contemplation of pointless spectacles designed to arouse admiration. He presented *practical, profound, rich lessons—* lessons derived from the visible world—to *teach* us that he can work miracles *in the invisible world of our heart* [OP, June 25, 1951, p. 3].

The visible world is a function of the invisible world, external reality is a mirror of internal reality. The point of knowing the world is knowing ourselves, because facts and events are really talking about us. Here we have the Protestant (and Catholic) version of Plato's allegory of the cave. The world is a cave, and visible happenings are shadows. The shadows point us in the direction of the light. Their only real purpose is to signalize some invisible essence. The world is a text to be read and deciphered so that we may grasp God's didactic activity and the *gnosis* of salvation.

There is a Zen saying: "The finger points to the moon, but woe to the person who takes the finger for the moon." Once one sees the moon, the finger is no longer needed. Once one glimpses the invisible the visible becomes unnecessary. Fixing our gaze on the visible world may distract our attention from the invisible realm towards which it points us. Perhaps that is why believers close their eyes when they pray. They want to erase the visibility of the visible world in order to contemplate the invisible face-to-face. The world is simply a stage for the drama of salvation. The important thing is the soul, and it hopes to hear some message about its own destiny when it looks at the stage.

Facts and events in themselves matter little to believers. What matters to them is the voice of God hidden in events. Facts are coded messages which God drops along the way to guide believers to their true destination.

Divine Causality and Human Activity:
The Problem of Freedom and History

If the Protestant universe is defined and bounded by an inexorable divine causality, what is the significance of human activity? Is it merely an expression of divine causality? That would seem to force us into pantheism. Are pantheism and divine providence synonymous?

As I have already indicated, Protestantism rejects such a solution because pantheism would eliminate the possibility of dualism. It would also do away with the moral conscience and the sense of sin. But Right-Doctrine Protestantism clearly nurtures a sense of duty, guilt, and morality.

There is really no logical solution to the whole question of the relationship between divine providence and human responsibility. Why? Because here we find ourselves at the junction of two irreconcilable worlds: the Greek world and the Hebrew world. The doctrine of providence is a response to the Greek quest for the *archē*, the one underlying principle behind diversity of phenomena. It reveals a human being obsessed with the question of the theoretical unity and oneness of the real. The many are resolved into the one. At the same time we have the Hebrew perspective, which ignores such theoretical explanations of an all-embracing sort. The Hebrew conscience is intentionally focused on the moral question as it shows up in history—in the conflict between good and evil, egotism and love, freedom and bondage.

Once we have the junction of the Greek spirit and the Hebrew spirit, we do not get a new synthesis but rather a mere juxtaposition of two models that cannot be united. This shows up clearly in a passage from the Westminster Confession of Faith:

> God from all eternity did by the most wise and holy counsel of his own will freely and unchangeably ordain whatsoever comes to pass: yet so as thereby neither is God the author of sin, or is violence offered to the will of the creatures, nor is the liberty or contingency of second causes taken away, but rather established [LC, n. 6.014].

Two logically contradictory assertions are brought together in the above passage: (1) everything that comes to pass, does so by divine necessity; (2) human beings are free. In the actual practice of life, of course, we do not have to be logically consistent. We can choose our practical recipes on pragmatic grounds and disregard the logic of all-embracing explanations. In this case the logical contradiction is resolved by a working formula:

> Pray as if everything depended on God;
> Work as if everything depended on you.

We face a paradox, because the two dictums cannot logically be held simultaneously. "Everything depends on God" and "everything depends on persons" are contradictory propositions. Either one or the other, but not both at the same time. Nevertheless, such a formula faithfully reflects the Protestant attitude towards life. How to solve the contradiction? The key is the phrase *as if*. The formula is a fiction. It does not truly express the reality; it is kept as an unsolvable paradox. The two elements are identical in the mind of God, but in our understanding they seem opposed and contradictory. There is no logical solution for us. The determinism of divine providence and the freedom of the human being must be affirmed and lived by faith, but their compatibility remains a mystery.

The doctrine of providence sets up a fixed and finished world. Appearances vary on the surface of an unalterable structure. There is no room for the notion of *process* in the Protestant universe, except insofar as we are talking about the passing parade of mere appearances. The underlying reality was set up at the very beginning, before historical time. The future is merely the revelation of what was already there in the past. There is no room for the new and unexpected, for the exercise of freedom, because that would destroy the certainty of a happy ending. The price of freedom is the end to all certainty, and that is terrible.

> Nothing is more seductive for man than his freedom of conscience, but nothing is a greater cause of suffering. And behold, instead of giving a firm foundation for setting the conscience of man at rest forever, Thou didst choose all that is exceptional, vague and puzzling. Thou didst choose what was utterly beyond the strength of men, acting as though Thou didst not love them at all—Thou who didst come to give Thy life for them! Instead of taking possession of men's freedom, Thou didst increase it, and burdened the spiritual kingdom of mankind with its sufferings forever [Dostoyevsky: 235].

To live freedom in a radical way is to experience reality as open and undetermined, as something waiting for my love to fertilize it or for my hate to kill it. Freedom and absolute knowledge are mutually contrary, and never harmonize. Thus in order to maintain absolute knowledge, one must build a fixed and finished world, a world without the unexpected and without surprises. In this world, doubt is permanently exorcized, and in its place dwell the certitudes that tranquillize the heart. Protestantism, as the affirmation of an absolute knowledge, cannot accept history as a process of the generation of new possibilities. Instead of making use of the category of *process*, Protestantism, quite the contrary, and consistently with its principles, prefers to understand history as a mere *de-velopment*, an unwrapping, an unfolding of a predetermined reality. History is not built. The future is not created. One journeys through history. One lives in a time that emerges from a past which already contains it.

That the future and the present are found ready-made in the past is clear from a reading of events. How is one to understand what is occurring today? The arms race? The Arab-Jewish conflict? The oil crisis? The ecological crisis? The value revolution? Natural catastrophies? The answer is not to be obtained by means of an internal analysis of the phenomena. The question Protestants ask themselves is: In what way do the events of time reveal the hour of eternity? History is seen as the hands of an invisible clock, marking how much time still remains to us. The line of death, which divides our individual lives into two times—the time of decision and the time of eternalization—no longer has a purely biographical function. When the final hour sounds, the line of death will decree the end of history as well—the end of unfolding, the end of seeming process, the end of transformations. And herewith will be inaugurated a perfectly fixed, balanced, and final universe. This is Judgment Day, Christ's second coming. How many hours remain? How much time do we have? Events are "signs of the times." The end approaches. Hence the importance that what is occurring be understood in the light of the prophecies. The prophecies are newspapers dated yesterday about the events of tomorrow. That is, in the past the future was already concluded. Interest in events is not an interest in their content. On the contrary, the question is to determine at what point of the development, the unfolding, of the historical process we find ourselves, in order to know how much time still remains to us. And this is done by a comparison of the present with the prophetical chronogram already established in the past.

Once again the spirit of Protestantism and the spirit of science collide. The time on which scientific rationality lays hands is abstract time, time empty of tension and intention. One second of time is indistinguishable from any other second of time. Chronological time is absolutely indifferent as to its contents: it is time without haste. This is the reason why, in science, time is measured mathematically. It is time without intention. It is time as *chronos*, time that extends toward the infinitely past and the infinitely future: time without beginning, time without end.[12]

The time of the biblical universe, meanwhile, results from a creative act. It is the product of an intention. And in its development, it functions as the means for the realization of that intention. Or more precisely: it is the creative intention that, in its self-manifestation, creates time. Time, then, would not be a fundamental *a priori* of perception; rather, it would itself constitute, from a point of departure in an even more fundamental *a priori*, the intention.

What may we conclude? That the Protestant concept of time is identical with the biblical concept of time? Are they not both teleological times, times oriented toward an end? Surely they are. But there is a basic difference to be noted. In the Old Testament, the intention that creates time is the *redemption of history*. Accordingly, what happens in history is of fundamental importance. The prophet looks to the past not in order to find there the ready-made plan of an inevitable future, but in order to discover the intention of the divine power, *whose realization depends* on the obedience or disobedience of human beings.

> Hardly ever does [the prophet] foretell a plainly certain future. YHVH does not deliver into his hand a completed book of fate with all future events written in it, calling upon him to open it in the presence of his hearers. It was something of this kind the "false prophets" pretended. . . . Their main "falsity" lay not in the fact that they prophesy salvation, but that what they prophesy is not dependent on question and alternative [Buber: 103].

The divine intention reveals itself *as* an historical event, the Exodus; but it constitutes an invitation, not an inevitable fate. God depends on human beings. This intention points towards an historical future of redemption and justice; that entails a transformation of all relationships between human beings: "They shall beat their swords into mattochs, and their spears into pruning-knives" (Isa. 2:4). The divine intention shows up in the form of a *utopia*, a new sociohistorical order; it assumes the *abolition* of the present order.

The influence of Greek thought on Christian theology eliminated the utopian elements from the Christian conception of time. Greek time was circular: the end discharges into the beginning. Without aim or purpose it was irredeemable. The problem, then, was to transcend time and save oneself in eternity. When this conception was combined with the Hebrew element, Christian thought became a curious hybrid. Unlike Greek thought, Christianity stressed that time had a beginning and an end. But like Greek thought, it also maintained that the aim of time was the abolition of time and entry into eternity.

Thus the Greek spirit won out because such an arrangement ruled out the appearance of a utopian mentality. Utopias belong to the temporal order, which now became insignificant. And along with the disappearance of the utopian outlook went the abolition of the prophetic aspect of the Christian religion. The prophetic outlook must simultaneously do two things: (1) believe in the redemption of history; (2) continually deny that this redemption is already present as reality. Redemption is a future horizon. History is the journey of a people toward that horizon, a journey marked by the dialectical interplay of awareness and hope. We are aware that the present is not yet redeemed: i.e., facts are not values. But we also have hopes for a new future.

In such an outlook conscious intention calls for some structuring of historical time. We cannot contemplate the creation of a new space except through the mediation of time. In the Greek-Hebrew amalgam noted above, by contrast, this temporal orientation of consciousness is replaced by a spatial orientation: i.e., the visible space of appearances over against the invisible space of essences. And since the two areas are already fixed and finished, human activity has no role to play in their creation. Dialectic gives way to dualism. Human activity does not create any new time or space; it simply effects *dislocations*, movements towards the more solidly organized space within a rigidly organized frame of time.

The prophetic and utopian outlook propose to create a new time and space by *negating* and *abolishing* the present. It assumes that the present is not the result of some divine causality but of options taken by human beings. And what was built by human beings can be demolished by human beings. In this perspective politics is this work of demolition and construction, a mediating tool between the present and the future.

In the Protestant universe utopia is already fully present in suprahistorical space. Hence politics is unnecessary. The only task is to *see* what is already there, finished and full-blown.

The above remarks might well seem to contradict all the stereotypes about the spirit of Protestantism: i.e., its disciplined asceticism, its work ethic, its pragmatism, and its obsession with activity. Am I suggesting that Protestantism is a contemplative religion? Not at all. I don't deny RDP activism in the least. What I am trying to point out, however, is how Protestants *understand* their activity. Framed within the doctrine of divine providence, this activity cannot be seen as creativity. It can only be interpreted as *witness*, as a revelation of the inner being and life of the believer.

Prayer as Contradiction

On this point, meanwhile, a problem arises that calls for elucidation. To the extent that the limits of their language denote the limits of their world, human beings who articulate the language of providence live in a fixed and finished universe. At the same time, these same human beings, at certain moments, parenthesize the language of providence, suspend it in a provisional silence, and articulate in its place the desiderative language of prayer.

What is prayer? It is a language which expresses a desire. In prayer human beings present God with their deepest anxieties and hopes. And that would be totally senseless if people did not believe that their wishes were capable of altering the course of events. The praying person seeks to abolish the power of for *this is the way things are* for the magic of *this is the way things ought to be*. But how can believers use both languages, or substitute the language of wish for the indicative language of divine providence and its workings?

One explanation offered is that the wish expressed in prayer is always subordinated to God's wish: "Thy will, not mine, be done." But then why mention one's own wishes at all? It would seem more sensible to say: "Thy will be done" without any reference to one's wishes. This explanation explains nothing, for it seems to render prayer superfluous and unnecessary.

Another proffered explanation is that prayer is essentially communion with God, not an effort to move God by some sort of magic. The fact is that prayer is often a simple act of thanksgiving or adoration. It asks nothing, it only says: "I give you thanks, O God."

But these explanations do not exhaust the list. Prayer is also supplication, petition, and a struggle with God. It is in prayer that human beings express their protests against things as they are, and their hopes that somehow a new causality will be set in motion and change the course of events.

If a medical doctor is a believer, he or she will use all the resources of science in diagnosing and treating patients; but he or she may also pray to God for guidance and success in treating a patient. If a mother sees her son leaving the Church, she will pray that God do something to save him. Despite the doctrine of double predestination, a husband or wife will pray for the conversion of a non-believing spouse. Indeed believers pray for all sorts of things: that the sick be cured, that wars cease, that churches grow, that enemies be reconciled, that rain should fall or that it should stop, that business be successful. They obviously feel that in some mysterious way their wishes can move God's supreme will, which would remain unmoved if they did not express their wishes in prayer. Their prayer somehow sets in motion some extra burst of efficacy that would not exist if they remained silent.

Prayer, then, reveals something surprising to us: a believer who does not believe in divine providence as an ironclad causality; and *another God* who heeds human desires and alters the course of events. In a rigorously deterministic universe, in which emotions are impotent in confrontation with reality, prayer is an impossibility.

We are confronted with a contradiction. The doctrine of divine providence says: "What happens is the effect of an inflexible, transcendent causality." Prayer says: "Human wishes are able to move mountains." Providence and prayer cannot be logically reconciled.

How are we to explain this contradiction? Here I must resort to tools outside the storehouse of Protestant reasoning. In *Totem and Taboo* Sigmund Freud suggested that there was a strong resemblance between the psychic life of primitive humanity, which used magic to achieve its objectives, and the psychic life of neurotics. Human desires are the motive force behind the use of magic, and early humanity had great confidence in the power of its desires (Freud d: 109). Wishes and desires are forces capable of changing the course of events. In a similar vein Bronislaw Malinowski suggested that magical behavior arises when reality interferes with the realization of desires (Malinowski: 79). The use of magic represents a refusal to accept the verdict of actual facts. As Bloch put it: "What is, cannot be the truth." Neurotics, too, think that their wishes can abolish the real world and create the world they are hoping for. Thus magic and neurosis are acts of rebellion by the pleasure principle against the reality principle.

Is there a resemblance between magic and prayer? Obviously. They differ only in form. In both instances human beings are motivated by the hope that their desires can, in some mysterious way, affect the real and alter its course. Like magic, prayer is the cry of the oppressed creature. It is a refusal to accept the cruelty of facts as final, a hope that human values can bend invisible necessity, a wager made on the pleasure principle as opposed to the reality principle.

What is the reality principle in the world of RDP? It is the doctrine of providence. Prayer is a murmured protest against an ironclad order obsessed with the "glory of God" and impervious to human happiness.

I see prayer as a Freudian slip in the RDP world. Repressed and prohibited, the language of prayer still slips out within the RDP discourse on providence. Prayer tells us that the rebel is not yet dead, that consciousness has not bowed completely to divine providence. The soul is still capable of expressing its desires in the face of necessity.

Unfortunately the relationship between the two types of language remains problematical and overlooked. They are logically contradictory, as I noted earlier. To the extent that RDP is obsessed with the glory of God, it cannot find any meaning in a language which articulates the wishes of human beings. There is no synthesis of reason and feeling here. Indeed, as I will show in the next chapter, the RDP ethic discredits personal feelings, disciplining and repressing them by means of a heteronomous code of reasoning.

I think this helps to explain the artistic poverty of Protestant worship. The creation of a work of art requires the artist to integrate forms of expression with personal feelings. Form and feeling come together. Catholics were able to create a liturgical drama, the Mass, in which both elements were combined harmoniously. We see nothing like that in Protestantism. Protestant worship tends to fluctuate between the extremes of excessive verbalization (cold rationality) and excessive emotionalism (amorphous heat). Protestantism itself oscillates between these two extremes: Right-Doctrine Protestantism on the one hand, and Protestantism of the Spirit on the other.

Conclusions

1. The Protestant universe is structurally identical to the medieval universe. The visible is explained by the invisible, the immanent by the transcendent, time by eternity. Catholics and Protestants inhabit the same world.

2. The structure of reality is fixed. No transformation of its essence can take place. Here we find a radical break with the modern world, which has replaced the category of essence with the category of function.

3. All points in time and space are split by a basic dualism: damnation versus salvation.

4. Dualism is resolved in the unity of divine providence (or, double predestination). Both salvation and damnation are effects of one and the same cause.

5. Human activity cannot be creative. It is movement within a fixed universe, a journey along roads leading to eternity.

6. Life is not an end, only a means.

7. This scheme functions ideologically insofar as facts are elevated to the status of values. They serve as the visible face of an invisible divine intention. Protestantism sacralizes tragedy.

8. Once visible facts and events are seen to be theophanies, tolerance and democracy become impossible. Tolerance and democracy presuppose that facts and knowledge remain ambiguous. Such a presupposition is ruled out in a universe of theophanies, one which is known absolutely by a certain religious community. There are many affinities between the doctrine of divine providence and a totalitarian theory of power and authority—a theocracy in this particular case. Tolerance would be possible if Protestantism postulated divine providence but admitted only imperfect knowledge. It would even be possible if RDP claimed absolute knowledge of the world but admitted that the world was open-ended and incomplete. But Protestantism absolutizes both poles: reality and its knowledge of reality. So, despite Protestant disclaimers, it seems to me that epistemology contains, in its articulation with the Protestant vision of the world, the seeds of authoritarianism embedded within it.

FIVE

BELIEVERS ARE DIFFERENT: THE PERSONAL ETHIC OF RDP

Morality as the Physiognomy of Salvation

As we have indicated, the recent convert is defined as the one who "does not yet know what he or she believes." The problem facing converts is to get beyond their condition of ignorance and take possession of the absolute knowledge demanded by the conversion experience. On the other hand, we have shown that the Church is defined as the institution which holds a monopoly on knowing. The solution of the problem of knowledge, therefore, demands that new believers forget the knowledge they bring with them, and substitute the knowledge that is codified and crystalized in the institution. Convert and Church unite in a relationship of subordination: the apprentice submits to the teacher.

We now leave behind us the process of world apprenticeship. Our new converts have now learned how reality is structured. They have mastered the content of Protestant discourse and its syntax. But they still lack another type of knowledge. The indicative mood does not suffice. It is not enough to know *that* the world is thus and so. One must also learn the imperative mood. One must know *how to behave* in this universe. We come to the realm of duty and morality.

The Protestant subordinates the question of morality to the question of salvation: "What must I do to inherit eternal life?" To ask this question is to look for a description of the *physiognomy* of salvation. The new convert has moved from the expression of emotions to a more precise knowledge of the RDP world, but salvation has not yet taken on a concrete face. It will become visible and objective only when it is embodied in behavior. In defining morality one is describing the Spirit-made-flesh. Here we get the phenomenology of salvation, the physiognomy of the "new being" and its life in the Spirit.

There must be no possibility of mistakes. The physiognomy of the Spirit must be described clearly and in complete detail. For this description will provide the elements that will enable the Church to separate true believers from false believers, the wheat from the chaff. The ecclesial institution must have criteria which will enable it to recognize those who are truly a part of it. The conversion experience will not suffice because its concomitant feelings and emotions remain buried within the subjective life of the individual. How to distinguish false from true emotions? Impossible. The acquisition of absolute knowledge marks an advance. True believers must profess the right doctrine. But even the criterion of absolute knowledge is not enough because not all those who profess orthodox doctrine are true believers. Absolute knowledge is a necessary criterion, but insufficient.

The physiognomy of the Spirit becomes clear and precise only when morality is added to knowledge. The only true believers are those who make the orthodox confession of faith *and* behave in accordance with the rules laid down by the Church. If one of these two elements is missing from the life of an individual, then he or she does not possess the necessary prerequisites for membership in the community. It is the union of knowledge and moral behavior which defines the ideal type of Protestant personality, the human being who is truly "in Christ."

Morality as a Function of the Collective Conscience

How do new converts learn what behavior fits in with their new life? How is their moral conscience formed? How do they become capable of distinguishing between good and evil?

Here again we find a process of apprenticeship. New believers do not know what to do. It is the Church that has a monopoly on ethical knowledge. It knows what is good and what is evil, so only it can offer commandments: "Thou shalt. . . . Thou shalt not." Just as the Church determines the indicative, so it determines the imperative. The earlier teacher-learner relationship is now extended to the area of moral apprenticeship. The ecclesial institution gives commands; the individual believer obeys them. At an earlier stage the cognitive awareness of individuals was negated so that they might be taught the Church's absolute knowledge of reality. Now the moral conscience of believers must be negated so that they can acquire the Church's knowledge of good and evil. It is in the collective conscience of the Church that believers will find the answer to the question: "What must I do to win eternal life?" The individual's ethical consciousness must be replaced by the collective ethical conscience. In other words, RDP morality starts off with the fact that the Church imposes itself on individual believers, becoming their living, vigilant, and powerful conscience.

It is time to offer some evidence for my assertions. Here is a question which someone asked a church theologian:

Q. Is it permissible for a believer to listen to a football game on the radio at home on Sunday?

The issue might seem to be of secondary importance, but it isn't for Protestantism in Brazil. Sunday is the "Lord's Day," and keeping it holy is absolutely central. Here is what the theologian replied:

A. On Sunday believers can and should do anything which ensures them, *in good conscience*, three harmonious things: mental and physical relaxation, personal sanctification, through worship of God, communion with him, and the practice of any good deeds which they have an opportunity to perform. . . . One sincere believer may find relaxation in listening to the radio; another believer, equally sincere, may not make use of the radio on Sunday [OP, May 25, 1953, p. 3].

The theologian's reply seems to negate what I have been saying. It suggests that the external form of behavior is not the critical thing—at least in this specific case. The important thing is that it be done "in good conscience." The theologian refused to give a definite yes or no answer to the question. This implies that the Church cannot impose its collective consensus on the conscience of the individual believer.

But the fact is that his answer was in direct conflict with the ethical norms of his Church, and hostile reactions were not slow in coming. Here are the adverse comments of two church leaders:

1. . . . although there are problems of conduct that should be left to the discretion of the individual, there are others for which *the Church has established principles of a general nature that are sufficiently clear to help [believers] in solving inner difficulties connected with those problems.* Now it so happens that the "Tele-Fatos" section of the same issue . . . reported the negative attitude of a certain Church towards two young women who were dancing. *The church session did not judge that the matter in question was one to be decided simply by the conscience of the persons involved—and it was quite right, in our opinion.* Hence the reply given by our distinguished colleague *does not seem to us to be in harmony with the consensus of the Church* regarding this issue.
2. In his reply we learn that the resolution of the problem is to be left to the judgment of each individual believer. We disagree. And I ask: What is the one and only rule of faith and practice for one who believes in Christ? Is it the Holy Bible or the CONSCIENCE OF THE SINNER? [OP, June 10, 1953, pp. 5–6].

The two replies agree on two points. First, both deny that the question of morality can be solved at the level of the individual conscience. They reject the idea that conscience is to be the arbiter of ethical decisions. Individual conscience is the CONSCIENCE OF THE SINNER. The Calvinist doctrine of the "total depravity of the human being" rules out the possibility that human beings might have any ability at all to distinguish between good and evil.

The second point of agreement follows from the first. It is that individual conscience must be subordinated to an authority which makes the final decision on ethical questions.

Ecclesiastical Discipline: The Juridical Shape of the Collective Conscience

Here some readers might pose another objection. Why do I assume that the two rebuttals really represent the spirit of the Church in question? Why don't I take the voice of the church theologian cited above as the official one? Am I generalizing on the basis of two statements alone?

No, I am not. I have cited the two rebuttals above as examples because they spell out the rationale of RDP morality, a rationale which finds embodiment in the institution of *church discipline*. The latter is the whole complex of mechanisms which, on the basis of a text universally accepted by the Church, catalogues punishable faults, receives complaints and denunciations against transgressors, and then doles out judgment and punishment. As the *Code of Discipline* makes clear (Chapter II, art. 9; see MP), punishment may take the form of a warning, exclusion from the sacraments, or expulsion from the church community. The institutionalization of church discipline means that the behavior of individuals is subjected to the judgment of church tribunals. It is the Church's way of saying that it has a monopoly on ethical knowledge. If individuals want to participate in the church community, then they must act in conformity with this knowledge. By arrogating to itself the right to impose penalties, the Church asserts its status as the conscience of the believer. A person's conscience may subjectively be at peace with itself, but guilt becomes objective through the imposition of punishment. Peace of conscience is no proof of innocence. Guilt and innocence are not determined by the feelings of individuals. They are determined by the logical relationship between individual behavior on the one hand and church norms on the other. And the norms are the ones affirmed by the collective conscience and institutionalized in church discipline.

This institutionalization of morality means that the ethical condition of the individual is essentially juridical. Individuals find themselves before a tribunal—an entity that is objective, alien, and coercive. It is objective because it is independent of subjective desires and intention. It is coercive because it has the power to punish and exclude people. It is alien because it ignores and denies the ethical judgments of the individual conscience.

Hence when I say that individuals find themselves before a tribunal in matters of morality, I am not indulging in a figure of speech. As soon as a sin is verified as such, it takes on the character of a petty or serious crime; and it is presented as such to the Church in the form of a written *complaint* or *accusation*. At that point the church community is transformed into a court of law that is to pass judgment on a defendant. As the *Code of Discipline* puts it (Chapter IV, art. 18; see MP): "The councils convened for judicial purposes function as tribunals." And what is the function of tribunals? To "try and pass judgment on" the guilty party, and then impose some ecclesiastical sentence as a penalty (ibid., art. 19). The mere reading of the relevant texts in the *Code of Discipline* will reveal the juridical nature of its underlying mentality. The ultimate point of reference for all RDP morality is the church tribunal, before which any believer may find himself or herself eventually.

The function of church tribunals is to punish sins. What is a sin? According to *The Shorter Catechism*, "sin is any want of conformity unto, or transgression of, the law of God" (LC, n. 7.014). Can we therefore conclude that the tribunals in question propose to undertake the task of punishing all sins? Obviously no, since that would be an impossible task. Why? Because all human beings, by theological definition, are sinners. If the church tribunals were to punish *any and every* want of conformity with the law of God, then they would dissolve in a process of self-punishment; for the church judges, too, are sinners. Thus church discipline must make some sort of distinction between punishable and non-punishable sins. Moreover, it must assume that those who hand out verdicts of *guilty* to transgressors are themselves innocent of the same offenses.

Note well what all this means. The institutionalized morality of the church community cannot start off from the liturgical confession of sinfulness by all believers. Insofar as the whole community shares a common guilt, the exercise of church discipline would be impossible. Only some sins can be punishable. Sins that do not fall into that category are morally indifferent insofar as church discipline is concerned. In other words, the latter sins are not serious enough to distort the *physiognomy* of salvation. Believers must continue to make their private and public profession of sinfulness, to be sure, but punishable sins indicate that such sinners are already living apart from God, that the eternal destiny of their soul hangs in the balance.

I was almost tempted to write that church discipline establishes the boundaries between the human and the inhuman, but I caught myself in time. This Protestant ethic ignores these categories. It would be far more correct to say that church discipline draws the line between grace and disgrace.

The Limits of the Permissible: Punishable Sins

Where are the punishable sins formally spelled out and defined? Nowhere. The definition of these sins comes down to a series of tacit conventions familiar to all. No codification is necessary. Disciplinary practice demonstrates a persistent regularity where punishable sins are concerned, such that it is possible to organize them in six distinct classes. The first class is composed of *sexual sins*. The second contains *violation of the holy day, the Lord's day*, Sunday. In the third we find the *vices: smoking, drinking, gambling*. Fourth come *crimes against property,* as theft and dishonesty. Finally, a fifth category contains *crimes of thought—heresies.* Interpreted in a negative way, the tacit conventions here are very explicit: whoever commits sins of the types listed above will be liable to punishment. Interpreted positively, they offer a moral profile of the believer: the believer is the one who *abstains* from sexual sins, from violating the Sabbath, from the vices, from crimes against property (believers are honest), and from thinking in disagreement with the Church. Abstention from such sins delimits the area of innocence and grace. Their commission situates the human being in the circle of guilt and disgrace.

Sexual Sins

A discussion of problems of sex is open to a series of misunderstandings. I should like to call the attention of my readers, especially my Protestant readers, to my purpose here. My intention is to *describe and analyze* the logic of this particular Protestant morality as manifested in the mechanisms of church discipline. I am at pains to adopt as objective an attitude as possible. I am not propounding a new morality. I am only describing the morality which this church discipline places before me. I am not asserting that it is correct or in error. I am merely making an analysis. My intent is simply to render explicit, clear, and articulate, what this Protestant morality accepts in an implicit way.

Protestant morality as defined by church discipline is concerned with only two things. The first thing is the *norm* to which the act under judgment is subject. The second thing is verifying whether the act in question does or does not transgress the norm. The whole process is akin to a syllogism. The major premise is the norm, the minor premise is the act, and the conclusion is the final judgment.

This sexual morality is governed by a very simple and completely unambiguous principle: *sex is permissible if, and only if, it takes place in marriage.* There is a categorical prohibition of sexual acts and sexual relations *before* marriage and *outside* the marriage relationship. Such sexual acts are sins that must be punished.

From the juridical standpoint, then, sexual morality is defined clearly and precisely; but a price is paid for this clarity. Overlooked and ignored are certain elements which are of fundamental importance to any moral act. Take sexual relations before marriage, for example. By lumping all such acts together as sinful, church discipline fails to distinguish between acts which may be very different in content. Sex relations with a prostitute may be purely genital and manipulative, totally devoid of love. Sex relations between lovers or engaged couples, on the other hand, may be expressions of great tenderness, affection, and love; they may occur in a context of interpersonal relations marked by responsibility and respect.

The same holds true even in the matter of adultery. For relations labelled adulterous may range from a chance encounter with a prostitute to long-standing and stable relationships. Consider the following case which was presented to an interpreter of the Church's thinking for an answer:

> *Q.* Many years ago this man left his legitimate wife and went to live with another woman. The man and this other woman have lived together as husband and wife for almost thirty years. Now this couple have undergone a conversion to the gospel message. Can they be accepted for profession of faith and baptism?
> *A.* No [BP, January 1962, p. 8].

In this situation church discipline exercises a preventive function. Instead of throwing a sinner out of the community, it prevents someone defined as a sinner from joining the community. Let's reformulate the whole question for the sake of greater clarity. This particular couple has lived as husband and wife for almost thirty years, even though no law obliged them to do that. We have every right to conclude that their relationship is an embodiment of freedom and love. Now if that is indeed the case, what must the couple do in order to join the Church?

Here is how the answer of the Church would go. From the legal standpoint, the situation of this couple is one of adultery. If people want to belong to the Church, their lives must conform to the norm. Hence this man and woman must break off the love relationship that has existed between them.

This Protestant morality in general, as exemplified in this particular case of sexual morality, gives priority to legality over love, to form over substance in life. It is an abstract morality, which refuses to consider the concrete specifics of a given situation. Set aside as irrelevant are love, fidelity, and responsibility as existential determinations of the moral situation.

> Believers divorced and remarried legally in countries which permit divorce can be received into our churches [BP, April 1960, p. 4].

But how do the two cases differ? Obviously, on the basis of a consideration of the elements of freedom and love, there is more to be said for the former than for the latter. Meanwhile Protestant morality rejects the former and accepts the latter. The reason? A purely formal one: the conformity of sexual activity with the norm that it only be permitted within marriage. And marriage, at least in this specific case, appears to have its legality defined not by evangelical principles, but rather by civil law. If civil law does not permit divorce, a separated couple is faced with a definitive prohibition as far as their sexuality is concerned. If, on the contrary, divorce is permitted, the Church has no objection. We are forced to the brutal conclusion that, *for this Protestant morality, civil law is the boundary of grace.*

It seems to me that it is sexual morality that gives the key to another Protestant disciplinary practice: that of considering dancing a sin, and of judging and imposing penalties upon those who dance. The documents of the Church's official bodies record a high number of disciplinary actions taken against persons who have attended dances. Here are the comments of two ministers:

> It is impossible for a normal male, holding a woman in his arms and feeling her body, to prevent the arousal of impure passions and sexual desire.

> The problem of dancing continues to vex the honor of church councils. As far as we know, all we have *to combat the sexual danger of dancing* is a pamphlet by Miguel Rizzo entitled *Dança e Psychanalyse* [OP, May 25, 1953, p. 12].

The rigorous Protestant disciplinary stance against dancing suggests that dancing, in its view, is a stylized and symbolic version of the sex act; to go to dances, then, is to expose oneself willingly to temptation and thus tarnish the purity which should mark every believer:

> *Q*. Can a believing student take part in the class dance . . . that is part of their graduation day?
> *A*. It is never permissible for a believer to take part in dances. It is an improper and worldly celebration *that only harms the senses* [OP, September 25, 1952, p. 4].

> *Q*. Is it permissible for believers to dance, and to take their children to family or school dances?
> *A*. Modern dancing—i.e., dances in general . . . in the neighborhood, clubs, dance-halls, or at school—do not fit under Philippians 4:8-9 and 1 Corinthians 10:31. They are to be avoided completely by believers [OP, August 10, 1956, p. 3].[13]

If simple dancing is punishable under church discipline, one can imagine how Protestants views the carnival celebration that is such a traditional part of Brazilian life. It is the

> apotheosis of prostitution . . . recreating the bacchanalia, saturnalia, and lupercalia of ancient pagan Rome [in which] the priestesses of Bacchus, the god of wine and drunkenness, ran frenzied through the streets, hair all undone, thyrsus in hand, filling the air with their lascivious songs . . . drawing after them crazed young men and dirty old men who were eager to satisfy their coarse appetites. . . . A pagan feast practiced *most enthusiastically in countries considered Catholic* [BP, February 1959, p. 1].

Here we meet another element underlying the Protestant ethic of sexual purity as defined by church discipline. It tends to associate sexual permissiveness with Catholicism. Church discipline for sexual sins, then, functions to ensure that "believers are different." But it also has broader implications and consequences. It tears converts away from their cultural roots, which are equated with "the world" or "impurity."

Do we find a positive doctrine of sexuality in this Protestantism? I must tell readers that when I asked questions along this line, I met with complete and total silence. I found no sermons on sex as grace, no Sunday-school lessons, no articles. It is very difficult to hazard an opinion about something that is not discussed at all. But we might also remember what Gunnar Myrdal said about silences:

> The hypothesis is that we almost never face a random lack of knowledge. Ignorance, like knowledge, is purposefully directed. An emotional load of valuation conflicts presses for rationalization, creating blindness at some spots, stimulating an urge for knowledge at others [Myrdal: 29].

Considering that Protestantism pretends to be a system of absolute knowledge, we might well wonder about its silence with regard to the positive value of sex. What unconscious values enforce silence in this area? The most likely hypothesis, it seems to me, is that the Protestant ethic makes room for sex only by way of *permission* and *concession*.

Sexual pleasure is not a grace. It has nothing to do with the essence of the human being. The function of reproducing is commanded, but sexuality as such is something accidental and transitory. So I would conclude from a church theologian's response when he was asked why angels don't get married:

> *A.* They are not entitled to "increase and multiply" as creatures (Gen. 1:28). . . . And up there in heaven no natural multiplication will be needed because the number of created beings will have reached its final limit [BP, September 1965, p. 7].

Here we have a reaffirmation of Augustine's teaching on sexuality. Sex is a means, not an end. Its purpose is to complete the number of those predestined by God for salvation and damnation (Augustine: 457). Thus two requirements come together in this sexual morality: (1) that sex be dissociated from eroticism; (2) that the function of sex be subordinated to the conscious intention of procreating.

What must be emphasized here is that this teaching about sex presupposes an anthropology. In this specific case Augustine is the determining influence on both Catholic and Protestant anthropology. And behind Augustine we find that strain of Greek thought which divinizes the intellectual functions of the human soul at the expense of the body's vital impulses. Anthropological disorder is equated with the predominance of the latter impulses over intellectual functions. To cure that disorder is to restore the predominance of intellectual functions and repress the impulses of the body.

Augustine's doctrine of original sin is a classic example of the myth of the fall being interpreted in Greek categories. And this is revealed most clearly in the realm of sexuality. When human beings experience sexual desire, rationality proves to be impotent in the face of vital instinct. Commenting on the fact that Adam and Eve covered themselves when they found they were naked, the Bishop of Hippo wrote: "Shame modestly covered *that which* lust disobediently moved in opposition to the will" (Augustine: 466; my italics). "That which" is obviously a reference to the genital organs. Prisoners of an inner disorder, human beings cannot subordinate their bodies to reason. They watch helplessly as the sexual instinct expresses itself in their experience of sexual desire. In fallen human beings desire has turned into the motive and aim of sexuality. How is harmony to be restored? By getting back to the original condition. Sexual pleasure must be dissociated from the sexual function:

> What friend of wisdom and holy joys, who, being married . . . would not prefer, if this were possible, to beget children without this lust, so that in this function of begetting offspring the members created for this purpose should not be stimulated by the heat of lust, but should be actuated by his volition, in the same way as his other members serve him for their respective ends? [Augustine: 464–65].

Buried beneath Protestant silence on sex as grace are centuries of talk about sex as shame. It is a silence that speaks; and what is speaking here is Neoplatonism, Augustinianism, and the whole Catholic spirituality of exalting virginity and imposing sexual abstinence on all those who would attain the loftier spirituality of the religious life.

The abolition of sex in heaven and the prohibition of sex to those closest to God mean something clear and unmistakable: God and sex are two mutually repelling poles. But it must also be admitted that behind the shared Protestant and Catholic shame of sex lie the words of Paul:

> It is a good thing for a man to have nothing to do with women, but because there is so much immorality, let each man have his own wife and each woman her own husband. . . . All this I say by way of concession, not command. . . . To the unmarried and to widows I say this: it is a good thing if they stay as I am myself; but if they cannot control

themselves, they should marry. Better to be married than burn with vain desire [1 Cor. 7:1–8].

Now if sex is simply a concession, if marriage is merely a remedy against a worse evil for those who cannot control themselves, then Augustine, Catholics, and Protestants are right when they say that one can only feel shame in speaking of sex or expressing it. As Augustine put it: "Lust requires for its consummation darkness and secrecy" (Augustine: 466). Protestant silence about sex is a way of expressing shame at the language level. Sex is spoken of in the dark and in secret, with a plea for forgiveness.

But then what do we do with the Old Testament? For in it sex is spoken about in direct and unmistakable terms. And this discourse reaches its climax in the erotic *Song of Solomon*, which is part of the canon of sacred books:

How beautiful you are, my dearest, how beautiful! Your eyes behind your veil are like doves, your hair like a flock of goats streaming down Mount Gilead. Your teeth are like a flock of ewes just shorn which have come up fresh from the dipping; each ewe has twins, and none has cast a lamb. Your lips are like a scarlet thread, and your words are delightful; your parted lips behind your veil are like a pomegranate cut open. Your neck is like David's tower. . . . Your two breasts are like two fawns, twin fawns of a gazelle, which delight in the lilies [Song of S 4:1–5].

Come, my beloved . . . let us go out early to the vineyards, and see if the vine has budded or its blossom opened. . . . There I will give you my love [Song of S 7:11–12].

Shame could not chant such a song. It was compelled to reduce to silence what the biblical poet praised: love for love's sake, pleasure for pleasure's sake, with no reference to procreation. That is why Catholic hermeneutics interpreted this song as an allegory of Christ's love for his Church. The bodies disappeared to make room for spiritual, asexual entities. Protestantism did the same thing. Here is an excerpt from an editorial in the official organ of the Presbyterian Church of Brazil:

What gives this particular song its incomparable merit over against other songs in the Bible? Surely it is the fact that it, more than all the others, is concerned with Christ—the Pearl of Great Price—who is supereminent in value as compared with the other things we prize in life [BP, November–December 1958, p. 12].

One cannot talk about sex as grace when church discipline defines it as a permitted concession. And the boundaries of this permission are set by marriage as civil law defines it. Neither sexuality nor love expressed in sexual self-giving constitutes the living essence of morality in this area. Instead the essence is found in a formal, abstract definition of marriage, which in turn becomes the basis of sexuality. Once the civil fact of marriage is established, the sex act is permitted.

But here certain questions must be raised. Isn't sex frequently immoral, even within marriage? We know it is not rare for marital relations to be determined by economic and social interests. We know they can be loveless relations in which people are used and manipulated. By the same token, sex relations outside marriage may be filled with love. But the logic of church discipline tells us that it is not love that makes sex legitimate. Indeed church discipline would abolish itself the moment it took the living content of an action as the determining moral factor. The exercise of church discipline essentially means the dominion of law. Actions are judged by their form, not by their content.

The meaning of Protestant sexual morality extends beyond the area of sexual activity, taking in the whole body as well. Like sexual activity, the body is moral insofar as it serves as a means to an end. What, then, determines the aims and ends of bodily activity?

Freud's clinical observations led him to conclude that the body set its own purposes, that the program of the "pleasure principle" decided the purpose of life (Freud a: 23). Nietzsche spoke about the body as a "great reason" (Kaufmann b: 146), as the ultimate value which everything else must serve. In other words, the body is its own absolute, as suggested in this striking passage in *1984*:

> On the battlefield, in the torture chamber, on a sinking ship, the issues that you are fighting for are always forgotten, because the body swells up until it fills the universe, and even when you are not paralyzed by fright or screaming with pain, life is a moment-to-moment struggle against hunger or cold or sleeplessness, against a sour stomach or an aching tooth [Orwell: 102].

In this perspective the utopian project of the Ego would be the liberation of the body from everything that blocks or represses its expression. The human tragedy is not that the body has liberated itself from rationality, but rather that it has been subjected to a repressive rationality and turned into a means rather than an end. The body is unhappy because the social arrangements of civilization have made it a function of rational structures that serve as the commanding norm. The erotic components of behavior, ranging in the broad sense from sexual pleasure to the pleasant contemplation of stars at night, do not constitute the basis of duty and morality. The body is moral only when it serves as a means to some end imposed on it from outside, only when it becomes an instrument in the service of some commandment.

The Protestant ethic of the body, as revealed in its sexual morality, embodies this latter view of the body as mere instrument. Its affinities with Kant's ethic are obvious. As Kant saw it, willing was moral only when it was determined solely by *duty*. The body's pleasure and happiness did not enter into consideration at all. The author of the *Critique of Practical Reason* did admit that feelings might happen to produce actions that were formally in accord with the command of duty; but such *accidental* agreement was of no significance. Morality demanded that action be *determined* by duty. Hence any action determined by the erotic impulses of the body was immoral, whether or not it happened to accord with duty.

Morality imposes an obligation on the will to systematically repress the body's vital instincts. That is precisely the logic of classic Calvinist morality. Max Weber saw clearly that the Calvinist ethic was a combination of *discipline* and *asceticism*. Discipline subordinates the body to certain ends, turning it into a mere means. Asceticism prohibits people from taking the body as its own end. The body is placed under a regimen of systematic self-abstention so as to produce an action which represses the body rather than expressing it. In love-play and dancing the body denies all alien rationality, acting in a way that gives expression to its impulses. So prohibitions of sexual activity for its own sake and dancing are merely specific applications of a universal norm: i.e., the body ought not express itself but rather repress itself. The greater the repression of the body, the closer one gets to God; the more the body expresses itself, the farther away one moves from God. Nietzsche glimpsed the implications of this type of spirituality, shared by some Protestants and Catholics: "The saint in whom God delights is the ideal eunuch. Life has come to an end where the 'kingdom of God' begins" (Kaufmann b: 490).

But we might well pose certain questions to Protestants: Doesn't your sexual morality imply that God is not the creator of sexuality and the body, of pleasure and the world? In your creed you profess that you believe "in the resurrection of the body." But here are you not joining those Greeks who profess belief only in the immortality of the soul, who see the body as an accidental, passing thing? How can you profess faith in the resurrection if the body itself is not an ultimate value? Why do you claim that God reveals himself in experiences involving pain and suffering, but not in pleasurable experiences? Is it, perhaps, that God is a sadist? If one follows this logic to its ultimate conclusion, then it leads to the uncomfortable position pointed out by G. S. Hendry:

> If, however, the utterly transcendent God, who stands over and against the world, and whose grace has to be dearly bought with moral effort and discipline, cannot be worshiped by means of anything that is

pleasant, the eucharist itself would be disqualified; for it is pleasant to eat bread and drink wine (Psalm 104:15) [Hendry: 31].

In the area of sexual morality and the ethics of the body we find the same thing that we found earlier in the RDP theory of knowledge. Life is replaced by language, the body by talk, and experience by a discourse which ignores experience. And if the essence of neurosis is the repression of the body by an alien rationality, then we must conclude that the Protestant ethic inevitably tends to produce neurosis. But this brand of Protestantism is merely one species in a larger genus that includes equivalent versions of Catholicism. And we may draw this general conclusion: any religion which imposes a regime of systematic repression on the body, in the name of a spiritual order, tends to produce neurotic personalities.

Sunday Violations

Many readers might find it odd that the use of a radio on Sunday would prompt a big debate. But that simply means that outsiders have no idea of the spiritual and moral importance attached by Protestants to keeping the Lord's Day. In an article I have already cited, the author put it this way:

We recognize the imperative necessity of providing the Church with a coherent, uniform, and certain teaching with respect to all matters of importance in the spiritual life of the flock. No one will deny that keeping Sunday holy falls under this category. . . . If we grant that a believer may listen to a football game on the radio on Sunday, because he says it makes him feel good mentally and physically and does not harm his spiritual life, then we do not see why he may not, on the basis of this principle, move on indefinitely to many other similar concessions. Listening to plays on the radio on Sundays, for example, certainly need not harm his spiritual life. And the same could be said for whatever other programs the believer likes and wants to hear. And if listening to such programs causes no harm, why should we say that seeing them would be bad? Some believers will say that they can attend a good football game on Sunday, get good mental relaxation, and do no damage to their sanctification. Others will say the same about a good play or a good movie. Obviously, then, once we grant the premise, we can easily be led to conclusions with the gravest consequences. Such believers will end up, not just bringing the world into church and home, but bringing church and home into the world [OP, July 10, 1953, p. 6].

Observance of Sunday would seem to signalize the purity of the Church and its separation from the world. But that is not the basic question. The second writer in that same issue had this to say:

"And do not fear those who kill the body but cannot kill the soul; rather fear him who can destroy both soul and body in hell" (Matt. 10:28). . . . It is the Lord whom we should fear, says Jesus. And he gave us a commandment which orders us to keep holy his day, just as he gave us commandments about avoiding covetousness, robbery, adultery [OP, July 10, 1953, p. 7].

Sunday must be observed because there is a commandment which says so. And obeying the commandment is a matter of salvation or damnation. A believer is characterized by the way he or she behaves on the Lord's Day; and behavior which transgresses the limits must be punished by church discipline.

So all agree that Sunday must be kept holy. But what does that mean exactly? What is permitted and what is prohibited? There is no consensus among Protestants on this question, so let me offer a few examples of how far some may go in trying to keep Sunday holy:

1. A North American missionary, noted for her dedication, insisted that believers should not open any correspondence that might reach them on Sunday. To open and read correspondence is to let mundane concerns invade the Sunday atmosphere of prayer and meditation.
2. Many consider the reading of nonreligious books, journals, and newspapers as a violation of the Lord's Day. Such reading is permissible only after midnight on Sunday.
3. I know at least one minister who regards sexual intercourse between husband and wife on Sunday as sinful.
4. One pious Elder was deeply scandalized to find out that the students of an evangelical school listened to the profane music of composers such as Beethoven and Chopin on Sunday.
5. At one evangelical school students were forbidden to take part in any recreation or sports on Sunday.
6. Several churches forbade youngsters to play ping-pong on Sunday.
7. One Elder used to offer this final word of advice and admonition to all candidates for profession of faith: "Now you are believers. No stopping to sip a cup of coffee or buy an ice-cream bar on Sunday" (because commercial transactions were involved).
8. A certain missionary was upbraided by a colleague for using a horse and buggy to go and pray at a little church on Sunday. The church was ten kilometers away. The problem, you see, was that an employee had to go and get the horse from a field. That is work. The missionary accepted the rebuke and thenceforth made the trip on foot.
9. Students who are believers cannot study on Sunday, even if they have exams the following day [OP, March 25, 1954, "Consultório Bíblico," q. 5.306].

But the best illustration of this Protestant attitude towards Sunday is a little story which appeared in the children's section of the Church's official magazine:

> Sunday, 8:30 A.M. Mama was getting little Peter ready to go to Sunday School. She urged him to get ready quickly and be on time. As Peter put on his cap, the Devil said to him: "Take your marbles to play with." Peter replied: "I don't play marbles on Sunday." The Devil said: "Not to play with, but just so you can finger them now and then." On his way, however, Peter met a buddy and did not resist the temptation to play marbles; and he played to win. One of the marbles rolled into the gutter. Peter went to pick it up, got his hand dirty, and buried his dirty hand in his pocket. He got to Church late and did not want to go in for the lesson. When the other kids came out, he asked for a copy of the lesson sheet and headed home. But he went slowly, sadly, and in a bad mood. When he got home, his mother asked him if it was a good lesson. "Yes," he replied, "but on the way home I fell on the sidewalk and dirtied my hand in the gutter." His mother asked him what the golden text of the lesson was. Peter replied: "I don't remember now, but God knows that I went to Sunday school." And with the hand in his pocket he counted the marbles he had won in the game. . . .
>
> Peter worshipped the marbles instead of God—he broke the first and second commandments. He spoke the name of God in vain—he broke the third commandment. He did not honor the Lord's Day—he broke the fourth commandment. He did not honor his mother because he disobeyed her—he broke the fifth commandment. He stole, because gambling is stealing; he lied; he coveted the marbles of another—he broke the eighth, ninth, and tenth commandments [OP, July 10, 1951, p. 6].

It strikes the eye that there is a big difference between the morality that regulates sex and the morality that makes rules for Sunday observance. The line between what is permitted and what is not is clear and simple in the former case. In the latter case there is an unending casuistry. Case after case is brought up in trying to define what exactly is permitted and what is not. The classic example of this approach is that of the Pharisees, who went so far as to prohibit the eating of an egg laid on the day after the Sabbath because it had been fashioned by the hen on the Sabbath itself. Since nothing could be made or done on the Sabbath, that was a violation of the Sabbath law!

We need not delve into the details of Protestant casuistry here, because church discipline has simplified the parameters of the permitted and the prohibited. Granting some possible variations, I would say that there is general agreement that certain activities are definitely sinful transgressions of the law governing Sunday observance:

1. All commercial activities are prohibited since they entail expenditure and profit-seeking. In cases of extreme need or situations specified by law, an exception may be made.
2. All recreational and entertainment activities are prohibited. Believers cannot go to the movies, football games, theaters, or clubs on Sundays.

In short, Sunday calls for the paralyzation of all activities involving production, consumption, and pleasure-seeking. *Homo faber* and *homo ludens* must give way to *homo religiosus*. I noted earlier that Protestants did not make any division between the religious and the profane, that all points in time and space were part of the journey to eternity. Now the division of the week into six work days and one day "set apart for the Lord" might seem to contradict my assertions, but in fact it does not. Every day of the week is part of the journey towards heaven. Sunday is an oasis, a time for meditation and communion. On Sunday people revitalize their spiritual energies so that they can faithfully carry out their religious vocation during the rest of the week. Sunday is the day of the Word, when sermons and study reaffirm and confirm the RDP ideas about reality. Repetition of the same language Sunday after Sunday helps to ensure a fixed and stable world. Just as marriage is the disciplining of sex, so Sunday is the disciplining of mind and spirit. That is why "spiritual exercises" are ordered for Sundays. As the *Shorter Catechism* explains:

> The Sabbath is to be sanctified by a holy resting all that day, even from such worldly employments and recreations as are lawful on other days; *and spending the whole time in the public and private exercises of God's worship*, except so much as is to be taken up in the works of necessity and mercy [LC, n. 7.060; my italics].

Notice that the command to sanctify Sunday by resting has nothing to do with any imperative to rest the body. In the latter case the imperative would be determined by the body itself, which would then have the right to decide its own way of resting. Indeed that is the logic of those believers who argue that a movie, a game, or a picnic would be a sensible way to rest; for resting is not inactivity but a change of activity. Sunday would then be a respite from the "forced labor" of weekdays and its repression of the body. It would allow for pleasurable activity that enabled the body to express itself.

For the Protestant, the dialectic between "six days you shall labor" and "you shall rest on Sunday" is not parallel to the dialectic repression-expression. All bodily activities stop on Sunday so that the whole time may be taken up by the spirit. To the repression of the body on weekdays in the pursuit of one's calling is added the repression of the body on Sunday so that the soul can express itself. The body has no rights, particularly on Sunday.

What is permitted and prohibited on Sunday has no connection with human biological needs. Sunday is not the creation of a natural, humanistic ethic. No expression or even sublimation of the body is permitted; and all that is left is repression. The Sunday imperative derives from the will of God, so human reasons have no place. Perhaps nowhere is the heteronomic nature of the Protestant ethic more evident than here.

Vices: Crimes Against the Body's Master

Believers do not have vices. That is one of the hallmarks of their Protestant character. Conversion to Christ means the end of smoking, drinking, and gambling. One Brazilian theologian had this to report during a trip to Europe: "In Alsace . . . no one is scandalized to see a seminarian smoking a nice pipe or a theology professor sipping his mug of beer" (OP, May 10, 1953, p. 1). The writer and his readers in Brazil *were scandalized* with the use of the pipe and beer. It might also be noted that the liturgical principles in force declare that "the elements of the Holy Supper are bread and wine, and the session must make sure that they are of good quality" (MP, p. 117). In reality, however, the churches use grape juice for the sacrament of the Eucharist.

I am not suggesting that abstention from vices is not salutary. I simply want to point up the reasons underlying this abstention. The reasons behind Protestant abstention from smoking and drinking are not medical or economic. They have to do with the conception of the body in philosophical and theological terms. That conception can be summarized in three points:

1. The body is a means for certain ends. Hence norms of behavior cannot be derived from bodily instincts and needs.
2. The corruption of the body—sin—involves an inversion of this correct order. The body becomes an end instead of a mere means.
3. The imperatives of morality seek to restore the correct divine arrangement by subjugating and disciplining the body. It must be turned into an instrument of God's will. For, as the *Shorter Catechism* tells us, the chief end of human beings is not pleasure or self-fulfillment but "to glorify God and to enjoy him forever" (LC, 7.001).

Here we find a whole philosophy of life. While it may be true that our life-program is determined by the pleasure principle, believers know that such a program is doomed to failure. Or, to be more exact, it is doomed to eternal damnation. So instead believers submit to a divine program: the will of God. As one put it:

By reading the Bible and praying I managed to discover God's plan for my life. I have never regretted doing the will of God, but I have always regretted what I do when I follow my own sinful will [OP, April 10, 1956, p. 5].

Believers are servants of a lord and master. Their will is his will. Their bodies do not belong to themselves—indeed nothing does. Nothing can be used for ends which human beings set for themselves:

All that I have—life, health, intelligence, possessions, money—belongs to God. He requires of me that I administer it all well. My talents are God's treasures [ibid].

I am not a proprietor, I am simply a steward or administrator. God is the owner and master, and I am responsible for what he has entrusted to me. This is the doctrine of *stewardship*:

What are you really doing with your life? Make no mistake: in living one is investing the immense capital which God entrusted to one [OP, September 25, 1953, p. 16].

The fact that this anthropology, this view of the relationship between God and human beings, is expressed in terms borrowed from economics is revealing. Economics is the logic of *exchange-values*, not of *use-values*. Money cannot be consumed as food can. It is devoid of human meaning and existential density. It has only a symbolic function. Money and capital are defined in terms of the *operations* which can be realized with them. Economic logic is the logic of abstract operations. It leaves no room for considerations of *value* in a human sense. In making an investment, an investor cannot ponder the human significance of that investment. From the profit standpoint, it makes no difference whether one invests in a business that grows roses or a business that manufactures weapons.

My talents, which serve for my self-expression in life, are God's treasures. They are God's money or capital. From the theological standpoint, then, the human being is viewed as a *potential field of divine operation*. God defines me as a means to his own ends. The role of the human being is to be a good administrator, a responsible steward. As a potential field of divine activity, I should be used in terms of my maximum profitability. In the parable, the servant who buried his talent was cast into the exterior darkness, where there was weeping and gnashing of teeth. So my body must be ever ready and available to its owner and master, God.

Now it should be clear why RDP opposes vices. A vice is a relationship between the body and some object in which the body is enslaved to the object. In such a case, the body cannot be used by a human being in terms of its maximum profitability for God. Vice is an obsessive pattern of behavior in which the body is possessed by some object as if by the devil. The person in question knows that the vice is irrational and enslaving, but his or her reason is impotent in the face of impulse. His or her body is incapable of disciplining itself and subjecting impulse to divine rationality. In such a person grace is not fully at work. The function of grace is to cure and rehabilitate nature. But if created nature is to be defined in terms of the submission of vital instincts to rationality, then a body in bondage to irrational impulses is obviously not yet fully under the power of God.

Anyone might oppose vice for medical reasons, for the sake of the body. But Protestants denounce vice because it defines the human being as a means to a divine end, as God's capital, as a field of divine operation. The primary concern is the health, not of the body, but of the soul. If medical reasons are brought into the picture, as they often are, they are merely *additional* reasons. The fundamental religious reason remains the same, however: my body does not belong to me, it belongs to God. In succumbing to vice I rob God, I commit a crime against my body's owner and master. Hence vice is a crime against the right of ownership. Since I possess nothing, I have no right to decide how to use what only *seems* to be mine. I must remember that *my body was entrusted to me only so that I might produce a return on it and make a profit for God.*

Crimes Against Property and the Norm of Total Honesty Always

Sexual morality, we see, unlike the ethics of the Sunday observance, has no casuistry to offer us. Innocence and guilt are determined in function of a clear and simple norm: Within marriage—defined civilly—sex is allowed; outside marriage it is forbidden. As for the positive content of sexual morality, we would have to say that it is to be encountered in that immense silence which, in its shame, renounces speaking of sex as grace.

As was true in the case of sexual morality, there is no casuistry with regard to theft. It is sinful to take possession of anything belonging to another in a surreptitious way. There is nothing more to be said. It could not be otherwise because theft is defined as a crime by civil law. All believers know that theft is prohibited, so we do not find any systematic or insistent talk about theft in Protestant literature. This almost total silence about theft, however, is the negative side of a trait which typifies the Protestant personality, and which is spoken about repeatedly and in clear-cut terms. The Protestant believer is honest, and all are proud of this fact. Theft is merely one instance in which the imperative of honesty is broken. The imperative itself must find expression in all of life's situations.

And what is honesty? The most important thing to note here is the fact that honesty goes far beyond matters of property and ownership. For the believer, to be honest is to tell the truth always. He or she must be a mirror of the facts always, whether it is a matter of speech or of action.

In filling out their income-tax statements, believers must tell the whole truth and nothing but the truth. Workers are honest insofar as their work hours are truly hours of work. In terms of the doctrine of stewardship, it is not the worker-employer relationship that matters here but rather the worker-God relationship. God in his providence placed his children in that particular situation, and the children of God must be absolutely faithful in administering their talents, their God-given capital. A secular calling is a sacred calling, and the Big Eye will not allow any act of deception. The same holds for Protestant students. They may not use any dishonest means to prepare their lessons or to pass their exams. Cheating is deceit and theft because one pretends to possess knowledge that one does not really have.

In every situation the believer is expected to behave honestly and truthfully. Hence he or she is also expected to have the courage to confess any transgressions of morality. The husband who has been unfaithful to his wife, the wife who has been unfaithful to her husband, the student who, in a moment of weakness, has become angry—in order to be restored to their condition of believers, must make a confession, since, in confession, deceit is dissolved: the innocent is revealed as guilty. Believers do not take bribes. Believers do not buy raffle tickets. They are entirely submissive to legality in all its forms—political, domestic, professional, etc.

This dovetails with the doctrine of divine providence. If the various orders of society are the product of God's will, and if God requires patient submission to his will, then true Christian behavior must entail acceptance of God's providential designs and functional adaptation to them. Lying in any form is an expression of *rebellion* against the will of God. Believers must tell the truth because what truth is, is the will of God. Their conscience must mirror the real, and their speech must enunciate what really is.

But how is truth defined? In this case truth is defined as the conformity of intellect and speech to the thing spoken of. As such, truth is one of the *a priori* elements of Protestant morality. It is an unconditional absolute, which is not in any way dependent on considerations of a practical nature.

Let me offer a concrete case. Suppose a doctor has just discovered that a patient is suffering from an incurable disease. What should the doctor tell the patient? The plain truth might hasten the end, creating an atmosphere of terror and paralyzing the patient in the amount of time left to live. Or, on the other hand, the truth might have a beneficial and liberating effect as the patient contemplates death face-to-face. A friend of mine who was in a Nazi concentration camp told me that he had never felt so free as when he was condemned to death during his stay there. Death dissolves many of the trivialities we deemed important: the desire for possessions, status, power, and so forth. It tells us discreetly that the only important thing is living. Only those who experience the terror of death can truly marvel at life. As Don Juan the Yaqui mystic, put it:

Death is the only wise adviser that we have. Whenever you feel, as you always do, that everything is going wrong and you're about to be anni-hilated, turn to your death and ask if that is so. Your death will tell you that you're wrong; that nothing really matters outside its touch. Your death will tell you, "I haven't touched you yet" [Castañeda: 55].

The announcement of approaching death can be a liberating thing, but the doctor does not know if it will be. His talk is suspended in doubt, and he can only wonder what his word will do to the patient. Hidden in his doubt is the certainty that his word should be something more than mere conformity with the facts, for it has the capability of giving new life to the patient or killing him. Insofar as truth is mere conformity between what is said and what is, it is an abstract truth. For it does not know or care what may possibly result once it is spoken. Another type of truth is at stake here: truth as a word that does good, that serves life and love. The doctor speaks amid the terror of uncer-tainty, not knowing for sure whether his words will do something good, will be real truth or falsehood.

Protestant morality rules out any such thing from happening because it defines truth as *conformity between what is said and what is.* What our words will do to the listener does not matter, so long as they conform to the facts. The speaker's obligation to be consistent and honest is the only important thing:

> *Q.* Is it permissible for a Protestant doctor to lie to a patient in order to forestall a worsening of his or her condition?
>
> *A.* No. It is not permissible for any believer, under any circum-stances or for any purpose, to lie to, speak less than the truth to, delude, or deceive anyone at all [BP, September 16 and 30, 1963, p. 5].

Notice that all consideration of purpose is prohibited ("for any purpose"). The ends do not justify the means, even when the ends may be goodness and love. Notice also that the real-life situation is put in parenthesis: "It is not permissible for any believer, under any circumstances . . . anyone at all." In other words, the imperative to tell the truth always totally disregards the contextual situation. Another example makes this still clearer:

> *Q.* Can a believing merchant, who has a certain kind of merchandise in his shop and is selling it at a reasonable profit, conceal that merchan-dise later, without saying that he does not have it to sell, in the hope that its price may increase in the market?
>
> *A.* Yes, because everyone may dispose of what belongs to him as he wishes and deems opportune. What the believer cannot and should not do is tell a lie. To have the merchandise in stock and deny it was there

would be a downright lie. . . . The believer should be frank and honest with a customer and say: "I do have that merchandise in stock, but it is not desirable or beneficial for me to sell it at the moment." Then everything would be correct and above board [BP, December 1963, p. 5].

The important thing is for the believer to be frank and honest. What does that mean? It means making sure that what one says is in conformity with what really is the case. The whole issue of business behavior and its impact on one's fellow human beings is subordinated to the right of property: "Everyone may dispose of what belongs to him as he wishes and deems opportune." In this case opportunity is defined in terms of the chance for a bigger profit. Economic activity is left to the mercy of avarice. No consideration is given to the human consequences of such an approach. As long as the believer admits openly what he is doing, everything is "correct and above board."

Here again we see affinities between the Protestant ethic and that of Kant. The latter had commented on lying in a small treatise *On a Supposed Right to Lie from Altruistic Motives*. This was a reply to Benjamin Constant, who maintained that the maxim, "It is a duty to tell the truth," if adopted and practiced consistently and unconditionally, would make any society impossible. Kant rejected this view: "To be truthful in all declarations, therefore, is a sacred decree and must be obeyed in an absolute way, limited by no expediency" (Lehmann a: 126).

In both RDP and Kantian ethics, then, the category of finality or purpose is to be totally ignored by human conscience. Ethics is not reflection seeking suitable means to attain certain ends. The intention or aim of an action has no role in conferring moral worth on the action. An action is moral when, and only when, the will behind it is determined completely by the imperative of duty.

Here we have the repression of the body in another form. After all, isn't it *the purpose* which makes human activity explicable when it is most intensely human? At certain levels, to be sure, the behavior of an organism is little more than a reaction to some stimulus, the effect of some cause or other. But what is the case when human beings decide to plant a garden, beget a child, write a book, or paint a picture? Aren't such actions organized around some aim or purpose? In their intentional activity human beings transcend the level of determinisms, look toward the possible, and bring into existence something that did not exist. Only here can they be free. When behavior is merely a mechanical response to a stimulus, it is a prisoner to that stimulus and cannot transcend it. So when all consideration of aims and ends is eliminated from the moral act, the logic of life is repressed in the name of some norm outside life. *Real life is oriented around purposes, but the latter are declared immoral in RDP and Kantian morality.* No room is left for liberty and creativity because the human moral action must be merely a response to a moral stimulus.

I am afraid that is what we find in the Protestant imperative to speak the truth and be honest always. Our talk must be the automatic verbal translation of the stimulus embodied in facts. The human conscience must submit to the hard data rather than transcending it. Perhaps this is another reason for the literary poverty of Protestantism. Its program comes down to that of Comte's positivism: "the subordination of imagination to observation" (Marcuse: 347). Words can only duplicate facts. Creative writing runs counter to the mental habits imposed by morality.

I followed a curious trail in this section. I began with theft and ended up with truth. But theft, you see, is merely one instance of the more general order to be honest always. To tell a lie is to deny someone what belongs to him or her: i.e., access to the actual facts. And facts belong to others, not by natural law or right, but by virtue of the fact that they are products of divine providence. What God has done cannot be masked or denied. Lying is not so much denying our fellow human beings something that belongs to them as denying God and what he created.

Thought Crimes: Heresies

Thought crimes are a fifth category of sins which are punished by church discipline. Heresies are not immoral acts, but they are even more serious sins. Heretics have not succumbed to fleshly weakness; they have rejected some absolute knowledge and denied its claim to truth, proposing a new truth.

I cannot analyze thought crimes here. Rather than having anything to do with ethics, heresy has to do with a more basic issue: truth and the freedom to dismantle one cognitive system in order to build a new one. I shall come back to this issue in Chapter Eight.

The Priority of Sins of the Flesh over Sins of the Spirit

My readers might be wondering at this point about sins of the spirit, of the human mind and heart, which cannot be defined as acts but which are inner dispositions: hypocrisy, selfishness, intolerance, lack of love, pride, etc. What role do they play in characterizing believers? Morality draws a clear boundary line which marks off the Church from the world. On one side lie holiness and salvation; on the other side, worldliness and damnation. Do sins of the spirit serve as markers on this boundary line? If so, how does church discipline deal with them?

Church tribunals are institutional ways of separating the wheat from the chaff. Once set up, however, their own mechanisms predetermine which acts form the boundary between salvation and damnation. The only capital sins are those which are juridically punishable. Inner dispositions of the human spirit evade such treatment because they do not take the form of actions. Civil justice cannot punish someone for his or her inner intention. In like manner, church tribunals must confine their activity to the realm of committed acts.

That is why the judicial process can begin only when a written complaint charges that someone did something. And the case must be proved by witnesses or by the confession of the accused.

So sins of the spirit cannot be punished. They cannot serve as boundary markers between the Church and the world. Believers are judged by what they do, not by what they are. This means that the practice of church discipline is ruled by the logic of *justification by works*. How ironic that is, since Protestantism began as a protest against that logic in the Catholic penitential system. It is a logic of debits and credits governing the relationship between God and human beings. Salvation goes to those who have credits, damnation to those who have debits.

The genius of Luther was to see that such a logic inevitably produces anxiety because it makes the destiny of human beings depend on their moral virtue. Rejecting justification by works, Luther affirmed that we are justified by grace. God's love is not a divine response to our moral surplus. It is a totally free act rooted in God's goodness and love.

Luther's vision was lost later on, however. As I indicated in Chapter Two, theology reduced grace to an artifice whereby God perpetuates the legal equilibrium of the universe. Law is the ultimate word, and grace is merely its instrument. Transferred to the realm of morality, this subordination of grace to law gave rise to a legalistic morality. Grace is now the power given to the believer to fulfill the law—not, as in Luther's and Paul's theology, liberation from the law! Hence violation of the law is evidence that the believer has moved away from grace; and such a person should be barred from participation in the sacraments.

Once sins are juridically defined as *acts* which break the law, sins of the spirit cannot possibly mark off the boundary between the Church and the world. So they are never brought before church tribunals. I have never heard of a case where a tribunal was convened to pass judgment on hypocrisy, selfishness, intolerance, etc. People with these attitudes can frequent the RDP world without any disciplinary action being taken against them. From a strictly juridical viewpoint, such attitudes are not incompatible with the RDP universe. A wife who commits adultery is punished; the husband who refuses to forgive her is not. A man who commits a theft is punished; the merchant who refuses to sell his merchandise in the hope of higher prices is not. People who dance are punished; people who take pleasure in sexual fantasies are not.

In short, sins of the flesh are considered to be more serious than sins of the spirit. A hypothetical case will make this clear. Suppose two people got up to pray publicly in Church. One says: "O God, pardon my pride, my impatience, my selfishness, my lack of love, and my hypocrisy." The whole congregation would murmur, "Amen," and many would admire the humility and spiritual sincerity of the person in question. The second person says: "O God, forgive me, because I committed adultery last week, went to a dance, and stole something." Such a prayer would cause scandal, and the church tribunal would be called to order at once. Nothing like that would happen to the first person.

An Ethic of Limits: The Imperative of Abstention

We now have some of the elements which will enable us to describe in more precise terms the spirit of this Protestant ethic.

Let us note, first of all, that it is an *ethic of limits*. Believers are confronted by a prohibition, a boundary line. Life is circumscribed by a cordon of prohibitions. What is permitted is defined vis-à-vis what is not permitted. That is why believers always begin asking ethical questions with: "Is it permissible . . ." Here are just a few samples:

Is it permissible for believers to play dominoes? [BP, November–December 1958, p. 10].

Is it permissible for a believer to shoot off fireworks to celebrate the election victory of his candidates? [OP, June 1956, p. 3].

Is it permissible for a believing family, at the request of their daughter's fiancé, to use kegs of beer at the wedding party? [OP, March 10, 1957, p. 3].

The answers to these questions do not interest me here. What interests me is the fact that the questions reveal a certain type of conscience, a certain spirit. The conscience of these people asks questions because it deems itself incompetent to answer those questions. Questions are addressed to an authority, which has a monopoly on ethical knowledge. Morality is not a question of conscience. The only thing that the individual conscience knows clearly is that there are limits and prohibitions. Thus RDP moral consciousness is not a consciousness of freedom but a consciousness of limits.

The whole problem of casuistry surfaces once again. The five categories treated above are not enough to cover the infinite variety of human situations that may crop up. Moreover, church discipline has defined sin in terms of isolated acts rather than in terms of human intention or individual conscience. So believers find themselves prisoners of innumerable ambiguous situations which *may* be prohibited—but they don't know for sure. In case of doubt, however, it is better and safer to abstain. If you abstain from acting, you don't sin. The thing you mustn't do is run the risk of sinning. I recall one believer who systematically abstained from drinking guaraná (a soft drink) in bars. Why? Because a fellow Protestant passing outside might think he was drinking beer. That would upset the passerby, and it is sinful to scandalize one's fellow believer.

If a certain morality defines sin in terms of acts that transgress a limit, it will inevitably lead to an ethic of abstention. People will refuse to act out of fear that the action, as yet undefined by church morality, might be sinful.

Permit me a slight digression in order to situate this morality more precisely. Here is a quote from Schiller:

> An animal *works* when a lack is the driving spring of its activity, and it *plays* when an abundance of force is this driving spring, when the excess of life spurs itself into activity. Even in inanimate nature one finds such a luxury of force and a laxity of determination which one might call . . . play [Kaufmann a: 28].

Here human activity is viewed in terms of the basic motive forces behind it. In one case the animal acts because it lacks something. It is poverty trying to become wealth, emptiness looking for fullness. In the other case it acts out of overflowing fullness. Lacking nothing, it acts to express itself. In the *Gay Science* (n. 370), Nietzsche uses the same polarity to analyze esthetic production: "Regarding all aesthetic values I now avail myself of this main distinction—I ask in every instance, 'is it hunger or superabundance that has here become creative?' " (Kaufmann translation).

If we pose the same question to the RDP personal ethic, we will find no response. Neither superabundance nor the awareness of a lack lies behind it. These two ethical criteria are grounded in real life, and I have already indicated that life is neither the starting point nor the goal of Protestant ethics. Instead life is confronted with a norm that stands as a boundary-limit. The important thing is not that life enrich itself and overcome some want, nor that superabundant life express itself, but rather that life stay within the limits set for it by Protestant morality. And why should believers be willing to restrict their lives in that way?

We have already referred to the conservative nature of the conversion experience. Once converted, believers vigorously refuse to expose themselves to any situation that might place their salvation experience in danger. Why? The crisis that has preceded the conversion has been painful and anguishing. Conversion has transformed the anguish into peace and joy. Necessarily, the convert will flee any contact with experiences that might shatter the harmony. Like the mice in Skinner's box, once they have learned that a certain lever produces a shock, they never touch it again. The mouse will be able to act out of want, out of hunger. It will go ahead and touch the lever that gives food. When it has eaten its fill, it will turn its attention to play. But its attitude of *abstention* from the lever that produces a shock cannot be explained by either of these two categories. It abstains out of fear.

Protestant morality dictates that the believer must abstain from sin. Hence the repeated "No" that characterizes it. But why do believers abstain from that which, from the point of view of the body, seems good, and pleasant? Why do they not express themselves in dance? Why do they not live Sunday as the day of the expression of the body? Why do they avoid love in order to belong to the Church? One pastor, a friend of mine, told me just several days ago of a woman who had lived for over forty years with a man who was separated from his legal wife. They had many children and grandchildren. They were converted. They gave up their cohabitation. Why? Why are life and love repressed when confronted with a prohibition that tells them "No"? Out of fear. In the Protestant universe, forbidden activities are linked to the "world," and the world is linked to hell. Thus, in order to win future life, and heaven it is necessary to deny life and earth. And therefore the momentary pleasure that such activities may produce does not compensate for the eternity of suffering which will follow them. This fear of doing a forbidden action is often expressed in terms of Christ returning at the very moment when one is engaged in it. If this were to happen, there would be no further occasion for repentance and the soul would inevitably go to hell:

> When you are at the movies, my brother, always ask yourself this question: If Christ were in the world, would he be here with me? [BP, December 1961, p. 12].

> If Christ returned and found a believer at the movies, I don't believe the latter would be acknowledged or accepted by Jesus [OP, June 10, 1958, p. 3].

This sort of question will fit any situation: If Jesus were here, would he act like this? If Jesus returned and found me doing this, would he accept me?

An Ethic of Principles:
The Priority of Imitation over Value-Creation

I know it is obvious by now, but let me repeat: the RDP ethic is an ethic of principles. What does that mean? It means that there exists a norm that is transcendent, divine, eternal, immutable, and valid for all situations without exception. This norm determines exactly how believers are to behave:

> The ethical standard on which people should base their conduct reveals *the existence of transcendent moral laws, fixed* by a *supreme authority*, which set before human beings the *goal of perfection* for *their lives* and placed in their consciences germinal notions that are perfectly contoured to the proportions of that goal [BP, September 1958, p. 1].

Let's take a look at this statement. First of all, behavior is regulated by transcendent moral laws fixed by a supreme authority. The laws are fixed, i.e., immutable. They apply to all situations, so they are universal. They are transcendent, which means that they do not arise out of experience. Morality is not the product of concrete human beings who create their own forms of goodness in varying cultural situations. Moreover, these laws are the goal of perfection for human life. Life does not determine its own goals. This dovetails perfectly with the Calvinist doctrine of the human being's total depravity. Because human beings are essentially corrupt, any goals they might set for themselves would simply embody that corruption.

The logical conclusion is that the human being cannot have an autonomous morality. I do not know what I ought to be. My perfection—what I ought to be—is fixed by a supreme authority. There is a permanent conflict between what I wish and what I ought to do in moral terms. This conflict cannot be resolved because the old self can never be completely rooted out of our real-life experience. This, then, is the condition of the believer as a moral being. He or she faces an ongoing conflict between personal desire and moral imperative. Personal desire must be repressed. RDP morality means neurosis, if Freud is correct. For either the believer represses desire and impoverishes life for lack of freedom; or else the believer expresses desires, transgresses the moral law, and suffers from guilt feelings.

Notice also that what is good *has already been fixed*. It comes down to us from the past. The present is forbidden to rethink inherited values, to contemplate a future. All that is permitted is the *repetition* of the past. That is why Nietzsche labelled those who think they *already* know what is right and good as the great enemies of the future: "The noble man wants to create something new and a new virtue. The good want the old, and that the old be preserved" (Kaufmann b: 156). The noble man sees the creation of new values as the only way to revitalize culture. To him the worship of old values takes the form of a repulsive dragon:

> In the loneliest desert . . . the spirit seeks out his last master: he wants to fight him and his last god; for ultimate victory he wants to fight with the great dragon.
> Who is the great dragon whom the spirit will no longer call lord and God? "Thou shalt not" is the name of the great dragon. "Thou shalt not" lies in his way, sparkling like gold, an animal covered with scales; and on every scale shines a golden "thou shalt not." Values, thousands of years old, shine on these scales; and thus speaks the mightiest of dragons: "All value of all things shines on me. All value has long been created, and I am all created value" [Kaufmann b: 138–39].

There is no escaping the fact: the road of creativity is closed off to all those who prostrate themselves before the dragon. To create means to bring something new to light. How can we do that if the transcendent moral laws have already been fixed? We can only accept them, and creativity must give way to *limitation* and *repetition*.

Suppose my action today were inspired by a vision of some future to be created. Say I took Nietzsche's advice: "Let the future and the farthest be for you the cause of your today," Zarathrustra exclaims (Kaufmann b: 1740). Future? That which is not, which is not yet come to be, which only exists in imagination and in hope, in aspiration and in desire. Acting in order to fecundate. Acting to "call into being those things which have not been" (cf. Rom. 4:17). Now, this type of activity can only be had if we suppose that reality is not terminated, that it has not been fixed—that it can be fertilized and transformed by love expressed in action. As we have indicated above, however, the Protestant universe is fixed. Divine Providence has predetermined it from all eternity. Thus human activity is never creation, but simple movement in immutable space and time. If creation is not possible, there remains only the possibility of *imitation* and *repetition*. Given the numberless variations in human situations, believers already have, in advance, the recipe for their comportment. There is no question of contextual behavior. Contextual ethics takes its departure from an absolute: one must love. But it knows nothing of the forms which love will have to take in each situation. Consequently, in each situation, one must ask, interpret, take risks. We never know whether the *intention of love*, transformed into activity will create goodness. There are no certainties. Only risks. Nothing is pre-defined. The ethics of principle, on the contrary, asserts that the situation is totally irrelevant for the moral choice. Moral activity should not be a response to a transitory situation, but the realization of an eternal principle. The basic question is not love and goodness: what does my action *create* in my life? Rather it is the relationship of conformity between principle and action.

Accordingly, given the norm that believers must always tell the truth, they must tell it even when they know that its result will be the destruction of love. What matters in the last analysis is not the situation concretely created by the act, which involves not only the act but a numberless multiple of persons as well, but the relationship of logical identity between the eternal principle and the action. And this shows us that in this Protestant morality the concrete results of one's activity for one's neighbor are of secondary importance, since they cannot be the motive for the activity. Believers do not act to achieve certain results. What matters to them is *the goal of perfection for their lives*. And they are perfect insofar as their lives are replicas of the goal fixed in advance from all eternity. Their activity is not creation but *witness* to God and his word. It is more important to obey God than to obey human beings, to submit to the preestablished norm. In that sense the Protestant ethic is fundamentally anti-humanist. In reflecting on the problem of action, it puts the human being in parenthesis and concentrates solely on preserving the structure of atemporal norms that ought to guide behavior.

The Functions of Ecclesiastical Discipline

The *Code of Discipline* defines the aims of church discipline as follows:

All discipline seeks to instruct the people of God, correct scandals, errors or faults, and promote the honor of God, the glory of our Lord Jesus Christ, and the welfare of those at fault [MP, p. 65].

One of the basic rules of sociological analysis is that one cannot accept at face value the explanations of behavior offered by those involved in a given situation. Like psychoanalysis, sociology is the art of suspicion. It assumes that behind the consciously articulated explanations and self-justifications of people lie certain hidden, unconscious components which affect their conduct whether they know it or not.

This is such a case. We cannot rest content with the direct response offered above. It may well be that the above statement about the aims of church discipline does represent the belief and intentions of the participants in the situation. But whether that is the real *function* of discipline is another question.

So we will probe into the functions of church discipline, recalling what Robert K. Merton has written about social function in general:

Social function refers to *observable objective consequences*, and not to *subjective dispositions* (aims, motives, purposes). . . . [When sociological analysis] mistakenly identifies (subjective) motives with (objective) functions, it abandons a lucid functional approach [Merton: 78].

The Sadomasochistic Complex

Let us notice, first of all, that discipline causes suffering. There is no discipline without suffering. That is why RDP church discipline is objectified in a *penalty*, a punishment. The sinner is brought before the community in a public way, then rejected by the community and separated from it. Some members of the community would protest this remark, of course. They would say that the community never rejects a sinner. For the purposes of my analysis, however, it makes no difference what individual believers may think or feel. The point is that church discipline is a juridical action by the community which forbids the sinner to participate in the sacraments. The sinner may be allowed to be physically present at a service, but the Church denies him or her the right to participate in the essential component, the sacrament.

What lies behind this act of punishment? It seems that all the participants in this situation, both the innocent and the guilty, agree that there is an indissoluble connection between transgression and vengeance. Only through suffering can the guilt of the transgressor be extinguished. This connection between transgression and punishment seems to defy our analytical capabilities. As I indicated earlier, Paul Ricoeur describes it as a "matrix of terror":

The invincible bond between vengeance and defilement is prior to any institution, any intention, any decree; it is so primitive that it is prior even to the representation of an avenging god [Ricoeur b: 30].

Ricoeur also calls our attention to the fact that this bond shows up even in the rational, philosophical discourse of Plato:

> Plato indicates the direction of this anticipation: true punishment is that which, in restoring order, produces happiness; true punishment results in happiness. This is the meaning of the famous paradoxes of the *Gorgias*: "the unjust man is not happy" (471d); "to escape punishment is worse than to suffer it" (474b); to suffer punishment and pay the penalty for our faults is the only way to be happy [Ricoeur b: 43].

Hegel picked up this line of thinking in the *Philosophy of the Right*, maintaining that crime is annulled by revenge, and that the latter subjectively reconciles the criminal with himself. Does some need to be punished—so that guilt can be expiated—really exist in the guilty conscience? The answer seems to be yes. How else can we explain the fact that many RDP believers, who have committed sins in absolute secrecy, voluntarily present themselves to church sessions in order to confess their sins and receive their punishment?

But let us suppose that the community refused to mete out punishment. Suppose it said to the sinner: "Your repentance is enough. God has already pardoned you." What is pardon and forgiveness, after all? Isn't it the dissolution of the causal relationship between transgression and vengeance? In our hypothetical case, then, guilt would be wiped out, not by suffering, but simply by love which grants forgiveness.

We are forced to conclude that church disciplining becomes possible only when two factors come together: first, a guilty conscience that *wishes to be punished*; second, a conscience that does not regard itself as guilty and that *wishes to punish*. We have the association of a masochistic component with a sadistic component.

The side representing masochism is freed from guilt by submitting to suffering. But what about those who produce the suffering rather than enduring it? Foucault and Szasz have called our attention to the function of societal institutions for the mentally ill. Besides segregating and treating the mentally ill, those institutions perform another function for those outside their walls. Insofar as we classify certain types of behavior as abnormal and certain people as crazy, we are telling ourselves that our own behavior is normal and that we are not crazy. In like manner, the church community which classifies, judges, and punishes sinners is reassuring itself that it is not sinful but blameless.

Guilt, Secrecy, and Feelings of Rejection

Another noteworthy fact about church discipline is that it precludes the existence of any secrets. We might compare it with the confessional, for example. In confession the relationship between penitent and priest is secret. The latter is prisoner of an oath of secrecy; he can never make public what the guilty soul has told him. In the exercise of RDP church discipline, however, the most secret sins become public. They are dragged before a tribunal, sentence is pronounced before the whole Church, and then a penalty is publicly imposed. Thus the RDP believer is confronted with the terrible certainty that he or she will be accepted by the community *only if* he or she does not transgress the limits of the permissible. The community is structured in terms of innocence.

Here we see a significant break with Luther's teaching that the church community is constituted solely around mutual acknowledgment of guilt. We belong to the community not *because of* but *in spite of*. Since we all are sinners, there is no way for the community to make a division between those who possess credits and those who have debits. So it is impossible for some to have the function of punishing while others are marked out for punishment.

Insofar as the community is structured in terms of church discipline, the inevitable result is anxiety. Sinners have only two alternatives. Either they make public their sin and then endure punishment and rejection; or else they keep their sin secret. Sinners are accepted only insofar as they do not reveal themselves. What I am must remain hidden under the mask of what I ought to be. To belong to the community, I must indulge in self-rejection at my innermost depths; but on the level of social relationships I am innocent.

As we noted above, the neurotic person is one who has a big secret that he or she does not dare to reveal for fear of rejection. The cure of neurosis comes with revelation, so long as it is met with acceptance. Community acceptance would undermine the foundations of self-rejection. However, insofar as the church community is constituted in terms of innocence, it establishes a necessary connection between confession and revelation on the one hand and punishment and rejection on the other. This community rejection only aggravates the self-rejection of the individual as embodied in feelings of guilt. If, on the other hand, the individual keeps his or her sin secret, it is with the knowledge that the community does not accept the deeper levels of his or her personality where guilt and repentance are at work. That, too, aggravates feelings of guilt.

I have seen statistics indicating that Protestants tend to commit suicide more than Catholics do. I don't know whether that is true or not, but let us assume it is for the moment. One explanation for this phenomenon offered by Durkheim ties in Protestant suicides with Protestant individualism. Unlike Catholics, Protestants find themselves alone, unsupported by the community. That does not apply, however, to Protestants in Brazil. The fact is that Brazilian Protestants are even more tightly bound to their communities than are Catholics. Indeed one can say that everyone knows each other in Protestant communities. So here the explanation for suicide would be the fact that masochistic feelings of self-rejection and self-destruction are aggravated by the massive presence of a community structured around innocence. Suicide is really the extreme and ultimate form of punishment. But there is one big difference: suicide is more gentle and agreeable because it frees the culprit from the fear of being exposed to the community's rejection.

Ecclesiastical Discipline as a Power Monopoly

Finally we must note the political function of punishment. Those who exercise the right to cause suffering and reject people are confirming the fact that they have a monopoly on defining correct behavior and orthodox thinking. Church discipline, in other words, serves the important function of social control. It blocks the rise of deviation in ethical behavior and thought. It is through church discipline that the hoary definitions of old impose themselves, that new definitions are squelched. Indeed new definitions are squelched the moment they crop up, long before they can acquire any power. Through the practice of church discipline the older generation, which has a tight grip on power, ensures that its ideology will be preserved and that deviant behavior will be systematically eliminated.

Theological Postlude:
Ecclesiastical Discipline and the Ethic of Jesus

A theological postlude is necessary here. Protestantism, as everyone knows, has always seen itself as a return to evangelical origins as they are found in the New Testament. This was its difference from Catholicism. The Protestant ideal was to reproduce in thought and action the pristine Christianity of the first believers. So we must ask: What is the relationship between the Protestant ethic described in this chapter and the ethic of the New Testament?

Let us summarize our conclusions up to now. First, the Protestant ethic assumes institutional form in the mechanisms of church discipline. Second, church discipline establishes limits and says no to certain types of behavior. If the frontier between the permitted and the forbidden is crossed, the transgression will be punished. Third, church discipline lays special stress on the five types of sins: sexual, breaking the Sabbath, vices, theft and dishonesty, heresies. Fourth, the juridical mechanism of RDP church discipline cannot deal with sins of the spirit; it must concentrate on sins of the flesh and acts rather than on intentions.

Now let us look at the New Testament and consider some of Jesus' commandments. Remember that the theory of the verbal inspiration of Scripture would consider them to be the very words of Jesus himself. The thing to note here is that many of Jesus' commandments are not taken into consideration by RDP. They do not constitute the boundary line between the permitted and the prohibited. Let me cite some New Testament passages here, even though some of them may have been noted earlier:

"If, when you are bringing your gift to the altar, you suddenly remember that your brother has a grievance against you, leave your gift where it is before the altar. First go and make your peace with your brother, and only then come and offer your gift" [Matt. 5:23–24].

"If your right eye is your undoing, tear it out and fling it away; it is better for you to lose one part of your body than for the whole of it to be thrown into hell" [Matt. 5:29].

"Do not set yourself against the man who wrongs you. If someone slaps you on the right cheek, turn and offer him your left. If a man wants to sue you for your shirt, let him have your coat as well" [Matt. 5:39–40].

"Love your enemies and pray for your persecutors" [Matt. 5:44].

"Pass no judgment, and you will not be judged" [Matt. 7:1].

Then Peter came up and asked him, "Lord, how often am I to forgive my brother if he goes on wronging me? As many as seven times?" Jesus replied, "I do not say seven times; I say seventy times seven" [Matt. 18:21–22].

"If you wish to go the whole way, go, sell your possessions and give to the poor, and then you will have riches in heaven; and come, follow me" [Matt. 19:21].

"Always treat others as you would like them to treat you: that is the Law and the prophets" [Matt. 7:12].

The above passages clearly indicate that we cannot derive an ethic of limits from the teachings of Jesus. The evil we ought to abstain from, the realm of the prohibited, is not what is decisive. What counts most is the good that should be done. Jesus commands goodness. It is positive goodness objectified in loving action, not evil from which we should abstain, that characterizes the children of the Kingdom. What distinguishes the good tree from the bad tree is not the fact that the former does not produce bad fruit; even a sterile fig tree does not produce bad fruit. But the important thing is to produce good fruit.

By contrast, church discipline focuses on the bad fruits that are prohibited.

What about Jesus' command not to pass judgment on others, to forgive seventy times seven? Doesn't that call for the elimination of any church discipline based on a tie-up between transgression and punishment? And what about the five types of sins that are the special concern of church discipline? Is there any solid foundation for this special concern in the New Testament itself?

There is no evidence that Jesus put any special emphasis on sexual sins. Indeed he told the pure that prostitutes would enter the kingdom of God before them (Matt. 21:31). Jesus was hardly a preserver of the Sabbath. When the Pharisees accused his disciples of doing unlawful things on the Sabbath, Jesus retorted: "The Sabbath was made for the sake of man and not man for the Sabbath" (Mark 2:27). Nor did Jesus put any special value on formal honesty in the RDP sense: i.e., conformity between what actually is and what one says. The Pharisees were paradigms of honesty in that sense, but Jesus found their behavior morally reprehensible because it was filled with presumptuousness and devoid of love. There are no references to smoking in the New Testament, but there are references to eating and drinking. Jesus was accused of being "a glutton and a drinker" (Matt. 11:19), and he did not bother to defend himself against such charges.

Jesus' habits with regard to bodily purity were very different from those of the Pharisees. The latter really were like people today who are totally free of vices. The word "pharisee" comes from the Aramaic word *perishin*, which means "separated." Opposing the syncretistic and modernist tendencies of the Sadducees, the Pharisees were determined to maintain their bodily purity at all costs; they would not eat or drink anything that might taint it. They criticized Jesus and his disciples for eating without washing their hands. Jesus' basic response to all this was: "Do you not see that whatever goes in by the mouth passes into the stomach, and so is discharged into the drain? But what comes out of the mouth has its origins in the heart; and that is what defiles a man" (Matt. 15:17–18). Obviously Jesus' concern for purity of the body was minimal by comparison with that of the Pharisees.

And what about orthodoxy? Right thinking and right doctrine were of little or no concern to Jesus. Interestingly enough, the orthodox are often the villains in his parables. In the parable of the Good Samaritan, for example, the priest and the Levite were incapable of showing compassion for the traveller who had been mugged and robbed.

Who were the big enemies of Jesus? Against whom did he direct his harshest words? Against those who were sexually pure, those who kept the Sabbath, those who had strict habits of bodily purity, and those who were honest and orthodox. Consider how this prototype of moral virtue becomes the villain in one of Jesus' parables:

"Two men went up to the temple to pray, one a Pharisee and the other a tax-gatherer. The Pharisee stood and prayed thus: 'I thank thee, O God, that I am not like the rest of men, greedy, dishonest, adulterous, or, for that matter, like this tax-gatherer. I fast twice a week; I pay tithes on all that I get.' But the other kept his distance and would not even raise his eyes to heaven, but beat upon his breast, saying, 'O God, have mercy on me, a sinner that I am.' It was this man, I tell you, who went home acquitted of his sins" [Luke 18:10–14].

The prayer of the Pharisee was not a farce. He would not dare to lie to God. He did abstain from sexual sins. He did avoid physical impurity, dishonesty, lawbreaking, and violations of the Sabbath. And, needless to say, he was orthodox.

According to Jesus' criteria, however, this very man who fits under the norms of church discipline is the very man who is regarded as the outsider. So we face a curious paradox. The Protestant morality of debits and credits has a moral logic that is the opposite of Jesus' moral logic. His morality commands that positive good be done, rejects the tie-up between transgression and punishment, and stresses pardon based on love. Instead of keeping a record of accountability, it considers the dispositions of the human heart. So two contradictory moralities confront us here: justification by works versus justification by faith; juridical morality versus an ethic of love and liberty.

SIX

LET THE INDIVIDUAL BE CONVERTED AND SOCIETY WILL BE TRANSFORMED: THE SOCIAL ETHIC OF RDP

A Reluctant Exercise in Apologetics

The Protestantism that we are examining here never articulated a social ethic spontaneously on its own initiative. Its concern was, and is, the salvation of the soul. The whole question of changing and transforming the world always seemed to be a perilous deviation. Its ethic is individual, not social. It defines the type of behavior that is appropriate for a believer as one who is saved. It describes his or her traits of character and sets the limits of proper behavior. A social ethic has no essential place in the RDP universe. A Protestant believer could say everything that ought to be said without once alluding to the necessity of transforming the world.

It was due to external pressures that RDP began to talk about social ethics. It spoke out on the subject because it was forced to. So the social ethic of RDP is a response to certain questions that began to threaten the calm operation of its traditional discourse.

Which factors provoked the Church to talk about social ethics? The first was the growing awareness of socioeconomic problems in Brazil during the decade of the fifties. Underdevelopment and economic dependence; poverty, inequality, and injustice. There were timid steps towards formulating something that might be called a project for Brazil.

This awareness of the whole sociopolitical problem went hand in hand with certain theological influences which came to Brazil for the first time from Europe rather than the United States. Up until then the main influence had been that of the United States. Its missionaries and forms of piety had had no real competitors. The new thinking from Europe was welcomed enthusiastically by Brazilian young people and seminary students. But of course these theological influences were indirect, since they were never advocated by the Church. Three theological influences deserve special mention.

The thinking of theologians such as Emil Brunner and Karl Barth. This thinking was forged amid the great crises which hit Europe in the twentieth century: World War I, the Russian Revolution, World War II, etc. These crises dragged the Churches into the mainstream of history whether they wanted to plunge or not. The passive attitude of Protestants in Germany as Nazism grew and took over the country raised serious questions about the political responsibilities of Christians. German Protestants had been silent at best, or actively supportive of Nazism at worst. Can the Church be silent when six million Jews are being exterminated, alleging that its competence is restricted to the spiritual realm? No. The God of Jesus Christ implies a radical no to any and all totalitarian authorities. Thus the relationship of the Christian with the political order cannot be one of passive accommodation. It must be one of critical-minded tension. It is significant that this school of theological thought came to be referred to as the "theology of crisis."

Biblical theology. Its revolutionary discovery was that Hebrew ways of thinking were radically different from Greek rationality. While a Greek thinker sought for the explanatory *logos* of reality as it is, the Hebrew prophet looked for signs indicating the dissolution of existing reality in the name of a new and hoped-for order as yet to be established: the kingdom or reign of God. The Hebrew prophet did not explain; he denounced. Instead of justifying the status quo, he proclaimed its end as a necessary phase in our journey toward the future. In his perspective the important thing was not individual perfection but rather active participation "in what God is doing to make the world more human." Thus faith in Jesus Christ has to find expression in social responsibility.

The ecumenical movement. This movement grew out of a concern over the worldwide divisions in the Church. At first the concern was based on missionary interest. How could the Church proclaim reconciliation between human beings if it itself was not reconciled within? Then political and economic problems entered the picture. How could the Church talk of unity in a world divided by colonial exploitation? After all, the very nations which were behind the mission movement—and the divisions of Christ's body which followed them—were a wealthy minority growing ever richer through the exploitation of the poor nations. The embarrassing fact was that the colonial penetration of European countries and the United States into Asia, Africa, and Latin America went hand in hand with their missionary expansion on those very same continents. Whether the Church wished it or not, it was caught up in the political and economic realities of our history. It could not choose between participating or not participating. Its only choice was between conscious, responsible participation on the one hand and unadmitted, irresponsible participation on the other.

So we began to hear clear, incisive talk about our national problems, along with hesitant and uncertain strains of new theological thinking. This talk was heard within the Presbyterian Church in Brazil, though it was confined almost exclusively to young people and seminary students. And it was this talk that forced the Church to spell out clearly its formula for handling the new situation.

But there was a basic problem. The presuppositions of social ethics, as forged in this situation, were in direct conflict with the presuppositions of the Protestant universe. Though not fully formulated, the new social ethic assumed that the problems of poverty, injustice, and well-being had priority over all other problems. The body had to be saved. Moreover, this new social ethic affirmed that the root of these problems was structural. People are not poor because they wish to be. They are poor because certain socioeconomic structures determine that some will be poor while others get rich. So the problem of poverty and injustice cannot be solved on the individual level, simply by convincing individuals to work in a responsible, disciplined way. Structural problems call for structural solutions. And underlying all this was the assumption that the Church should be one of the instruments used to create a new world of justice and well-being.

Even the most superficial analysis will reveal how heretical those assumptions would be for RDP. To the latter, the basic question is the salvation of the soul, not the body. How can one transform structures when they are the result of divine providence? The task is not to transform structures but to transform individuals. The only task the Church can set itself is to save souls, to transform hearts. The structural problem is not within its jurisdiction. It falls under the power and responsibility of the magistrates appointed by God.

I have given this background information to show that the Church in Brazil did not begin to talk about social ethics on its own initiative. It was forced to take up the issue. And its intention was one of defense and apologetics. Faced with a new vision of the faith which was implicit in the new social ethic, a heretical vision, it had to reaffirm the orthodox vision. The RDP Church spoke about its social ethic only in order to disqualify the claims of any and every social ethic.

The Inevitability of Poverty

One aspect of any real problem is the fact that it can be solved. If we face some painful situation which we know from the start we cannot solve, then it does not take on the nature of a problem. Instead of vainly trying to apply our theoretical and practical energy to it, we must simply endure it with patience and resignation.

Real social ethics assumes that poverty is a problem that can be solved. While it may never be solved completely, there is no reason why the situation of the poor should be accepted as an inevitable destiny. But what if we accept the RDP doctrine of divine providence? If history is the effect of a divine cause, then one must conclude that poverty is the will of God:

That is why the inspired Legislator of the Hebrews wrote in *Deuteronomy*: "The poor will always be with you in the land" (Deut. 15:11).

We find these words echoed by our Lord: "You have the poor among you always" (Matt. 26:11). So the good news he came to announce did not mean that poverty was going to be banished from the world. *On the contrary*, his teaching was: "Even when a man has more than enough, his wealth does not give him life" (Luke 12:15). Not because God likes poverty, but because of weakness or certain morbid conditions, caused by sin, with which many come into the world and from which they cannot free themselves. . . . Would the world be a Paradise if all were equal physically, mentally, and economically? That's like asking if the body would be a body if it were all eyes. In the aggregate of its members *the body must have some that are less worthy and decorous*, though all are useful to the community, in their place and for their function, so long as harmony and interdependence prevails. [BP, September 1962, p. 3, editorial].

Before I analyze this passage, I must point out that the Hebrew legislator was treated a bit unfairly. His words were foreshortened. Here is the full verse in Deuteronomy:

The poor will always be with you in the land, and for that reason I command you to be open-handed with your countrymen, both poor and distressed, in your own land [Deut. 15:11].

As cited in BP, the text justifies poverty as a fated necessity. It cannot be eliminated. You just have to accept it. The verse in Deuteronomy says exactly the opposite. The reality of poverty is turned into a command to exercise brotherhood and love: "I command you to be open-handed. . . ." I don't want to get into exegesis here, but it is rather interesting that the writer of the editorial deliberately left out most of the verse he quoted.

The editorialist tells us: "The good news he came to announce did not mean that poverty was going to be banished from the world. *On the contrary*, his teaching was: 'A man's wealth does not give him life.' " The editorialist is telling us that in his view of the gospel message there is no connection between *life* and *economics*. Economic transformations have nothing to do with the life promised by the gospel message. Or, to put it a bit more radically, turning the elimination of poverty into a central problem comes down to establishing an essential relationship between life and economics; and that is heresy.

What are the causes of poverty? The editorialist tells us that they are due to "weakness or certain morbid conditions, caused by sin, with which many come into the world and from which they cannot free themselves." In other words, behind poverty lies sin as the causative factor. Could the same logic be used to explain wealth? I think so. The wealthy are those who are free from the bad conditions and who can, through work, accumulate riches. So the poverty of the poor ceases to be mere economic misfortune or disgrace. It is interpreted as moral and spiritual disgrace. Notice that there is no mention of structural determinants. The curse of poverty and the blessing of wealth are viewed in terms of the moral and spiritual condition of the given individual.

Notice that although the editorialist begins by denying that poverty pleases God, he ends by justifying it in functional terms. Poverty has a function in the harmonious life of the whole. And something that is functional should be maintained. The harmonious functioning of the whole body requires that there be less worthy and decorous members.

What, then, would be the only proper attitude for those who suffer from poverty and misery? The editorialist does not tell us in so many words, so let me pursue his logic to the end. The poor, aware of their proper function as less worthy and decorous members, should adopt an attitude of patient submissiveness towards the situation in which divine providence has placed them. Indeed, their attitude should be one of gratitude and thanksgiving. They should, in other words, equate their *condition* with their *vocation*. Providence has called them to poverty. And of course the same thing can be said of the rich. By this means one would arrive at

> the comforting assurance that the unequal distribution of the goods of this world was a special dispensation of Divine Providence, which in these differences, as in particular grace, pursued certain ends unknown to man [Weber b: 177].

So we get a romantic vision of poverty that is functional for both the rich and the poor. The latter humbly accept their situation as a blessing. The rich, asserting that the poor will inherit the earth, assume an air of unhappiness when they compare their lot with that of the poor. Consider the following description of Jeca-Tatu, a generic name for the poor Brazilian hillbilly, somewhat akin to Li'l Abner in the United States:

> Ah, what I wouldn't give to be Jeca-Tatu, barefoot, stripped to the waist, working out in the open air under the healthy virgin rays of the sun! I would love to be Jeca-Tatu, bone-weary from work, voraciously chewing down a raw plate of beans and cassava, accompanied now and then by some rice, meat fat, or a little hash soaked in fat! [BP, March 1964, p. 3].

Needless to say, those words were not written by Jeca-Tatu!

To be perfectly truthful, I must say that such sentiments are rarely expressed openly. My point, however, is that such a view is perfectly possible and orthodox within the framework of the Protestant universe. It does not in any way contradict the basic doctrines of the Church. Its publication in the Church's official organ did not provoke any hostile reaction from the defenders of right doctrine.

Our conclusion, then, is that poverty is not a basic problem for this brand of Protestantism. It does not really matter that a person is poor. What is of crucial importance is the subjective way in which he or she lives this poverty. The proper attitudes are resignation, patient submission, gratitude, and the certainty that all things work for the good of those who love God.

I must also point out that the behavior of Protestants does not always reflect the cold logic of their theological interpretation of poverty. Like other brands of Protestantism, Brazilian RDP has its gallery of anonymous heroes who gave up everything to serve the poor. Doctors, nurses, teachers, ministers, and missionaries have plunged into the interior and lived lives of poverty and privation to serve the poor and the marginalized. That page of the story must not be forgotten. But the fact remains that poverty is a secondary issue at the level of articulated ideology and theology. It is the salvation of souls that really matters, and even those totally dedicated to the poor are convinced that care of the body is merely a prelude to the care of souls.

The Moral Root of Social Problems

Now we come to a second issue: How does RDP interpret the nature of the whole social problem? As I noted earlier in this chapter, the new social ethic of the fifties saw social problems as structural ones and called for structural solutions. Brazilian RDP could not possibly agree with that view, as the following citation makes clear:

> The basis for reforms—where does that basis lie? There is only one answer: in the human being. People have been misled and disillusioned by the majority Church, now seeing what was wont to be called a "spiritual power" . . . poking its nose into agrarian reforms, tax reforms . . . and every other type of reform, without realizing that the sphere of such power is different. . . . We are certain that no basic reform will take place until the human being has been reformed. And this latter reform, which we refer to as transformation and regeneration, lies in the specific realm of faith [BP, August 1 and 15, 1963, p. 1].

State and Church are two separate spheres set up by divine providence. The State looks after material matters, the Church looks after spiritual matters. In the idiom of classic Catholic theology, the Church rules over the supernatural whereas the State rules over the natural. In Luther's formula, the Church constitutes the "kingdom of grace" whereas the State constitutes the "kingdom of law." The assumption is that structures are inert, lifeless pigeon-holes without soul or dynamic movement. It is regenerated and transformed human beings in key positions that will give them life and improve their quality:

> Forms of government may change, the people's representatives may change, and the outer veneer of things may be changed. But if corrupt and corrupting human beings continue to hold the reins of institutional

power, there is no reason to hope for any improvement. Everything will soon plummet into the abyss. The basic problem is this: the HUMAN BEING. We need human beings of character more than anything else. We need human beings who "fear God and respect their neighbor." We need people willing to run the risk of serving. . . . If we place people of that caliber in key national positions, then the shape and direction of things will change as if by magic [BP, May 1962, p. 3; editorial].

The urgent task is to reform the world. And we believe the only way to accomplish that enormous task is for each individual to reform himself or herself in line with the teaching of the Bible, and to surrender to Jesus Christ immediately [BP, October 1959, p. 2].

There is no doubt that the causes of every crisis are moral causes [OP, February 10, 1953, p. 8].

This basic stance follows quite logically from certain premises that I have already pointed out. The real cause of everything that happens, the primary cause, is the invisible, vertical, spiritual relationship between God and the universe. In our specific case, here, it is the relationship between God and society. Other explanations of a scientific or sociological nature are merely descriptions of secondary causes, and they remain on a very superficial level. The core of the whole matter is to be found in the spiritual and moral relationships that exist between God and individual human beings. We can hope for the transformation of society only insofar as each individual member of society undergoes conversion and transformation. That means conversion to Christ, of course. A new social order can only come through the mediation of true religion.

The Spiritual Mission of the Church

What, then, is the mission of the Church according to RDP? As we noted above there are two spheres of competence. Temporal authority is entrusted by God to civil magistrates. Spiritual authority is the competence and mission of the Church. And since the real cause of social crisis is moral and spiritual in nature and origin, the truly revolutionary factor in society is the Church, insofar as it rigorously restricts its ministry to the spiritual sphere. Thus it must work only indirectly to try to transform such areas as politics and economics; its true work is going to the deeper spiritual roots of every problem. The relationship of the soul with God is what is of ultimate importance, and the corruption of the spiritual sphere is the only ultimate explanation for social crises. That is why, as we shall see again later, the big culprit responsible for poverty, underdevelopment, and injustice is the Catholic Church:

We must confront this revolutionary world with the redeeming message of Christ. Amid the political turmoil of our day the Church must maintain a transcendent position. . . . The orientation of the Church must be focused on Christ and the principles of Christian morality, with no concern for involvement in political factions or ideological blocs. The most effective program of action for the Church is preaching the transforming gospel of Christ [BP, January 1963, p. 8].

The Church works directly for the spiritual rehabilitation of human beings, and INDIRECTLY for the improvement of their moral, economic, and social level. The early Church contributed to the abolition of slavery, but *it did so only indirectly*. It let the gospel message, as received and lived by people, work slowly like leaven in the dough. The Apostle of the Gentiles did not rail against that system as it flourished in the society of his time, nor did he condemn it openly. Instead he offered this advice: "Slaves, obey your earthly masters with fear and trembling, single-mindedly, as serving Christ" (Eph. 6:5). Jesus, too, put the spiritual life and the material life on two different levels, urging us first to seek the kingdom of God and its justice. He told us that all other things would be given to us *secondarily*, by way of addition. . . . Let us beware of the winds of strange doctrines that are already blowing strongly in certain corners of our Church [BP, September 1962, p. 3; editorial].

That final remark is very revealing. It points up the polemic and apologetic purpose of everything that has gone before. "The winds of strange doctrines" are blowing in the Church, and the writer's interpretation of the Church's mission is meant to counter them.

Not being interested in exegesis here, I want to focus on the ideological function of the writer's formulated interpretation. What does it mean? Is the writer trying to tell us that we help to transform situations of injustice precisely when we accept them? Yes, it seems to me. The slave's obedience to its master, "as serving Christ," is allegedly the spiritual instrument for transforming masters and liberating slaves. Slavery and other unjust institutions could not and should not be abolished by active rejection on the part of the slaves. They are to disappear as the hearts of the oppressors are transformed. Here we see a radical dualism between the spiritual order and the material order. The Church works in the spiritual order. In some miraculous way this work in the spiritual sphere has indirect effects on the material sphere. So believers are encouraged to behave patiently in society as Paul advised, certain that spiritual forces are at work:

There has been a lot of publicity lately about the work of certain people in opening up hillside roads and improving slums in Rio. . . . However, if the emphasis placed on this work is meant to imply that this is the mission of the Church, then in all fairness we would have to label municipal officials as the first and foremost heroes of the faith. . . . The Church is supposed to form personalities like Christ, who will serve as the salt of the earth and the light of the world. There were many social injustices in the Roman Empire. The early Christians did not band together to combat those injustices (including slavery). Instead they bore loyal witness to Christ, and the Roman Empire with all its despotism collapsed [OP, November 10, 1956, p. 2].

Once again we see an instance of apologetics and polemics. Who were the people who went to improve the hillsides and the slums? They were young people in the youth movement. Instead of using vacation time for their own pleasure, they organized work brigades in needy localities. They did manual labor during the daytime, and at night they met to study the Bible and see how its message related to their personal work and experiences. Their overriding theological inspiration was the doctrine of the Incarnation as expressed by Paul:

> Let your bearing towards one another arise out of your life in Christ Jesus. For the divine nature was his from the first; yet he did not think to snatch at equality with God, but made himself nothing, assuming the nature of a slave'' [Phil. 2:5–7].

God revealed himself as a servant, as someone who comes down to render service. How, then, are we to vivify the presence of God among human beings? By following the same course of incarnation. Christians must go down where human beings are suffering and make God's presence real by rendering service to those human beings. Something as simple as those youthful work brigades really embodies a new way of understanding the faith and an ethical revolution. The youth brigades imply that individual perfection is less important than silent presence geared around service. And they also call into question the mission of the Church as it has been traditionally interpreted. They suggest that the Church of Jesus Christ has the mission of being the servant of human beings. It cannot live in and for itself. It must empty itself, be present among human beings, and render service to those who are suffering.

That is obviously heresy. That is why the writer of the cited article challenged the publicity surrounding the youthful work brigade. If the mission of the Church were to do that sort of work, then municipal authorities would be the first and foremost heroes of the faith. The real task of the Church, says the writer, is to create personalities like Christ. The object of its work is the human heart, not hillsides and slums. The early Christians never worried about social justice. They transformed hearts, and the transformation of Roman society ensued. The old doctrine is reaffirmed, as it is in the following remark:

> The precise concern of the minister, and of the Church of course, is the business of souls. Their great obligation is to care for souls and their immortal interests [OP, April 10, 1955, p. 1].

One thing is clear from all this. Protestants make no use of structural categories to understand social phenomena. Perhaps the most basic insight of all sociological reflection is the fact that individuals are not autonomous entities. Their behavior is explicable in terms of the social structures to which they belong. When sociology makes use of such categories as role, function, collective consciousness, class, production relations, and caste, it is saying that the logic of individual behavior is subordinated to the logic governing the structures in which individual behavior is socially located. Sociology does not see any explanatory function in the category of the individual. Instead it seeks to shed light on the whole complex of relationships which make the individual what he or she is.

Now here we encounter a curious contradiction. If my earlier analysis is correct, RDP does unwittingly accept the sociological point of view in its ecclesiology. The relationship between the believer and the Church is marked by the systematic subordination of the individual to the collective conscience of the church community. The Church lays down the rules for correct thinking and correct interpretation of the sacred texts. It tells the believer how reality is structured and what the correct norms of moral behavior are. If the believer revolts against this collective conscience, he or she will be punished by church discipline. Individual conscience has no right vis-à-vis the absolute knowledge of the Church. The case is very different, however, once believers step beyond the boundaries of the Church and enter the world. Structural reality disappears, and society becomes nothing more than the sum of the individuals which make it up. The quality of society is not provided by structures, but merely by the interaction of individual personalities. The Protestant defines society in psychological rather than sociological terms. Just as the various forms of psychological therapy tend to deal with individuals on a one-to-one basis, so RDP seeks to change society by transforming its members one by one. Here we have a contradiction which, in fact, rules out any social ethic. The RDP social ethic under consideration here is really the negation of social ethics.

Progress and Underdevelopment: God's Blessing and Cursing

It is now time to get more specific about RDP social ethics. Its approach can be summed up in a syllogism:

Major premise: All social crises are the result of spiritual and moral crises faced by individuals.

Minor premise: Protestantism, as absolute knowledge of God's will, is the solution for those individual moral and spiritual crises.

Conclusion: Protestantism is the solution for all social crises.

Protestants maintain that the Reformation marked a return to the pure truth of the gospel message, which the Catholic Church had buried under man-made traditions over the course of time. This return to the spiritual truth explains why Protestantism has always been associated with freedom, democracy, and economic progress as those traits are to be found in the most developed and affluent nations of the world. By the same token, the Catholic Church's corruption of the gospel truth explains why Catholic countries are economically backward and opposed to democracy:

> The Reformation, . . . being a return to primitive Christianity, gave rise everywhere to the spirit of freedom and resistance to absolutism. It tended to foster the growth of republican and constitutional institutions. Protestantism acknowledges only one authority in religion: the Bible. It does not bow down to the authority of some human being as does Catholicism; the Protestant examines and discerns things for himself. Having established a republican organization in the Church, Calvinists and Presbyterians took the logically consistent step of transporting the same principles and habits into political society [BP, November–December 1958, p. 8].

> The Reformation is the great inspiration behind modern democracy. . . . The ideal of the new democracy—social democracy—is to be found in germ in Calvin's ideas about the sovereignty of God. Human beings, who are merely stewards of material goods, must use them for the welfare of their fellow human beings rather than for their own benefit [BP, October 1959, p. 10].

> The Reformation saved the Christian religion itself from irremediable and fatal discredit. The movement was inspired and directed by the Holy Spirit of the Lord. And from the Reformation would come the fundamental principles and guideposts of modern democracy and all the achievements that have emancipated the human spirit. The secret of its power lay in its fidelity to Scripture [OP, October–November 1954, p. 3].

However, the reasons for the progress of Protestant countries are not explained in purely sociological terms. Protestants are not simply adopting the thesis of Max Weber. Theological and spiritual reasons underlie the fact that Protestant countries are wealthier than Catholic countries. Wealth is a divine blessing conferred on those who are faithful to God, just as underdevelopment and poverty are a curse on those who disobey God:

> God promised to punish the children of idolatry down to the third and fourth generation. The same God shows mercy to the thousands of those who love him in Spirit and in Truth, and who keep his commandments. That is why nations with greater evangelical influence are in the vanguard of material and spiritual progress: Switzerland, Germany in

the Protestant Corners [sic!], England, the United States, in areas faithful to the pilgrims, Scotland, Finland, etc. And that is why pagan or neopagan nations—Portugal, Spain, Austria, Paraguay, Russia, etc.— live under the threat of terrible hecatombs and miseries. By neopagan nations we mean those nations where the authorities, elite, and common masses do not have the freedom to read and become familiar with the Sacred Scriptures, since they are dominated by Roman traditions [OP, August 10, 1957, p. 7].

I can't explain how Russia could be considered a country dominated by Roman Catholic traditions, but that is what the above passage says. In any case, the point here is the underlying logic of the author. Economic progress is not explained in economic terms. It is a blessing conferred by God on those who are faithful to his truths.

The above explanation is a spiritualized version of other analyses that have sought to explain why Protestant countries, as a matter of fact, are more affluent than Catholic countries. The most famous analysis is that of Max Weber, of course, but it is never invoked by the Brazilian Protestants. If I were asked why, I would propose two complementary hypotheses. In the first place, Protestant logic does not harmonize with sociological explanations, as I mentioned above. Moreover, in its popularized version, Weber's thesis has often been viewed as explaining capitalism as an outgrowth of Protestantism. Insofar as capitalism is equated with a materialistic and exploitative mentality, Protestants could hardly accept such a view. Much more appealing to Brazilian Protestants is the approach used by Emile de Laveleye in his book entitled *Do Futuro dos Povos Católicos*. He simply points up the connection between Protestantism and progress on the one hand, and Catholicism and backwardness on the other.

It is worth including here a lengthy book review which appeared in the official organ of the Presbyterian Church of Brazil. It is a review of a book by F. Hoffer entitled *L'imperialisme protestant*. Both the book and the review express very well what these Protestants think of themselves and of Roman Catholics:

It is an impressive book, perhaps the most impressive of modern treatments of the subject. He begins his study by pointing up the decisive influence that religion has on the destiny of nations. . . . North American civilization is essentially a Protestant civilization. "And the imperialism for which some reproach the United States is, to tell the truth, a Protestant imperialism, if by that one means not efforts at domination by a religion which has always spurned political action, but rather the natural expression of the vitality of a people so impregnated with religion that they cannot isolate it from the spiritual forces that have ensured their greatness!"

Thus all the progress and might of the United States, all its culture, is explained by the magnificent Protestant inheritance it received from its ancestors. Catholicism could not produce a civilization or a culture of the kind to be found in North America and countries of Protestant origin. "Rome is the heir of Imperial Rome, and the great epochs of Catholic peoples lie in the past. Catholicism is the religion of ancient peoples who are in decline, whereas Protestantism is the religion of New, Young Peoples."

The author offers another criterion for comparing the influence of these two factions of Christianity. He states that the more faithful a nation is to its Protestant tradition, the more developed it is. It is exactly the opposite with Catholicism: "Thus the Scandinavian nations, more than 99% Protestant and strongly attached to their religious traditions, are those which, as is generally known, have the highest standard of living; on the other hand, among Catholic countries, those where the Church exercises more influence—such as Spain, Portugal, and Ireland—have the lowest standard of living. . . . The situation would seem to be that Protestantism is the impulse behind the development of modern civilization whereas Catholicism exerts an inhibiting influence on it."

After showing how much North American civilization owes to Protestantism, the book ends with a warning to that nation. While it is combatting external manifestations of totalitarianism in Europe and Asia, it is not noticing the growing and well-orchestrated infiltration of the most dangerous tyranny—tyranny over conscience—so well represented in the methods, procedures, and systems of the Roman Apostolic Church [OP, January 10, 1952, p. 4].

Where Roman Catholicism Stands

The social problem finds its solution in religion, since the latter is the ultimate explanation for the situation of a given society. What would be the best possible society? What would be the Protestant utopia?

The best possible society would be one in which all were Protestants. A Protestant society would be free, democratic, and affluent. It would be free and democratic because "free inquiry" and the political organization of Protestant Churches require that. It would be affluent because a sense of individual responsibility, required by the doctrine of stewardship, and God's blessing on those who are submissive to his will, would produce the maximum of economic well-being.

The Catholic Church, on the other hand, is the antithesis of freedom. Its teaching is a corruption of the gospel truth. So countries under its domination will not be able to produce democratic forms of government and will not be blessed with wealth by God:

The philosophy of the Roman Church is totalitarian in nature, since it believes itself to be the exclusive depositary of truth. . . . There should be freedom only for the truth. For error there should be only tolerance, and only to the extent that there is no possibility of decreeing its total extinction [BP, March 1965, p. 3].

Where the Catholic clergy dominate, there is still danger today for minority rights, freedom of conscience, freedom of worship, free inquiry, and the other franchises of authentic democratic civilization [OP, February 1949, p. 1].

What is Romanism? Is it not that perfectly organized machine which sovereignly rules over the destiny of various countries, imposing its inflexible will on them, reducing contrary ideas to subservience, and exercising exploitation in all its forms? The structure, program, and aim of the papacy are totalitarian to the core . . . as is Canon Law itself. That is why the Roman Church lives in conflict with political governments of the people, especially with those governments which constitutionally defend democratic rights and the rights of conscience of free citizens [OP, August 10, 1953, p. 6].

Even today threats, excommunications, lying, calumny, and oppression are the "democratic" methods of that Church which is Christian only in name! How many difficulties must be faced by an honest Catholic who is obliged to harmonize the democratic principle with the methods of the Roman Church! [OP, May 10–25, 1955, p. 4].

According to this line of interpretation, the totalitarian character of the Catholic spirit explains why Catholic countries are an easy prey for communism:

The Roman Catholic Apostolic Church poses as a champion in the fight against communism. But if we study the matter we will see that the Roman Church, in the countries where it is dominant, offers the indispensable preconditions for communism to flourish: i.e., ignorance, poverty, corruption, and injustice. In Europe, then, many countries which are overwhelmingly Roman Catholic have fallen under communist domination. If Italy, Spain, Portugal, and France have not yet been engulfed by communism, that is due to the substantial aid they have received from the United States, a nation with a Protestant majority. Roman Catholicism prepares people for communist totalitarianism. . . . The totalitarian structure of Roman Catholicism leaves nothing for communism to do. That is why Catholic countries are much more threatened by communism than Protestant countries are [OP, May 25, 1956, p. 1].

Communism does not succeed in nations that are Protestant in origin and formation, such as the United States. It did not win out in Protestant Finland, Sweden, and Norway, which are under the shadow of Moscow, but it succeeded in dominating the Romanist nations of Central Europe and is exercising its terrible influence on other Roman Catholic nations on this side of the iron curtain [OP, September 10, 1953, p. 2].

This conviction that Catholicism and communism are two embodiments of one and the same totalitarian spirit was carried to the President of Brazil, Castelo Branco. In an open letter to him, one local Church informed him:

The Roman Catholic Apostolic Church, Illustrious Marshall, is the only one responsible for the political crisis that Your Excellency is now overcoming with wisdom and firmness. That Church, mistress of an historic past, after four centuries of brazen interference in government affairs, has been unable to give a dynamic thrust to the faith which it professes, creating in this Land of the Holy Cross the favorable preconditions for the thriving of atheistic materialism [BP, June 1964, p. 3].

Now readers must recognize the fact that this particular Protestant interpretation of Catholicism did not arise out of nowhere. Behind it lies a bitter experience of suffering and persecutions. It must also be noted that in the past the Catholic hierarchy of Brazil depicted Catholicism as the bulwark of the social order, and Protestantism as a factor of disintegration. Here is an excerpt from Father Negromonte's comments in *O Globo*:

The spiritual decadence of the West began to accelerate when Protestantism broke up the religious unity of the West. One sees, therefore, that Protestant countries are the most corrupt ones. They lack both the intellectual backing of the truth and the supernatural strength of the sacraments to restrain passion and foster virtue [OP, November 27, 1957, p. 1].

A similar line of argument was offered by the Cardinal Archbishop of Rio de Janeiro, Jaime Câmara, when he sought to justify the persecution of Protestants in Colombia. Here is a comment he made in *O Jornal* (December 8, 1956):

Catholic unity has undoubtedly been the most solid foundation of nationality. . . . In Bogota we again see the rise of a group of Protestant propagandists, associated with hoodlums as usual. As experience tells us, Protestant propaganda in Latin America does not tend to foster the numerical increase of sincere and respectable Protestants. Instead it leads to the loss of all religious faith, or the loss to communism of all those who accept teachings that are basically contrary to the dogmas of Catholicism [OP, December 10, 1956, p. 1].

The fact that Câmara refers to "Protestant propagandists" is revealing. He thus gives a purely secular and political cast to the religious activities of Protestant ministers, missionaries, and adherents. His ideological-theological stance prevents him from seeing Protestantism as a branch of the Christian Church. To him Protestantism is anti-religion, the destruction of the faith. He groups Protestants with hoodlums and communists—i.e., with those who are in conflict with the social and political order. Catholic unity, on the other hand, is the most solid foundation of nationality. It recommends itself to authorities and the people as a factor fostering social integration and political cohesion.

Father Negromonte argued similarly. He made Protestantism responsible for moral corruption and spiritual disintegration in the West. Protestantism, after all, is the very antithesis of spiritual truth. So one should conclude that Protestantism is a subversive force that ought to be repressed.

The Protestant polemic against Catholicism, then, has been part of a minority's struggle for survival amid constant threats. This struggle has profoundly marked the character of Protestant thinking and Protestant institutions in Latin America. The Catholic Church forced Protestantism to play its game, so the latter has assumed features of the very enemy it is combatting. In reacting against Catholic aggression, Brazilian Protestantism allowed the Catholic initiative to shape it as a negative image of Catholicism. Erasmo Braga, one of the most brilliant intellectuals produced by Brazilian Protestantism, put it this way: "Protestantism is a negative image of Catholicism, with all the inconveniences of a negative." If Brazilian Protestantism continues to be anti-ecumenical today, Catholics must remember that it was of their creation. Willy-nilly, Brazilian Protestantism is a child of Catholicism. Persecution and polemics have inhibited the development of more creative institutions in Protestantism, turning it into nothing more than anti-Catholicism.

Notice, for example, that Brazilian Catholics and Protestants are in complete agreement about the basic rules of the game. They fight each other because they agree about the nature of the basic problem at stake. Both agree that religion is the basis of society. Both see social problems as a by-product of the religious faith one adopts. For both, then, the question of social ethics reduces itself to a matter of being loyal to the faith that one's group professes. Sociological, economic, historical, and political analyses become unnecessary.

The Protestant United States: A Social Utopia

We have seen that the RDP social ethic establishes a connection between Protestantism, democracy, freedom, and progress. Inevitably, then, RDP must eulogize the United States as the supreme example of what Protestantism can do for a people or a nation.

Why the United States? As we saw in the various texts cited earlier in this chapter, countries with a Protestant majority tend to be mentioned as a group when one is trying to establish the connection between Protestantism, democracy, and progress. But the relationship between Brazilian Protestantism and the United States is a very special one. Brazilian Protestantism was the result of missionary work by North Americans in the nineteenth century. The first missionaries came from the United States. From there came the economic subsidies that enabled the nascent Protestant Church in Brazil to survive. From there came the lyrics and melodies of the hymns that Brazilian Protestant communities learned to sing. Of course, this phenomenon was not peculiar to Latin America alone. Just as Latin was and still is the universal language of Roman Catholicism, so North American melodies identify Protestants all over the world. Protestants, who have "found salvation in Christ," know that they owe this to the United States. Even if people knew nothing of Brazil's past history, they would notice the North American influence on Brazilian Protestantism by merely reading the names of the most famous Protestant educational institutions in Brazil: e.g., Mackenzie, Bennett, Granbery, Isabela Hendrix, and Gammon. Thus a connection has been established between Protestantism, the United States, democracy, and progress. The United States—as a political, economic, and cultural model— stands out as the utopia implicit in Protestantism.

Just as Brazilian Protestants think that Protestant believers are different in their personal ethic, so they maintain that North Americans are different. One of the best-known preachers of the Presbyterian Church of Brazil gave a public lecture in which he compared the American mentality with that of the Brazilian. To illustrate his point, he told how newspaper vendors in U.S. cities leave out a pile of papers and a money box so that customers can pay their money and take their own paper. "Now you know what would happen if that was Brazil," he concluded, "because Brazilians . . ." North American are honest, Brazilians are not. One Brazilian woman, recalling her recent visit to the United States, remarked: "What an extraordinary country! You feel that its people are moved by a superior power." In short, the lifestyle in the United States matches the aspirations which Brazilian Protestants have introjected.

One person who has analyzed the process of conversion to Protestantism in Brazil notes that this conversion process means breaking with our Brazilian cultural traditions and adhering to Anglo-Saxon cultural traditions. And that goes down to the smallest details. In one of the largest Protestant seminaries in Latin America, the table manners of the students are made to conform strictly to U.S. etiquette. So much so that the students had to eat bananas with a knife and fork. Such small details are like Freudian slips: they reveal the large ideological structures which remain unspoken. In this case they reveal that U.S. culture is viewed as superior to Latin American culture.

It could not be otherwise. After all, Latin American culture is saturated with Roman Catholic influence whereas North American culture embodies the Protestant spirit. In Brazil, then, conversion to Protestantism logically entails a break with our cultural roots. Wherever the Protestant missionary movement took root in Latin America, the "natives" learned that their culture was pagan. Breaking with the native culture was one proof of conversion. Thus the missionary movement may well have been the primary vehicle of cultural imperialism. When John R. Mott, the great leader of the missionary and ecumenical movement, made his first trip to Latin America, he jotted down a rather significant remark in his diary: "What opportunities for evangelization! The Protestant Church should turn the Monroe Doctrine into its model for missionary policy on this continent."

It is important, then, for Brazilian Protestants to stress the superiority of the United States over Brazil. They must point up what Protestantism can do for a people. Notice the following incident which is recounted and then commented on:

> Louis Serrano sent a letter to *O Globo*, recounting a curious incident which occurred on a bus in Hollywood. The driver stopped the bus, got off, and returned with an old blind man on his arm. He helped the blind man sit down. The passenger offered his wallet to the driver, who took out the exact price of the bus fare and returned the wallet to its owner. Serrano writes: "No one but I was amazed that the bus driver had the old man's wallet in his hand and took out only the price of his bus fare!"
>
> This happened in the United States, where no one but the Brazilian journalist was impressed by a fairly commonplace incident. It happens every day. And to what is it due? To the influence of the gospel, thanks be to God [OP, November, 10–25, 1957, p. 6].

It is equally important for Brazilian Protestants to defend the United States against those who attack it:

> *Q.* Is there racial segregation in the United States?
> *A.* Yes, there is social separation between whites and blacks in the United States; but today the Churches and believers in general are eliminating these racial customs that are contrary to the teachings of God's Word. Unfortunately, blacks themselves are generally the first to not want any connection with whites. Thank God, President Truman, being the loyal adherent of the Gospel that he is, is doing away with the separation in question. The Roman Church also implements the same social separation. So it cannot throw stones at the Protestants who have tolerated this error in the United States [OP, July 10, 1951, p. 3].

This reply is most revealing. The question was a simple one, and it could have been answered with a simple "yes." But the respondent sniffed out the polemical implication of the question: "You Protestants point to the United States as a model of what Protestantism can do, don't you? But doesn't racial segregation exist there? Look at Brazil, a Catholic country. Here segregation does not exist.''

The response above can only be understood against this polemical back-drop. No, it is not whites or Protestants who are to blame. Blacks are the main ones who don't want any connection with whites. You Catholics should keep your mouth shut because you too are guilty of segregation. Who is solving the problem? The Churches and believers in general, and a Protestant president loyal to the gospel in particular.

To sum up this chapter, then, the Protestant social ethic adds nothing to what has been said earlier. The Church spoke out because it was threatened by a new way of thinking. It reasserted that there are really no social problems, that the true problems are moral and spiritual. Society will be transformed by the conversion of individual souls. One need only look and see which countries of the world are rich and prosperous: i.e., those which have Protestant majorities. They embody the Protestant *promise* to all underdeveloped, poor nations. If a nation is converted to Protestantism, it will be miraculously transformed.

We find ourselves back where we started. The social ethic brings us back to the beginning: the experience of conversion.

SEVEN

THE ENEMIES OF BRAZILIAN RDP

Defining One's Identity in Terms of Enemies

A remark of Hegel's will lead us into our subject here: "In defining living things, their characteristics must be derived from the weapons of attack and defense with which these things preserve themselves from other particular things" (Marcuse: 72).

I know who I am when I know who I am against. When I assert myself, I am implicitly denying everything that denies me and threatens me with annihilation. Identity presupposes conflict. And, by the same token, conflict creates identity.

It makes sense, then, that situations of danger tend to produce social cohesion. Faced with some natural disaster or an external political threat, enemies shake hands and make political alliances, however fleeting they may be, to confront the common enemy. War produces much more of a sense of national unity than does peace. It is easier to persuade a nation to make heavy sacrifices in order to destroy a common enemy than to persuade that nation to build a peaceful world where there will be no enemies. In war domestic enemies march to the same drum-beat. When the war is over, the marching stops and all withdraw into their own private world. The barricades go up against those who were buddies in the trenches. Wartime friends become enemies once again.

That is why oppressed minorities have an ability to affirm their identity which their persecutors frequently do not possess. Here we also find the social rationale for military rituals in peace-time: the liturgies and mythologies of warfare can re-create the atmosphere of war in times of peace. They resuscitate dead enemies and call potential enemies to life. They exorcise peace, and hence abet social cohesion.

Brazilian RDP has a very clear picture of its enemies. Indeed the definition of its enemies is part of the way in which it knows and understands itself.

Now the first step in attacking an enemy is to *define* it as the enemy. In this way a community points out who should be avoided and feared. The enemy is someone who desires my destruction, someone with whom I cannot dialogue or cooperate. The participants in a dialogue define each other as companions in a common search; so do people engaged in cooperative efforts. Dialogue and cooperation dissolve our old definitions of the enemy. There may be some enemy outside the sphere of dialogue and cooperation, but the participants inside cannot be regarded as enemies.

But are such redefinitions functional when the identity of a community is at stake? To put the question another way: if a community has defined its identity in terms of combatting a certain enemy, what happens when that enemy becomes a friend? The community in question loses its reason for being, its function, its identity; it is doomed to disappear. How could St. George survive if the dragon he was fighting were to turn into a beautiful damsel? There are situations where the transformation of an enemy into a friend is more dangerous than the enemy's attack. Indeed it is always the case where the identity, mission, and function of a certain community depends on some enemy. Then the latter must be preserved as an enemy at all costs. Efforts within the community to redefine the enemy come down to subversion and treason. That is why the Inquisition maintained that the existence of witches was denied only by those who were secretly affiliated with witchcraft. To deny witchcraft was witchcraft. To deny heresy is heresy.

These preliminary observations were necessary so that readers might understand what happened in Protestantism during the past twenty-five years or so. Protestantism sought to redefine its enemies, to subvert the old definitions of the church community. Its fate was sealed, of course. But right now we must ask who exactly the enemies of Protestantism are. To answer that question we need only make an internal analysis of the RDP universe, as I have been doing in this book. The enemies, then, would be those who relativize or deny the absolutes on which its vision of the world is based.

Four enemies stand out. The first is the Catholic Church, which denies the RDP formula for salvation, its theory of knowledge, and its ethic. The second enemy is theological modernism or liberalism, which denies the possibility of absolute knowledge and the construction of faith into a worldview. The third enemy is worldliness, which rejects the morality of discipline and repression. The fourth enemy is the Social Gospel, which focuses on the social transformation of the world instead of eternity and the hereafter.

Those are not the only enemies which threaten Protestant identity, but they are the favorite targets of RDP attacks and polemics. Other enemies would include spiritualism and all types of religion which reject the dualism of salvation versus damnation, or the notion that faith in Christ is the only way to get to heaven. Communism is also an enemy because it is a materialistic and atheistic ideology which denies transcendence and overlooks the fact that human beings do not live by bread alone. It is anathematized in the same way that the Social Gospel is. However, neither spiritualism nor communism threaten Protestantism in any direct way. Spiritualist sects are small minorities. They lack the aggressiveness of the Catholic Church and tend to be tolerant, so they represent no physical danger to Protestantism. Neither has communism posed any real internal or external threat to the Church. So spiritualism and communism are only marginal enemies in that Church's struggle to survive and maintain its identity.

The First Enemy: The Roman Catholic Church

Protestantism has been in Brazil for slightly over one hundred years. Its history during that period has been characterized by fierce polemics with and against Catholicism. I have already cited samples of that contest, but those samples were confined to issues of only secondary importance: e.g., the relative influence of Protestantism and Catholicism on the fate of nations. The crucial issue, however, is the truth of the gospel message. Even when considering the historical function of Protestantism and Catholicism, RDP Protestants are careful to point out that the success and affluence of Protestant countries is *due to their fidelity to divine truth*. By the same token, Catholic countries are backward because God curses those who corrupt the truth. Protestantism is submission to Christ, Catholicism is rebellion against Christ. As the Westminster Confession of Faith puts it:

> There is no other Head of the Church, but the Lord Jesus Christ: Nor can the Pope of Rome, in any sense be head thereof: but is, that Antichrist, that Man of sin and Son of Perdition, that exalteth himself, in the Church, against Christ, and all that is called God [LC: n. 6.130].

So the real question is not whether Protestantism conduces to progress and Catholicism to backwardness. The point is that the conflict between Protestantism and Catholicism reveals the metaphysical conflict between light and darkness, salvation and damnation, truth and falsehood. It is the truth that is at stake, and the sociopolitical aspect is merely a symptom of a larger issue.

Wherein lies the Catholic error? It does not lie in any secondary matter. It is not that Catholic hermeneutics mistakenly interprets this or that particular passage in Scripture. The error is fundamental:

> Romanism is not some parallel branch of Christianity alongside the Evangelical Church—it is a divergent branch. Stemming from the same source, the two are completely separated today on essential points. One of these points is the Bible: i.e., the rule of faith and practice. We are not going to say that the principal error of the Roman Church against the Bible is the fact that it teaches doctrines which differ from those of the Bible. That is no small matter, of course. Neither is the fact that it hampers the reading of the Word of God and attacks so-called Protestant Bibles as false. Those are all big mistakes, but they flow logically from the fundamental error of the Roman Church. Its fundamental error lies in placing the authority of the Church above the authority of the Bible [OP, March 10, 95, p. 1].

One of the most pernicious errors in this area is the Roman Church's assertion that the Bible alone does not suffice as the rule of faith and practice; that it must be complemented by tradition through the living magisterium of the Church. This means that in the last analysis it is the teaching of the Church, which alone is authorized to correctly interpret both the Bible and tradition, that is turned into the rule of faith and practice [OP, December 25, 1951, p. 5].

The conflict is situated on the level of the theory of knowledge, where it comes down to trying to identify the final authority to which both knowledge and behavior should submit. In the eyes of Protestantism, truth has become objective in a written document which is not to undergo any additions or subtractions. The Catholic Church, on the other hand, affirms that the same Spirit which inspired the Scriptures continues to live in the Church. Thus the wisdom of the text cannot be separated from the wisdom of the church institution. When the Church reads and interprets the Scriptures through its magisterium, it is really the Holy Spirit engaging in self-interpretation. For Protestants, one of the clearest proofs of the improper subordination of the inspired text to an ecclesiastical institution is to be found in the fact that the Catholic Church felt qualified to add new books to the Hebrew canon:

The one who added books to the Bible was the Roman Church, and its apocryphal books are indeed apocryphal—i.e., devoid of authenticity and divine character [OP, March 10, 1955, p. 2].

Let me inject a critical aside here. In chapter three, where I analyzed the theory of knowledge, I pointed out that there was really no difference between Protestantism and Catholicism in the *actual way* in which scriptural texts were read and interpreted. The results might differ, but the hermeneutic approach did not. The RDP reading of the Bible is mediated through authoritative texts, the Confessions, which perform the same function that the magisterium does in the Roman Catholic Church. Believers go so far as to deny that the councils which prepared the Confessions were affected by historical and social conditionings; so their formulations are divine and absolute in character, for all practical purposes.

Here we might well ask: Why is it that Protestants do not see that their hermeneutic approach and that of the Catholic Church are identical? One reason is that the mechanisms of interpretation are given clear institutional form in the Catholic Church, whereas they are masked under the illusion of free inquiry in Protestantism. Another reason is psychosocial in nature and goes a bit deeper. Remember what Myrdal said about ignorance being just as functional as knowledge, and indeed sometimes more functional than the latter. If Protestantism is to preserve its sense of identity, it must define its relationship to Catholicism in terms of radical opposition and enmity. This necessity does not allow Protestants to take cognizance of the fundamentally identical way in which they and the Catholic Church approach the biblical text.

In the eyes of Protestants, their conflict with Catholicism must be radical and total. And the greatest symbol of what they oppose in the Catholic Church is the dogma of papal infallibility. The Protestant principle of *sola scriptura* is the antithesis of the Catholic principle of papal infallibility. It is the voice of God versus a human voice.

Herein lies the fundamental error of Roman Catholicism. Once the authority of the biblical text is shifted to the church institution, all the other errors follow logically: e.g., the mediation of Mary and the saints, the sacrilegious repetition of Christ's unique sacrifice in the Mass, transubstantiation, the idolatrous use of images, purgatory, Masses for the dead, priestly mediation, auricular Confession, a magical view of the sacraments, indulgences, moral laxity, the dogma of the Immaculate Conception and the perpetual virginity of Mary. These errors are secondary and derivative. They flow from the real root error: subordinating the Scriptures to the mediation of tradition and the Church's magisterium.

Someone unfamiliar with institutional behavior might well imagine that the ecumenical overtures of the Catholic Church after Vatican II would have been a reason for jubilation among Protestants. Catholics stopped defining Protestants as enemies and now called them brothers and sisters. Before this ecumenical period, Catholic historiography was characterized by a systematic effort to demoralize the Reformation, to depict it as the product of the sick and morally corrupt personality of Martin Luther. Now Protestantism underwent a metamorphosis in the eyes of Catholicism, and a new history was written. Catholics acknowledged their guilt for the schism that rent Christianity. Moreover, the Catholic Church moved to take account of some of the Protestant criticism of it, to incorporate Protestant ideas. Churches were emptied of statues of the saints. The altar, with a priest whose back was turned to the people, was turned into a eucharistic table where priest and people looked at each other face to face. Latin was replaced by the vernacular, and the Bible took a central place. Catholic writer Gustavo Corção was absolutely correct in his accusation: Catholicism turned Protestant.

One would have expected Protestants to have rejoiced over what was happening. They were getting much more than anyone had ever dreamed of. Rather than the conversion of Catholics, they were seeing the transformation of the Catholic Church itself.

No rejoicing took place. Why? Because RDP needs Catholicism as an enemy in order to maintain its sense of identity and mission. Institutions function according to a peculiar logic of their own. They come into being in order to resolve certain problems. Once they are solidly established, however, their preservation and continuing life require that problems not be solved. The problems must persist, otherwise the institution would have to disappear; and no institution programs its own destruction. Protestantism came to Brazil to solve a problem: i.e., Catholicism. Its mission is to convert Catholics to Protestantism. But suppose that Catholicism itself underwent conversion. What would happen to Protestantism? It would lose its function. The dragon must not be transformed into a beautiful damsel. Protestantism's sense of identity, requires that Catholicism not be protestantized. Catholicism must remain the enemy it always was.

So the ecumenical overtures of Catholicism had exactly the opposite effect on RDP than one might have expected. Catholic reform and renewal posed even more of a threat to it than did Catholic persecution in the past. The persecutions had been functional for the persecuted Protestant community, shoring up its cohesion and sense of identity. Once the enemy disappeared, however, there was no one to fight against.

Ecumenism entails a transformation of definitions. Enemies are redefined as friends. But as I indicated above, the redefinition of the enemy on the battlefield of radically opposed metaphysical viewpoints is equivalent to subverting the very structure of reality. Someone who tries to redefine the enemy must be regarded as a traitor. For he or she is opening the gates to a Trojan horse. And that is precisely how RDP viewed those who tried to redefine the Catholic Church as a sister religion:

> We were aware of the fact that in the United States and Europe there were many "Protestants" infatuated with the Church of Rome—to the point of considering it a "Christian Church," "one of the Christian denominations," a "sister Church," and so forth. But we did not realize that such optimistic Protestants existed also in our Brazil. In this magazine . . . we read an article by some seminarian from the South (published by special condescension of the editorial board), in which Romanism is called a "sister religion" and thus placed alongside Protestantism and under the paternity of God.

The writer of this article then proceeds to justify the title of "sister church" when applied to other Protestant denominations. But can the same title be applied to the Catholic Church?

> It is a very different case with Romanism. There everything is achieved through Mary. We would not even have Christ himself without Mary and her consent.

In the last analysis the critical issue is the fact that Protestantism, faithful to Pauline Christianity, defends justification by faith whereas the Catholic Church preaches salvation by works:

> The great Teacher of the Nations [Paul], when faced with the alien, spurious gospel of the Judaizers that salvation was by faith and by works, did not indulge in optimistic or accommodating circumlocutions. He was clear and categorical: "When you seek to be justified by

way of law, your relation with Christ is completely severed" (Gal. 5:4). Earlier in the same letter he wrote: "But if anyone, if we ourselves or an angel from heaven, should preach a gospel at variance with the gospel we preached to you, he shall be held outcast" (Gal. 1:8). Here we see the following about the doctrine of salvation by faith when combined with the doctrine of salvation by works: (1) it is declared anathema; (2) those who teach it are severed from Christ (can they still be Christians, then?); (3) those people have fallen from grace. How can people who pervert the gospel of Christ in this way be considered members of a "sister religion"? . . .

Now in our midst we find people who claim to know our teachings, yet who declare that Marian Romanism is a "sister religion" of Protestant Evangelicalism. We are left open-mouthed. . . . When Protestant seminarians who think that way finish their studies and are ordained ministers, to whom will they go to preach the gospel of Christ in this "Christian" country? What good news will these young men have to announce to all those "brothers and sisters" of theirs, who already belong to a "sister religion" . . . of theirs? Signed, AMICA VERITAS [BP, January 1959, p. 8].

This citation deserves analysis. Note that it begins with shock and astonishment. The writer is faced with something absolutely new and unexpected that is ruled out by the logic of his system. He knows that in other countries there are "Protestants" infatuated with the Roman Church. The use of quotation marks indicates he thinks the use of the word "Protestants" is dubious. For a Protestant by definition is someone who views the Catholic Church as an enemy. A Protestant who considers it a sister religion is a square circle, a logical contradiction in terms. The writer's astonishment lies in finding the same attitude present in Brazil, since it was voiced in an article which was published earlier in the same magazine (October 1958, p. 5).

The author of the earlier article was a certain seminarian from the South of Brazil. The roots of the evil are here revealed. First, it is the opinion of a seminarian, a young man who has already deviated from the solid, orthodox thinking of the past under the influence of new winds of doctrine coming from Europe and the United States. Second, this seminarian comes from the *South* of Brazil. At that point in time the church magazine was published in the North of Brazil, in Recife, and it was run by men from the North. The history of the Presbyterian Church of Brazil shows an ongoing tension between the North and the South. The North has posed as the champion of orthodoxy: the South has struggled to prove it is equally orthodox at all costs in order to preclude schism. In this case the evil comes from the South, from a seminarian whose theological education has led him badly astray. The article was published "by special condescension of the editorial board," which thus showed special "tolerance toward error." What does "special condescension" mean? That those in error do not have the right to speak? That they speak by special permission rather than by right? In this case the heresy is the seminarian's calling Romanism a "sister religion." But only those who have the same father can be called brothers and sisters, so the seminarian is suggesting that God is the father of Catholics as well. Protestantism denies that. Romanism is anathema; it is severed from Christ and fallen away from grace.

Thus Protestantism's whole reason for being is called into question. If such seminarians really believe what they say, they will have no function to perform when they are ordained ministers. Protestantism needs Catholicism as an enemy in order to define its reason for being. Then comes the final touch: "What good news will these young men have to announce to those 'brothers and sisters' of theirs, who already belong to a 'sister religion' . . . of *theirs*?" The person who denies the existence of witchcraft is a witch. The person who denies heresy is a heretic. Protestants who call the Catholic Church a sister Church are not Protestants; they are Catholics. Hence they are anathema, just as Catholics are. Towards members who baptize the enemy into a friend, the Church must have the same attitude it has towards the enemy. And the course of events followed this logical necessity.

March 1959: an article entitled "The Old Tactic of the Chameleon." It is the conclusion that interests us here:

> Clearly that Church continues to be collectively an apostate as Church, even though there are sincere souls in it and even though some of its leaders are eager for the truth. As an organization, however, its modern reformist tendencies are merely a disguised effort at survival, especially in Brazil, where the reforming influence of Protestants is being felt without slackening. It is a very old tactic, indeed the tactic of the old saurian among our fauna known as the chameleon, who assumes the color of the branch on which it perches [BP, March 1959, p. 9].

In other words, Brazilian Protestantism must not redefine the enemy as a friend *on the basis of superficial indications* of reform by the enemy. Catholicism essentially remains an apostate, and its reforms are designed merely to camouflage that apostasy and ensure its ongoing survival.

April 1959: an article entitled "Utopia." The writer has already made a direct reference to Pope John XXIII:

> One day the bitter said to the sweet: "Let's unite to do away with the bitterness of life." The sweet smiled and said; "I see no qualities in you for a union with me." Slavery once said to Liberty: "Let us join our links to free the people." Replied Liberty: "I am free. I have no links or chains." In 1959 John XXIII said to Christianity: "Let us unite to save humanity." Replies Christianity: "You have always been my enemy. Do you think I do not know your wiles? Light does not unite with darkness" [BP, April 1959, p. 8].

May 1959: an editorial entitled "Ecumenical Council" referred to:

> . . . an Ecumenical Council of his Church, which is to meet in Rome, and which will discuss matters of the utmost relevance for Roman Catholicism. . . . From Rome there may come novelties in the area of ecclesiastical discipline. There may be promises of concessions to Protestants in exchange for their return to the papal corral. They may promise to abolish obligatory clerical celibacy, the use of Latin in public worship, auricular confession, and—who knows?—the cult of images. Indeed the Protestant side may be allowed to have its own rite. That would be nothing new, of course, since there are already other approved Catholic rites besides the Latin one in use in the East. But in the area of dogmatics, where Rome regards itself as "infallible teacher," it will not retreat one millimeter—of that we are certain. At the entranceway to dogmas, the Pope will have a clearly inscribed sign put up: *non plus ultra*. Confronted with this, what will the so-called dissident Churches do? Will they capitulate? Will they lay down their arms and bow to the papal yoke? [BP, May 1959, p. 12].

The function of definitions is to rule out the unexpected, to determine exactly what kinds of behavior can be expected from the thing defined. What is the Protestant conception of the Catholic Church as revealed in the above passage? What *can it expect* from Catholicism? First, many modifications and concessions in the area of ecclesiastical discipline. The objective of such concessions would be to get dissidents to return to the papal fold. Here we have the central point in the Protestant interpretation of the ecumenical movement. If the Catholic Church is an apostate at bottom, how can it claim to reform itself? No institution can deny its very essence. Hence reform can only be a trick or wile of the apostate Church, designed to impose its domination on others. It is precisely in its essence that the Catholic Church cannot be reformed. And its essence is its claim to be an "infallible teacher," to possess absolute truth, to offer the "perennial philosophy." So, as Protestantism defines Catholicism, the latter can change its color on accidental matters in order to impose its dominion on the essential thing: thought.

The RDP presupposition here is that institutions cannot be reformed. The Holy Spirit may be at work in the hearts of sincere Catholics, and even in priests who seek the truth. But the Holy Spirit does not act on institutions. So when Catholics discover the truth, they do not reform their institution. Instead they leave it for an institution where truth is to be found: the Protestant Church. It is a war situation. To accept the Catholic invitation is to lay down arms and submit to the papal yoke. Thus the ecumenical overtures of the Catholic Church, which seem on the surface to be an invitation to fellowship, are viewed by Brazilian RDP as a new phase in the age-old war. The tactic is more insidious and subtle, but the objective remains the same: to subject the mind and will of those who separated from the Catholic Church to the power and authority of Rome once again.

June 1959: article entitled "Romanism and Ecumenism":

> The Roman Church, was, is, and always will be—*ad aeternum*—Rome. The word comes from its glossary. Times change. Rome never changes. The Church of Rome insinuates itself, engages in mimicry, fits in with the times, and adapts to circumstances—but it does not change. It continues to be itself. Since it proclaimed itself infallible, it cannot possibly change. Even though it has gone astray, it cannot admit to being in error. Infallibility cripples its movement and extinguishes its impulses for recovery.
>
> What does the Roman Church want through its pope? It simply wants this: that we return to "Holy Mother Church," confessing that we are prodigal sons, reciting our humble, repentant *mea culpa*, and asking pardon for the immense sin of not having returned sooner to the bosom of Romanism. If the sacerdotal prayer of the Lord is to be fulfilled, there cannot be doctrinal divisions. There will be "only one Romanist flock" and "one single shepherd," who will be, infallibly, "the pope." We are to accept, without a murmur, historical Romanism with its immense load of blemishes, stains, and unpardonable faults. We are to trample on the corpses of the many martyrs who gave their lives so that we might enjoy truth and liberty. We are to confess, as some phony Protestants have already done, that the Religious Reformation was a mistake and that its Reformers did nothing but "divide the body of Christ." We are to reject the Bible and return to idolatry, thus making ourselves "doubly worthy of hell." . . .
>
> In the ranks of Protestants today we certainly do find a foolish sentimentality that is trying to treat the Roman Church as a "sister Church." It is nurtured by the childishness of some, the love of novelty in others, and the incredulity of still others. Ecumenism and apostasy are words that should be different in meaning. . . . Papal ecumenism is Romanization, and Romanization is apostasy [BP, June 1959, p. 5].

There is some logic to the above argument, and Catholics must recognize that they are also guilty in this matter. If an institution defines itself as infallible, how can one believe it is capable of repentance? Repentance is possible only for those who can make mistakes. And it was Pope Paul VI himself who described the form of the Church as eternal: ". . . the same today, as yesterday, and as she will be tomorrow . . ." (June 30, 1968). Indeed one cannot live "as if it were possible to dispense with the Church, since she is derived from the constitutional principles established by Christ himself" (August 7, 1969). In offering his interpretation of the aims of Vatican II, the same pope said: "The first and most important transformation that the Council intended . . . was . . . moral, personal, and inward renewal" (Alves: 56–59).

So the form remains the same, simply acquiring new vitality.

The problem is whether the ecumenical spirit can be reduced to the logic determined and controlled by the church institution. The fact is that rebellion against the institution had already begun within the Catholic Church itself. Protestantism closed its eyes to the new forces at work within the Catholic institution, forces which have been struggling to arrive at a new understanding of faith and the Church. It preferred to stay within the ecumenical logic espoused by the institutional Catholic Church. That was very convenient for Protestantism because it enabled RDP to keep its own view of Catholicism as a hierarchical, monolithic bloc incapable of reform. In that context ecumenism obviously could mean nothing but the return of Protestants to the Catholic Church. And ecumenism in that sense was synonymous with Romanization, and hence with apostasy.

November 1959: an editorial entitled "Reformation and 'Separation' ":

Today, as the pope cries out to those he calls "dissident Christians" and summons them back to his sheepfold, we can only answer from here: Let his Holiness return to the purity of the gospel; let him lead his Church back to pristine Christianity as it is presented in the New Testament. Only then can we extend him the right hand of our fellowship. Having done that, let him end up by coming down off his throne, allegedly of divine right, and putting himself on the same level as the other members of his clergy. Let him cease his pretensions about being the Vicar of Christ on earth. After he has done all that, then let him come and talk to us [BP, November 1959, p. 16].

Here is another article from December 1960:

There is one type of ecumenism that is very appealing to us. It seeks to bring closer together all the truly evangelical Churches, i.e., those which regard the Bible as the sole rule of faith and practice. . . . It is a very different matter when people try to extend our hand of fellowship to the apostate Church of Rome, the so-called Orthodox Church, and heretical sects that call themselves evangelical. Then we rear up and protest: we cannot possibly jump into that Babylonian boat. The Protestant advocates of this broad, undigested ecumenism like to quote a phrase from Calvin in which the great theologian expresses his willingness to travel through the whole world if that could foster the union of all Christians. What he wanted, without doubt, was to proclaim the riches of Christ to the whole world. . . . And who would be any less anxious than he was? But we find it impossible to see in his words a willingness to view apostate Romanism as a part of the Body of Christ, a part of the Church of God. To proclaim the gospel message and the glories of Christ is one thing; to sit down around a table with unbelieving papists and discuss things about the Kingdom of God with them, as if they were our brothers and sisters in the faith and children of the same God, wholly united with us in sentiment, is something totally different, something quite impossible to do [BP, December 1960, p. 5].

April 1961: an article entitled "Jesus Christ and the Ecumenical Wishes of Pope John XXIII":

What would be the real aims of the Supreme Pontiff in Rome?. . . . The Roman Curia proclaims and declares: in the eyes of the papacy the unification of Christianity means the pure and simple submission and obedience of all the Churches to the Supreme Pontiff in Rome, the sole vicar of Christ on earth, according to the infallible understanding of the Curia itself. . . . A flood of questions . . . rushes into the minds of those who ponder and think about this thrilling matter. For us, however, the matter is clear and admits of no doubt. The obstacles to the spiritual, fraternal union . . . of all those who claim to be Christians are insurmountable . . . because it is impossible to combine harmoniously bodies that are fundamentally different in substance and accidents. Whether we like it or not, Evangelical Protestantism and Roman Catholicism are two essentially different religions.

In his masterly work entitled *Nossa Crença e a de Nossos Pais*, David S. Schaff brought out this fundamental difference more clearly than anyone ever has. It is well to reiterate his points here, so as to offer guidance to the Christian conscience:

1. Protestantism views Christianity as being mainly a spiritual disposition and attitude; Romanism regards it as profession and obedience.

2. Protestantism takes Christ as the way that leads to the Church; Romanism makes the Church, the Church of Rome, the sole truth leading to Christ.

3. Protestantism sovereignly exalts Christ; Romanism exalts the Church above everything else.

4. Protestantism is scriptural; Romanism is ecclesiastical.

5. Protestantism says: "Where Christ is, there is the Church." Romanism . . . says: "Where the Church of Rome is, there Christ is."

6. Protestant Christianity is Pauline, and open to admit new lights wherever they may come from; Romanism is Petrine, and satisfied with old conceptions.

7. Protestantism stresses faith as the test of Christian profession; Romanism gives preeminence to submission to priestly prescriptions.

8. Protestantism glorifies freedom of conscience: Romanism exalts authority and tradition.

9. Protestantism is a community of believers made up jointly of ministers and lay people; Romanism is a community of priests, in which lay people are included at a secondary level.

10. Protestantism welcomes the rational and the natural; Romanism excites the wondrous and the ecstatic.

11. Protestantism is Christianity on the march; Romanism is ossified medievalism.

12. Finally, the motto of Protestantism is: "Truth, wherever it may lead." The motto of Romanism is: "*Roma semper eadem*—Rome ever the same" [BP, April 1961, p. 9].

An analysis of the above contrasts would not further my purpose here. I think my point has been illustrated well enough. Protestant identity depends on defining the Catholic Church as forever irreformable and inimical.

When an institution is organized to solve a certain problem, it must be able to point a finger at the problem. The Inquisition was created to put an end to witches, among other things. But what if witches did not exist? What if those strange women were merely midwives skilled in the use of herbs, or perhaps people with mental problems? Then there would be no reason for the Inquisition to exist. Institutions make sure that the problem they are trying to solve is a real one, and so the Inquisition defined witches and found them. Protestantism needs Catholicism as an apostate and enemy to justify itself, and it finds Catholicism as such.

The Second Enemy: Theological Liberalism and Modernism

Things get a bit more complicated in the case of this second enemy. The Catholic Church is a visible enemy, and its churches are all around. It is part of the everyday experience of any Brazilian. Any believer can sense its presence and its menace. Theological modernism, which is used interchangeably with theological liberalism here, poses a problem because it is invisible. There is no institution, no objective organization, no uniform body of elaborated doctrines. Instead theological modernism is an *attitude* towards the sacred texts. It is a typically Protestant attitude because its cradle was Protestant Germany. Hence it is a *domestic* enemy. Whereas the Catholic Church can be seen by anyone, theological modernism can only be seen by those who have specialized their theological sight.

It is not my purpose here to offer an historical analysis of the movement. I am interested only in how it is defined by RDP believers. Their definition of it is all their own because they apply the label of modernist to theologians who would be considered orthodox and conservative in Europe: e.g., Karl Barth.

Theological modernism is characterized by the fact that it accepts the modern scientific worldview as its starting point. Science serves both as a theoretical point of reference and as a methodological tool in the interpretation of the sacred texts.

One of the first manifestations of theological modernism was the movement that came to be viewed as the quest for the historical Jesus (see Schweitzer). Towards the end of the eighteenth century, influenced by the critical and rational bent of the Enlightenment, some people began to take notice of the fact that the Jesus of church dogmas was the product of a long series of successive interpretations. That naturally gave rise to a question: What might Jesus really have been like? The quest for the historical Jesus was an effort to free him from the dress and makeup which his followers had added to him over the centuries. It sought to get back to the original Jesus as he really had been. That was an effort that any Protestant, even the most conservative, could applaud. After all, the Reformation had a similar intent, didn't it? It sought to recover the Christianity of the New Testament, which had been disfigured by Roman Catholic tradition.

But there was a basic problem. The new movement assumed that *the sacred texts, too, were an interpretation.* In the biblical texts certain individuals offered *their* witness, *their* interpretation, as to who or what Jesus had really been. Thus the New Testament texts were not a photograph of Jesus; they were different paintings in which the emotions and perspectives of the artists were intermingled. To reconstruct the historical Jesus, one had to *mistrust* the texts. The indicative mood of the text seemed to refer to the object; in fact it referred to the perception of the author. The critical tools of scholarly science had to purify the text of the various layers of interpretation laid down by the authors. Only then would the historical Jesus emerge.

David Friedrich Strauss was perhaps the most typical representative of this attitude and approach. He looked at the documents from the perspective of scientific scholarship. In that perspective there was no room for exception, or miracles, or anything that contradicted the regularities verified in our experience. But the New Testament was full of miracles: the virgin birth, cures of sick people, and magical transformations of nature (water into wine, resurrections, etc.). How were those texts to be explained? They were myths: creations produced by emotion, imagination, and fantasy. Though the indicative mood of the passages pretended to describe something as really having happened, that was not the case. As such, the passages had to be rejected.

In this case the modernist attitude entailed radical criticism of the indicative mood in the scriptural texts. What remained? What remained was the imperative mood, the ethical discourse and teaching of Jesus. If you take away all the myths, you are left with an ethics which universal reason should recognize as permanently valid. The teachings of Jesus constitute the core of the gospel message, and reason can accept and affirm them without any problem. Thus the imperative mood was salvaged from the debris of the indicative mood in the biblical texts. The Jesus of dogma was destroyed but Jesus, the moral teacher, was restored. Scholarly science, the loftiest expression of modernity, became the servant of faith to the extent that it made it possible to separate the accidental from the essential in the biblical texts.

Now no matter how fine the reconstructed historical Jesus might be, he dealt a mortal blow to the Jesus of dogma. The Jesus of dogma is a metaphysical entity. What matters in his case is not his history but his function in the cosmic drama. Jesus the savior is one who performs the task of mediation in a universe sundered by sin. The historical Jesus, by contrast, is a human being who serves as a moral model and an ethical teacher. These two Jesuses cannot subsist side by side. The important thing for traditional orthodoxy is the Church's teaching *about* Jesus. In the quest for the historical Jesus, the important thing is the teaching *of* Jesus. The underlying assumption which emerged in the process was that there was complete discontinuity between what the Church taught about Jesus and what Jesus himself taught. If that assumption was true, it meant the collapse of the universe inhabited by both Catholics and Protestants. It meant the end of traditional Christian metaphysics. So it is not surprising that Protestants should view theological modernism as one of its worst enemies.

Moreover, critical analysis of the scriptural text left no place for the doctrine of the verbal inspiration of Scripture. The function of that doctrine is to guarantee the absolute credibility of the Bible's indicative discourse. If it says that something happened, it did happen. This eliminates all possibility of error due to human mediation. In all biblical propositions the speaker is the Absolute Subject who knows absolutely. But what happens when we use the same critical tools on the Bible that we use on other texts? The assumption is that the biblical documents are like other documents; that they are one *species* of text in the larger *genus* of written texts. Since all texts are products of the human spirit, they are all conditioned by history, culture, society, and the psychology of their authors. The door is opened to relativism, and the Bible has no right to a privileged place vis-à-vis documents belonging to other religions of the world. Certainty is destroyed because the Bible has been stripped of its objective foundations.

A modernist would ask some such question as the following: "Why give a privileged place to the Lord of the Bible rather than to some other text?" His or her answer might be: "Because *I myself have made a decision* favoring the Bible. The Bible answers questions which my mind and heart raise." Thus authority shifts from the objectivity of the text to the subjectivity of the human mind and heart. In short, the final authority in matters of faith is the human spirit, not the Divine Spirit.

Here we might well raise this question: Isn't this conclusion the inevitable consequence of free inquiry? Must we not admit that theological modernism, not orthodox Protestantism, led free inquiry to its ultimate conclusions? RDP recoils at the threat, which would make it impossible to distinguish orthodoxy from heresy. Modernism denies that there is some absolute standard by which to differentiate correct thinking and knowledge from incorrect varieties. But if faith and salvation are questions of knowledge, then isn't modernism an enemy of salvation itself?

The hermeneutic program of modernism entails two tasks or phases in dealing with the text. The first of these is demythologizing the biblical text, to use Bultmann's term. Modernists eliminate from the text everything that contradicts the modern scientific view of the world. They maintain that *the ob-*

ject of faith is not a worldview, a mythological description of the cosmos and the universe.

What, then, is the object of faith? Here we come to the second phase of modernist hermeneutics. Rather than saying how the world is structured, claims modernism, faith and the gospel message are addressed to human subjectivity. The gospel message seeks to change *the human person's way of being in the world*. Faith has to do with the structure of the human spirit. Demythologization is the task which must be done first so that human beings can understand the spiritual message of the biblical text, a message which deals not with the theoretical structuring of the world but with the existential structuring of the human spirit. The biblical text is a response to the existential question raised by human beings. What is authentic living? What is freedom? What is the meaning of life and death? The biblical message cannot contradict science because it is not concerned with what *is*. It is concerned with what *ought to be* in the realm of human subjectivity. Its goal is not new knowledge but rather *metanoia*, a change of mind and heart in the human being.

Remember that Protestantism saw the Catholic Church as an enemy because it subjected the biblical text to the twofold mediation of tradition and the church magisterium. Well, modernism also subjects the biblical text to a twofold mediation. It sees biblical texts as the writer's *interpretation* of events. They are witnesses who give testimony. It also says that today's reader examines those texts and comes up with an *interpretation* of the writer's *interpretation*. So there is no possibility of an objective exegesis (Bultmann: 289–96). For modernism, then, there is no absolute knowledge because there are no objective absolutes such as the text itself, tradition, or the magisterium. The only absolute is the human spirit itself, if you will; but instead of being an absolute, it is a risk, a wager, a leap of faith. That is why theological modernism is the common enemy of orthodox Protestants and Catholics.

In the previous section we saw that Protestants traced the innumerable doctrinal errors of the Catholic Church back to its root mistake: its doctrine of Scripture. The same holds true for theological modernism. Despite its theoretical fruits, there is something wrong with its epistemological roots. Even a seemingly orthodox theology may turn out to be modernist and heterodox when examined closely under the RDP microscope. For, according to Brazilian Protestantism, the doctrine of the verbal inspiration of Scripture is the criterion which distinguishes truly orthodox theologies from modernist ones.

Consider the attitude of Brazilian Protestantism towards Karl Barth, for example. From the twenties to the fifties Barth was undoubtedly the most influential theological voice in Protestant circles. His theology marked a radical break with the liberalism which dominated European theology in the first two decades of this century. The breaking point came with his commentary on the *Epistle to the Romans* in 1919. Influenced by Kierkegaard, Barth structured his theology around the "infinite qualitative difference between time and eternity,'' and hence between the human spirit and the Divine Spirit. Thus the word of God was not a response to the existential questions of the human being; instead it marked the abolition of those questions. There was no continuity between reason and faith.

On this basis Barth launched an attack on the notion of the *analogy of being*, a central notion in Catholic theology which affirmed continuity between the structure of creation and the structure of the creator. The analogy of being provided the basis for a natural theology whereby human beings could ascend from reason and the world to eternity and true knowledge of God. *Nein* (No!) was the title of a short booklet in which Barth rejected the proposal for a natural theology made by his colleague Emil Brunner. The word of God did not answer human questions; instead it denied their validity. God was not the outer limit of human reason, the greatest possible object of human knowledge. He was not an object of human knowledge at all, and revelation was not the logical and ontological crown of the world. Divine revelation was the negation of all that. So it is not reason that constitutes faith. Instead theological rationality comes along when human reason collapses, when the human spirit hears and heeds the word of God.

Clearly Barth's thought broke with earlier theological modernism and liberalism. It might be expected that Brazilian Protestantism would have chosen him as an ally. That did not happen. There was almost total silence about him and his work until the 1950s in Brazil, even though he had been on the theological scene since 1918. When it was no longer possible to ignore Barth, RDP theologians began to speak out. They condemned him as a liberal theologian and modernist. Why? Because of Barth's teaching about the word of God.

Barth's view of the word of God was solidly rooted in the Hebrew concept of *dābār* ("word"). God's word was the *divine creative act* in and through which God reveals himself. It is an event, a happening, not a proposition *about* God. The word of God is "God present." Hence the written word in Scripture can only be a *witness* about the living divine word, a *sign that points to it*. By itself the sign is lifeless. According to Barth, then, we cannot say that the Bible is the word of God. However, it can *become* the word of God insofar as it becomes the vehicle through which a human being experiences the power of God.

Barth thus made the authority of the text subordinate to the authority of the divine act in which God reveals himself in a living way here and now. The authority of the text derived from the faith-experience. Rather than an authoritative text creating faith, it was the faith-experience that recognized the text as authoritative. Rather than the letter creating life, it was life recognizing its horizon of meaning in the text. Needless to say, RDP theology detected the danger of subjectivism here once again. It made no difference that Barth's theology was radically orthodox and staunchly opposed to theological modernism. RDP classified him as a modernist because his teaching about the word of God deviated from its view of the verbal inspiration of

Scripture, the doctrine on which absolute knowledge and certainty of Protestantism are based.

Fear of theological modernism also showed up in another area. It was perhaps the principal reason why the Presbyterian Church of Brazil consistently refused to join the World Council of Churches (WCC). The WCC stemmed from the efforts of Protestant Christians to remedy the scandal of division. Only slowly would the Catholic Church come around to considering the same issue since it had always considered itself to be *the* Church of Christ, united under one head. Its traditional ecclesiology offered only one solution to the problems of splintered Christianity: the Protestant denominations would have to *return* to the unity of Catholicism. Protestants were forced much earlier to ponder the reality of their dividedness vis-à-vis the New Testament idea of the Church as *the* Body of Christ. Thus the Protestant ecumenical movement took concrete shape in modern times about fifty years before ecumenism emerged in the Catholic Church. And I might note in passing that a Brazilian Protestant, Erasmo Braga, was active in the effort which led to the creation of the World Council of Churches.

But there was a problem. What was to be the criterion for participating in the WCC? What was the minimal theological formula that identified Christians as such? The decision regarding this confessional formula was a crucial one. In choosing a formula, you were automatically defining what was essential; and you were tacitly suggesting that everything else was secondary. The WCC opted for the following confessional formula: "Jesus Christ, God, Lord, and Savior." It thus was saying that the essential element of the faith was a confession about Jesus Christ; and it was tacitly implying that *what one thinks about the Scriptures is not essential*. Faith in Christ, not faith in Scriptures, is what defines the Christian. Any Church that professes Christ to be God, Lord, and Savior belongs to the Ecumenical Church, whether or not it believes in the verbal inspiration of the Scriptures. Thus modernism, in and of itself, is not an attitude opposed to faith.

The reaction of RDP was predictable. The WCC did not define modernism as an enemy whereas RDP did; and any friend of their enemy had to be considered an enemy too. The WCC was an institution that would give refuge "both to faith and to unbelief" (BP, November 1961, p. 3). Hence it was most important that the Presbyterian Church of Brazil not join the WCC as a member. To become a member would be equivalent to betraying the faith! The Church could not maintain an attitude of intransigence towards modernists on the home front and an attitude of tolerance on the international front.

Now another organization was coming into being around the same time. Various fundamentalist groups, which generally shared the intellectual positions that I have been analyzing in this book, decided to organize an "orthodox" organization as a counterpart to the "modernist" WCC. Their entity was the International Council of Christian Churches (ICCC). The Presbyterian Church of Brazil now found itself in a dilemma. Its intellectual affinities were with the ICCC. However, it had had some painful encounters with representatives of the ICCC mentality, who were tirelessly ferreting out heresies and modernist tendencies in their midst. Moreover, some leaders of the Presbyterian Church of Brazil had been sympathetic to the WCC and had been involved with it. Affiliation with one or the other of the two institutions would provoke a serious intramural crisis.

What did the Church do? It opted for what it called a position of "equidistance." Note that this did not represent any intermediary theological position. There was no intermediary position between WCC "modernism" and ICCC fundamentalism. Equidistance here was a purely practical stance: nonaffiliation with either organization in order to avert an internal crisis within the Presbyterian Church in Brazil. All this was explained and justified in an important editorial in the Church's official organ. I will present excerpts from that editorial and comment on them:

> We are living through a period of great agitation, in which the forces of evil are trying to undermine the foundations of the Church. . . . Some humble souls and sincere believers are careless and unwary, so that they are affected by winds of doctrine, let their convictions grow faint, lose their love for the Bible, and give up their submission to it. Others, more solidly grounded in the inspired Word of God but also unprepared, are rebelling against their Church because they hear that it has lost its fidelity to Scripture and is open to the influence of rationalism.

The first group of believers mentioned above are those who allegedly have been influenced by modernism. The second group are obviously those affected by fundamentalist accusations against the Church. To hold to a position of equidistance between ICCC truth and WCC error, wouldn't that come down to tolerance of error? Such was the fundamentalist accusation or implication. The editorial proceeded to uphold the orthodoxy of the Church and to reject fundamentalist accusations against it:

> In successive meetings of its General Assembly, the Presbyterian Church of Brazil . . . reaffirmed its orthodox, conservative, doctrinal position of fidelity to the Word of God. . . .
>
> Hence the Presbyterian Church of Brazil cannot be accused of laxity or neutrality with reference to the doctrinal issue, much less of being under modernist influences. . . .
>
> Amid the international struggles between the two international ecumenical bodies—one liberal and modernist, the other intransigently fundamentalist (the latter, in our opinion, in defense of the true thesis)—the Presbyterian Church of Brazil has adopted an equidistant position, due to local circumstances [OP, July 25, 1951, p. 1].

To interpret this text: Equidistance is not doctrinal neutrality. The Church is in agreement with the fundamentalists that the WCC is a modernist liberal organization. It is further agreed that the fundamentalist ICCC is on the side of truth. The ICCC, and the Church in its official expression in this editorial, have a common enemy. Thus they both define the situation in an identical way; they inhabit one and the same world.

The doctrine of the verbal inspiration of the Scriptures, in its first moment, is the decisive factor in the definition of the Catholic Church as an enemy. A Catholic-Protestant ecumenism cannot exist.

In its second moment, the verbal inspiration of the Scriptures is the decisive factor in the definition of the Protestant ecumenical movement as an enemy: it is modernist. The WCC, in its minimal theological formula, defines faith as a *confession concerning Christ*. Everything else is secondary, nonessential. Faith is an attitude toward a Person, not toward a book. Now the orthodoxy we are analyzing demands a text as point of departure—for the construction of absolute knowledge and absolute certitude. Faith ceases to be a confession regarding a Person, and becomes comprehensive, totalitarian, knowledge—the knowledge of a worldview. Ecumenism, therefore, would only be possible in the presence of agreement not only on the authority on which this knowledge is assented to—the inspired text—but also on the worldview logically deriving from the text.

The Third Enemy: Worldliness

The Catholic Church and theological modernism are enemies because they subvert the question of truth. They undermine right thinking and correct knowledge based on faith. But that is not the only front on which the battle between salvation and damnation is fought. On the left side of the wide road to damnation one will find a large building called the "Tavern of Worldliness." On it is displayed a banner with the inscription: "The World and the Flesh."

When I discussed the RDP personal ethic in chapter five, I underlined its repression of the body. The logic of the body is the logic of the pleasure principle. To follow that logic is to head down the wide road to damnation, to heed the world and the flesh. Worldliness is a lifestyle in which these realities exert a more powerful attraction than God's commandments.

Worldliness is a way of living, not a doctrine or a collection of dogmas. It is not concerned with truth. It implicitly affirms the supremacy of instinct, impulse, biology, and eroticism over the cognitive faculties of the human being. As a heresy, it is unconscious and unarticulated. It has no theory and it does not want one. It knows that the call of instinct is more powerful than any argument.

The danger of worldliness is in proportion to the strength of the body's call. Young people are obviously its favorite prey. So the Church must offer young people suitable channels of sublimation, otherwise the desire for pleasure will draw them outside the Church into the pathway towards the world and damnation:

> If we do not offer young people sound, pure, licit diversions, and ones that are even needed for good health, they will go out and look for them in the profane, worldly milieu. . . . They need such forms of recreation as ball games, ping-pong, track and field, picnics, swimming, physical exercises, parlor games, parties, literary competitions, get-togethers, comedy skits and plays, so long as such events do not take place on Sunday or in halls of worship, and so long as they do take place in Church-approved areas and under the supervision of the minister and the local session [OP, April 10, 1958, p. 2].

It is revealing that the writer of the article assumes that young people will seek diversions outside the Church if the latter does not provide them. It is also revealing that the problem seems peculiar to young people, not to the whole membership of the Church. The implicit assumption is that young people are the most vulnerable to the call of pleasure and instinct. So the Church has the mission of serving as a protective "hot-house" to prevent young people from entering the world. I put quotation marks around the term because that was the word used by young people themselves in the middle of the 1950's to express their resentment at the way the Church had described the situation and was dealing with it.

As I indicated above, worldliness is not a doctrine with ideologists and theologians to champion its case. Start a debate with it and no one will leap up as its spokesman. The battle with worldliness must be waged on the practical level. Concrete steps must be taken against worldliness when it rears its head. The panoply of church discipline is the war weapon to be used against such an enemy and its victim, the body. The latter is responsive to pleasure and to pain. Fleshly attractions promise pleasure, church discipline promises pain. Church discipline offers a preview of hell, showing offenders that the pursuit of pleasure means the pain of punishment in this life. And the latter is a foretaste of eternal punishment. In a thesis on "Eternal Punishments," one leader of the Church argued that they are necessary because otherwise worldliness and immorality would run rampant.

Now if the "world" is an enemy, believers must remain distant from it. But worldliness is not an idea, so it cannot be combatted by ideas. It is a sickness, a virus, a kind of demoniacal possession. Isolation and quarantine are the proper remedies. The Church defines itself as the milieu where behavior is controlled by God's commandments. There the body is repressed and controlled by church discipline. The "world" is everything outside the church milieu, where morality and its logic does not rule.

Catholicism and modernism are enemies of the Protestant construction of reality. Worldliness is an enemy which undermines the Protestant construction of behavior.

The Fourth Enemy: The Social Gospel

In a certain sense the Social Gospel can be considered the fruit of theological modernism and its spirit. The Social Gospel stresses the imperative as opposed to the indicative. It is interested in the moral teachings *of* Jesus rather than in the Church's teachings *about* Jesus (i.e., christology). The name of the movement suggests its hermeneutic program. Its point is that the ethic of Jesus is not an ethic of individual purity and perfection. Instead it is an ethic which lays down the basic principles for a social order that is just and fraternal. When we read the gospel message, says the Social Gospel, we should look for its social implications.

The titles of two books by Walter Rauschenbusch, a leading U.S. advocate of the Social Gospel, reveal much about the movement's orientation: *Christianizing the Social Order* (1912), and *The Social Principles of Jesus* (1916). In those books he deals with such topics as: the solidarity of the human family, the social ideal of Jesus, private property and the common good, the cross as a social principle, and the case of Christianity against capitalism. Here are two pointed excerpts from *Christianizing the Social Order*:

> The Kingdom of God is the first and the most essential dogma of the Christian faith. It is also the lost social ideal of Christendom. No man is a Christian in the full sense of the original discipleship until he has made the Kingdom of God the controlling purpose of his life, and no man is intellectually prepared to understand Jesus Christ until he has understood the meaning of the Kingdom of God [Rauschenbusch a: 49].

Rauschenbusch indicates that the meaning of the Kingdom of God finds its highest expression in the teachings of the Old Testament prophets.

> The prophets were religious reformers demanding social action. They were not discussing holiness in the abstract, but dealt with concrete present-day situations in the life of the people. . . . They demanded neighborly good will and humane care of the helpless. But their most persistent and categorical demand was that the men in power should quit their extortion and judicial graft. They were trying to beat back the hand of tyranny from the throat of the people. Since the evil against which they protested was political, their method of redress was political too. . . . They all had a radiant hope of a future when their social and religious ideals would be realized.
>
> Emancipation from foreign tyranny, peace and order throughout the land, just and humane rulers, fertility of the soil, prosperity for all, a glorious capital city with a splendid temple in it—it was the social utopia of an agrarian nation. Hardly an ingredient of human life is missing in their ideals, except the hope of immortality. . . . The more their

moral demands were baffled by brutal power, the more they threw their hope back on God for fulfillment. . . . This reign of God for which they hoped was therefore a social hope on fire with religion [Rauschenbusch a: 51–52].

I need hardly point out that traditional and orthodox Protestants were horrified by this interpretation of the gospel message. To them the gospel message was one of salvation for individual souls after death. To the Social Gospel movement, on the other hand, the kingdom of God was a socio-political utopia to be realized at some time in the future in history. Traditional Protestantism saw reality as a fixed structure which could not be transformed; Christians were simply to pass through it as pilgrims on the way to eternity. The Social Gospel movement felt that the biblical message demanded a radical transformation of social structures so that a just and fraternal order might be established. Traditional Protestants looked above and beyond this world; members of the Social Gospel movement looked ahead to the future of this world.

The Social Gospel movement as such never reached Brazil. Its echoes did, however, and RDP was horrified by its radical adulteration of the gospel message as it understood that message. Few Brazilian Protestants have read the works of Rauschenbusch, but they all know that the Social Gospel is something evil. It transforms the faith from a system of absolute metaphysical knowledge into a program of political action. Thus the most central tenet and message in the RDP worldview is lost: i.e., the eternal salvation of the individual soul after death.

The Social Gospel denies the central problem around which the Protestant universe is structured. The question of knowledge and its solution are rejected in favor of the gospel imperative. The Social Gospel rejects the RDP structuring of the world and the centrality of an individual ethic centered around personal perfection. The transformation of society is the ethical task that comes first.

No wonder, then, that Brazilian Protestantism has seen the Social Gospel movement as the symbol of everything opposed to its faith, even though it has had little or no direct experience of that movement. Indeed it has often used the name to pin it on people who began to show concern about the social responsibilities of the Church. It was a label for heresy. It is bad enough when there are enemies outside the Church, although they do help to cement the social cohesion of the in-group. But what happens when members of the Church itself begin to speak the language of the enemy? There is panic, and talk of infiltration and treason. That is precisely what happened. And those who tried to redefine its enemies were thrown out.

EIGHT

TRUTH AND DOGMATISM

We have come to the end of our journey. We have followed the RDP spirit from its start in the conversion-experience. We have noted the process whereby the emotional discourse of the new convert is transformed into a discourse propounding a body of absolute knowledge. We have considered the *a priori* categories around which RDP constructs its world: its space and time, its maps and its calendars. We have seen that the dualism which runs through that world is resolved in the unity of divine causality, which is explained in the doctrine of divine providence. We have examined the moral order of RDP, and how it finds expression in the discourse and practice of church discipline. We have seen that its individual moral ethic, focused around the salvation of the soul and the repression of the body, is actually a denial of anything that could really be called a social ethic. Finally, in the last chapter we saw how RDP's definition of its own identity entails a definition of its enemies as well.

I think readers can now easily see the affinity between the spirit of RDP and the spirit of medieval Catholicism. Both struggled with the same problem, constructed their worlds in answer to the same basic question: "What must I do to be saved?" I see no way of avoiding the blunt conclusion of Ernst Troeltsch cited earlier:

> Protestantism . . . was, more than anything else, a simple modification of Catholicism, in which the Catholic formulation of the problems was retained, while a different answer was given to them [Troeltsch a: 59].

But I must go a bit further than that simple conclusion. While Troeltsch's conclusion establishes the Protestant approach in a basic way, it does not point up some of the oppositions and implications involved. In this last chapter, therefore, I wish to spell out certain points about the RDP spirit, their roots and implications, and where we might go from there.

194

Dogmatism and Intolerance

It was no mere accident that I dealt with RDP epistemology right after the conversion-experience. More than once I indicated that conversion is not the core of the RDP spirit, since the new convert is still raw material who must be molded to that spirit. *The core of the RDP spirit is its obsession with truth.* As Kierkegaard said, *what is said* is of little importance. What determines the Protestant spirit is *how* it expresses its knowledge. RDP assumes that salvation is a function of knowing the truth. It must logically conclude that its knowledge *is* the truth, that it is an absolute and final knowledge which must be upheld without vacillations or concessions. Doubt is a symptom of damnation. Its discourse and real being coincide, hence it holds a monopoly on truth. It possesses a body of knowledge that is totally objective and absolute.

Moreover, truth has temporal and ontological primacy over goodness in the world of RDP. Its indicative discourse allows for no relativism whatsoever, whereas biblical imperatives can be relativized. So the proper order moves *from knowledge to salvation to morality*, and this order cannot be reversed or changed. Only those who possess the truth can be saved, and only those who are saved can conduct themselves in the correct moral way. In Catholicism grace is mediated through the sacraments, which work *ex opere operato*. Their effects do not depend on the conscious state of the minister or the recipient of the sacraments. In RDP, by contrast, grace is mediated through knowledge of the truth. Those who do not affirm its truth are separated from grace.

At first glance this obsession with truth would seem to be an extraordinary virtue. In my opinion, it is this obsession with truth that gives the Protestant spirit its extraordinary consistency, its willingness to draw the ultimate conclusions from its premises no matter how bitter those conclusions may be. That same obsession with truth can be found in the Protestant ethic, which does not hesitate to repress the impulses of the body in the name of a higher truth. Like Kant, the Protestant ethic is determined to speak the truth no matter what the price may be.

I said that "at first glance" such an obsession with truth seemed to possess great merit. But the dark side of this obsession is RDP's intolerance towards anything it defines as error vis-à-vis its absolute truth. A fundamental opposition undergirds the world of absolute truth: orthodoxy versus heterodoxy, correct thinking versus heresy. And since orthodoxy is bound up with the crucial problem of the eternal salvation of souls, *absolute truth must be intolerant.* Only doubters can be tolerant. When love of truth is identified with actual *possession of the truth*, the advocates of truth must be intolerant towards those who have a different way of thinking.

John Huizinga has called our attention to a curious fact. Society always tends to be more tolerant of those who *cheat* in the social game than of those who simply *refuse to play* that game (Huizinga: 111). When we cheat, we basically are agreeing to play a game and trying to win at it. Those who refuse to play the game do not make an effort to win at it because the game does not interest them. The Inquisition, for example, did not punish people who committed moral faults. Robbery, adultery, and murder were matters for the secular courts. The Inquisition was concerned with the much more serious crimes against orthodox thinking. Its enemies were those who denied the validity of the rules of the game as they had been set up. Those who indulged in immoral behavior did so in secret if they could, and they felt guilty of disobeying the rules and deviating from the norm. When they confessed their sins, they were admitting that the rules of the game were right and that they had broken those rules.

Things are very different with heretics. Instead of cheating, they openly contest the rules of the game. They denounce those rules and proclaim their alternatives. Unashamed, they do not try to keep their ideas secret. Indeed they would like everyone to accept their ideas as the real truth. Note the following comment of a medieval historian, Walter Ullman, on the attitude of the Inquisition towards heretics:

> Publicly to hold opinions which ran counter to or attacked the faith determined and fixed by law was heresy, and the real reason for making heresy a crime was—as Gratian's *Decretum* had explained it—that the heretic showed intellectual arrogance by preferring his own opinions to those who were specially qualified to pronounce upon matters of faith. Consequently, heresy was high treason, committed against the divine majesty, committed through aberration from the faith as laid down by the papacy [Szasz: 4–5].

The confrontation between orthodoxy and heresy is, at bottom, a conflict between opinions regarded as true by the majority and opinions regarded as true by some individual. Heresy is a rebellion of *one* against the *many*. Or, to put it in a more revealing way, it is a rebellion of the *weak* against the *strong*. Why? Because individuals are always weaker than groups or institutions are. The heretical individual denies the claim of a certain community to absolute knowledge. Heretics are telling the many that their construction of reality and their organization of thought are wrong; that their truth is a lie. So heresy is not simply an intellectual act, it is also a political proclamation and denunciation. As Szasz points out:

> The fundamental conflicts in human life are not between competing ideas, one "true" and the other "false"—but rather between those who hold power and use it to oppress others, and those who are oppressed by power and seek to free themselves of it [Szasz: 63].

Heretics are people who reject truth as defined by a given society. They reject a truth which is functional for a given setup of political power within an ecclesiastical institution; and they do so in the name of a higher truth. Heresy displaces or shifts the center of the sacred from a sociopolitical consensus to the more solitary experience of one individual or a few individuals. The latter affirm that they, not the community, are on the track of the truth. And in so doing, they deny the sacred pretensions of the collective consciousness. They are not ashamed. They do not repent. Only those are ashamed, and repent, who consider themselves in error, thus asserting the truth of the collective consciousness. Heretics, on the contrary, assert that it is the institution which ought to be ashamed and repent, for it is in error. Heresy's intent is ever to subvert a worldview, and therefore to build the world in a new way. But for an institution which equates absolute knowledge and salvation, which makes salvation dependent on truth, the heretic's preaching implies that the institution is on the side of perdition. This is why Giordano Bruno and Michael Servetus had to be burned at the stake, by the Catholic inquisition and the Protestant inquisition respectively.

We pointed out at the beginning of our investigation that Protestant discourse repeatedly declares that *free inquiry* is essential to the spirit of Protestantism. What does "free inquiry" mean? Free inquiry is the freedom of the individual conscience to read and interpret the sacred text, in opposition to the truths of the collective consciousness, and in a manner that is rebellious toward established orthodoxies. Free inquiry is systematically invoked, in polemical situations, against Catholicism. The Catholic is told, "Actually it is your individual conscience that establishes its own truths, even if they are opposed to Catholic orthodoxy." In reality, it is only when this happens that the individual can be converted from Catholicism to Protestantism. If it fails to happen, the subject's consciousness will forever remain the prisoner of Catholic definitions of truth.

But we also note that, once converted, individuals find themselves prisoners of a system of absolute knowledge, which is to be affirmed without doubt and without concessions. We are before a global, closed system: knowledge that cannot be contradicted by any experience. Discourse becomes its own point of reference. No experience exterior to it can be appealed to in order to criticize it. Everything verifies it; nothing gives it the lie. *Discourse* and *being* coincide.

Now if this is how the matter stands, we are forced to conclude that, while the Protestant spirit may begin with free inquiry, it crystallizes in the abolition of free inquiry. Free inquiry is permission for heresy. It allows *one* person to affirm a truth which opposes the truth of the *many*. If Protestantism were consistent with its "institutes," with the foundations of its moment of birth, it would have to constitute a social organization open to divergent readings of the text. It could not select uniformity of reading—confession of right doctrine—as the criterion for participation in the community.

We are making an analysis of the Protestant ethic as defined by the discourse and practice of ecclesiastical discipline. We find that it is built upon the negation of the body. The body must be disciplined by a norm of absolute knowledge, which is opposed to it in a heteronomic relationship. As we analyze the form in which Protestants know reality, we find, in precisely similar fashion, that the Church demands believers submit their thinking to a norm that is accepted as orthodox. Correct thinking, in parallel fashion to correct behavior, is the one in which human beings discipline their thought in such wise that their discourse be simply repetitive: the individual repeats the discourse of collective consciousness.

The heretic, meanwhile, is the one who rejects this. Heretics take free inquiry seriously. They do not forget the initial "institutes" the moment they are converted. They have the courage to stand on their own two feet when they speak. They refuse to repeat. They dare to say what is new. They presume that truth has not been exhausted in the past. They reject dogma. They propound new worlds. They proclaim new visions. They cry values. They do not move respectfully among the pillars of a world already built, seeking short cuts for their pragmatic intentions. They commit no fraud. World-destroyers they are, iconoclasts. They refuse to look upon discourse as identical with being. And if the divine is beyond discourse, truth cannot be affirmed as a possession. Truth is a horizon, the object of a search.

But how can the seekers survive in the midst of people who have already found the answers? Their continuing search suggests that the answers have not yet been found. Their effort to create new values can hardly dovetail with the feelings of those who affirm they already possess all true values. The theme of conflict between searchers and possessors of truth was a permanent one in the thought of Nietzsche, as we find in *Thus Spoke Zarathustra*:

> O my brothers, who represents the greatest danger for all of man's future? Is it not the good and the just? Inasmuch as they say and feel in their hearts, "We already know what is good and just, and we have it too; woe unto those who still seek here!" [Kaufmann b: 324].

The fate of the seekers at the hands of such people was clear and inevitable to Nietzsche:

> O my brothers, one man once saw into the hearts of the good and the just and said, "They are the pharisees." But he was not understood. The good and the just themselves were not permitted to understand him: their spirit is imprisoned in their good conscience. The stupidity of the good is unfathomably shrewd. This, however, is the truth: the good *must* be pharisees—they have no choice. The good *must* crucify him who invests his own virtue [Kaufmann b: 324].

The orthodox try to preserve the old, whereas heretics seek to destroy the old and replace it with the new. The orthodox fear the new and the unexpected because it threatens their salvation; heretics seek the old as merely the way to something new, as a provisional stage that is meant to be surpassed. The orthodox see a fixed and finished world; heretics see an incomplete world that is still in motion.

Those who focus their attention on preserving the past are condemned to live in the past and lose the future. The world of orthodoxy was created by living human beings at some point in the past. Those people died, however, and the orthodox inherited their world as an eternal memorial and mausoleum. The orthodox use that world as a jail in which to imprison the living. This whole approach is described by Leszek Kolakowski in terms of "priesthood":

The priesthood is not simply a cult of the past seen through contemporary eyes, but a survival of the past intact in the present, an outgrowth of itself. It is not only a certain intellectual attitude toward the world, but a certain form of the world's existence—a factual continuation of a reality which no longer exists [Kolakowski: 36].

Why isn't it just an intellectual attitude towards the old? Because power is involved. Kolakowski's priest—my orthodox believer here—is not just someone who loves the old; he or she is someone who has the power to maintain the old here among us, thus determining the world of the living. Heretics, by contrast, regard the heritage of the past as a tool to be used by the living for the construction of new meanings and new worlds. The dead past thus comes to life. It becomes a tool rather than a prison.

Heresy and orthodoxy are words created by the orthodox. And, as I just noted above, the orthodox are those who have the power to impose their own ideas. Heresy and orthodoxy have very little to do with truth and falsehood. They are terms which indirectly identify winners and losers. And as far as I know, there has been no situation in which winners have shown any interest in giving up the power they have won. Power seeks to perpetuate itself, and this perpetuation extends to the ideas which confer a divine aura on those who hold power. Victory is interpreted as truth, defeat as falsehood. Thus the polarity between orthodoxy and heresy is a polarity between the triumphant many and the defeated few. The orthodox many, in this case, have their eyes fixed on the past, whereas the defeated few have their eyes on the future.

Love of truth—of truth defined as absolute knowledge which we already possess—comes to light as the origin of intolerance and dogmatism. Necessarily, those who have all truth, the truth necessary for salvation, cannot tolerate those who lay claim to constructing a new truth. *The fate of those who pretend to possess the truth is intolerance.* No other option remains to them. One can opt for doubt or for certitude. But once the option has been made, the consequences follow inevitably, with the precision of syllogistic deduction. Those who doubt are condemned to tolerance. How could it be otherwise? If I doubt, I acknowledge myself to be someone who is not in possession of the truth. Available to me are only images seen "indistinctly, as in a mirror" (1 Cor. 13:12). My discourse does not show forth the possession of truth; it is a search at most. And if I am searching, it is because I have not yet found. The truth is not in me. Perhaps it is in another. The need to listen supervenes. Discourse "without vacillations or concessions" is forbidden. I vacillate; therefore I concede. By contrast, if I do not doubt, it is forbidden to listen. Why listen if I already have the truth? *A priori* the possibility of my conversion to another truth is forbidden. That would be tantamount to eternal perdition. The heretic—the one who does not consolidate with my discourse—is necessarily a voice to be silenced, as being necessarily on the side of error.

Now we can proceed to our last remark concerning the spirit of RDP.

The Fear of Difference

In the late fifties and early sixties there was a breach in the closed rationality of RDP discourse. Protestantism tried to redefine the enemies of the Church. That was treason in the eyes of RDP believers, as I noted in previous chapters. I do not intend to describe the conflict in detail here, since that is a task for the historian. Instead I will simply describe some important traits of the new spirit which surfaced within the ranks of RDP.

It was an ecumenical spirit in two senses. First of all, it recognized that it did not have a monopoly over truth. It felt at home with intellectual relativism and doubt. Second, it was open to the Catholic Church as a sister religion and a companion in a common search. True, it said, Catholicism is full of errors; but so is our Protestantism.

This new spirit gave priority to existential truth over intellectual truth. Good deeds meant more to it than did dogmatic propositions. In its eyes the gospel message was not a series of propositional truths to be affirmed "without vacillations or concessions." Instead it was a lifestyle characterized by love and service. The new spirit was not concerned about upholding the verbal inspiration of Scripture or its factual inerrancy. It was open to examining the biblical texts in the light of historical and textual criticism.

The new spirit was not too concerned about personal moral virtues. Gospel morality, it said, cannot be defined in terms of the conformity of behavior to some abstract, universal norm. The important thing is love, and there are no ready-made formulas for love. If "truth" does not create goodness in action, it disqualifies itself. Ethical truth is not to be defined in terms of an equation between behavior and stipulated rules. Ethical truth exists only when action contributes to the good. Thus this spirit in Brazilian Presbyterianism subordinated the old indicative discourse to an imperative discourse.

It also rediscovered the goodness of life and the world, seeing the gospel message reveal its power to the extent that it helps us to create a humane and just social order. The new spirit found its inspiration in the biblical prophets. The world is the destiny of human beings by God's will. The realities of the after-life are entrusted to God's goodness; and human beings are freed from obsession with the hereafter so that they can devote themselves to transforming the world into a sacrament of God's kingdom.

This new spirit could not survive. Instead of covering every stage of the conflict between orthodoxy and heresy, I have selected two texts which embody the attitude of the old "truth" towards error. The first is an article entitled "The Presbyterian Church and Modernism," which was published in March 1963:

> From the beginning of Christianity heresies have arisen and accompanied it, as a shadow accompanies the body, as evil dogs goodness, as darkness follows light; the two antagonistic principles will go together until the consummation of time. Heresy will always exist, though perhaps dressed in new clothes. Since its essence remains the same, the Church must be vigilant and unflagging so as not to be strangled by it or suffer considerable damage. . . . "Modernism" carries inside it the whole panoply of immorality and impurity, the full cortege of the world. The modernist is a worldling in the guise of a Christian, Satan's fifth column in the Church of God. . . . The Presbyterian Church is already suffering from the deleterious influence of "modernism." In its seminaries, or at least in some of them, there are modernist professors, hence modernist students. They are openly preaching their heterodox doctrines, causing great confusion in believers. Tolerance in cases of this nature is a crime against the Church. . . . To these people the Church is nothing but a refuge for old fogeys; for incompetent, retrograde fossils; for archeological skeletons who belong in a museum of theology and doctrine. It is not the milieu for those who breathe only in the modern atmosphere with its new airs and new concepts. Their lungs open only to the pure air of new biblical interpretations, however absurd and ridiculous. To be consistent and honest with themselves, they should leave it in peace and go find the milieu that pleases and suits them. . . .
>
> The Church, according to Paul, is a living organism, a body. Like any living body, it is subject to maladies. Modernism is the pitiless and fatal cancer that is attacking the Church. It, like cancer, must be stamped out right at the start. The Church must confront it before it is too late, before all effort proves to be vain. We must not allow its poisonous roots and tentacles to spread through the whole body of the Church before we try, and fail, to cure it. Surgery is always painful but necessary. . . . Before the Church is engulfed by the overpowering wave of modernism, it must be held back and unhesitatingly put down. . . . Conciliation with error is a crime; conciliation with heresy is worse than a crime. It is connivance with those who are doing the work

of the Devil and trying to destroy the Church of God [BP, March 1963, pp. 6 and 2].

In the same issue there was another article entitled "A Decisive Hour":

Two currents clash, two mentalities collide, two ideological conceptions meet head-on. On one side . . . is the faction represented by the
classic and traditional ministry: secure in its theological convictions;
loyal to the age-old, but not for all that, anachronistic creeds of the
Presbyterian faith; at one with the Church and its straight causes; dedicated to preaching the gospel message. . . . It is the Old Guard of the
glorious past of sacrifice and dedication. . . . On the other side are
lined up restless spirits who are ill shaped, revolutionary, iconoclastic,
and presumptuous. They flutter and tremble at every hint of not being
up to date. They are opposed to the past, ignoring it or showing no
interest in it. They flit about to suck in the strangest currents of doctrine
so long as the latter are recent and up to date. In this melancholy market
of theological negativism they are indifferent, if not hostile, to our confessional paradigms, which they regard as outmoded and obsolete. . . .
Polarized by political, economic, and social themes, and looking for
some illusory utopian panacea, they are crying out against the piety and
orthodoxy of our ancestors in the faith. They are replacing the traditional conceptualization of biblical Christianity with the serpentine categories of a jargon molded in the semantics of suspect or spurious
sources. The apostles of this new gospel display the paradoxical marriage of an ethic and a theology . . . which represents the sacrifice of
truth. . . .
   There is no way to reconcile such differing points of view. They are
opposed, mutually exclusive positions. Another approach besides con-
ciliation is needed . . . though it be drastic and lamentable: the extirpation of this cancer which is defiling the wellsprings of life and attacking
the very life of the organism in which it is spreading. . . . Prompted by
the zeal which faith demands of us, the love which the Church merits
from us, and the loyalty we owe to Christ, we must rid the Church's
body of those who are undermining its foundations and misdirecting its
steps. In my opinion, it is already late, perhaps too late, for this cathar-
sis [BP, March 1963, p. 10].

The two texts were not written by the same person, but they are extraor-
dinarily similar. Note the use of the body as a model of the Church, the stress
of heresy as a cancer, and the use of surgery as a solution. Those who disagree
with the age-old doctrines are emissaries of Satan, whose only aim is to undermine the Church of God. The two texts are good examples of talking
without vacillations or concessions. The uniformity of their diagnoses and
proposed solutions suggest that the issue had already given rise to a consensus

in the Presbyterian Church of Brazil. Indeed the texts proved to be prophetic. The dissident discourse in that Church was silenced. In April 1964, the editorial board of the Church's official publication, which until then had given room to both discourses, was shaken up. The "heretics" were no longer able to address themselves to the church membership. Thus began the surgical process, which is still at work today. I cannot treat it in detail here. Let me just say that the extirpation of the "cancer" was thorough, eliminating institutions and individuals from the Church. Here we have an example of social behavior which perfectly illustrates my thesis: those who affirm truth in absolute form, without leaving room for doubt, are destined to dogmatism and intolerance. Anyone who *possesses* the truth is condemned to be an inquisitor.

Political Conservatism

Nothing would seem to be further removed from the modern spirit. Yet, just as my thesis asserts the affinity of the RDP spirit with the medieval spirit, so it also affirms the affinity of the RDP spirit with the spirit of the modern world.

Orthodoxy calls for a rigid body of truths that must be affirmed absolutely. But what body of doctrines inspires the modern spirit? Isn't it true that ideologies are now collapsing, that we are seeing "the end of ideologies"? Almost every day we are surprised by unexpected signs of political pragmatism, both in capitalist and communist countries. In cases of political pragmatism, old enemies are transformed into new friends. This seems to suggest that the political identity of nations no longer depends on ideological constructions.

But let us move slowly here and not be deceived by surfaces. Political pragmatism *seems* to suggest that we are entering a more pluralistic world with a variety of options. As Alvin Toffler puts it:

> The people of both past and present are still locked into relatively choiceless life ways. The people of the future, whose number increases daily, face not choice but overchoice. For them there comes an explosive extension of freedom [Toffler: 301].

The individual will be left free in many areas, notes Toffler: "We leave him free in all other matters—as he leaves us free to be atheist or Jew, heterosexual or homosexual, John Bircher or Communist" (Toffler: 99).

Ideas are not important. Ideological criteria for separating error from truth are fading away. Indeed so are the ethical criteria enabling us to distinguish between good and evil. Everything becomes ephemeral, and society is coming to live under the spirit of "planned obsolescence" (Toffler: 67-71). What is good for the present is not assumed good for the future.

But Toffler himself recognizes that ideas and things are becoming transitory *precisely so that the economic system itself may remain*. As he explains it in terms of disposable ink cartridges: "By making the ink cartridge expendable, the whole structure is given extended life at the expense of the substructure" (Toffler: 61). Surface pluralism is needed to ensure deep-level solidity and permanence. Just as in the case of Protestantism, "free inquiry" is the bright ideological face of an underlying dogmatic rigidity. The immense fluidity of modern society thus seems to be a device designed to ensure continual refinements and alterations in the *operations* which are required to maintain the social system as a whole.

In an earlier day Mannheim pointed out that pragmatism, insofar as it focused on solving specific problems, implied tacit acceptance of the overall structures involved. So I am led to conclude that modern society is built on an unprofessed dogma: i.e., the immutability of its socio-economic system. And this dogma elevates the system to the status of absolute truth. The redefinition of enemies implied in the ideological laxity of political realism, in its pragmatism, is really akin to certain superficial kinds of "ecumenical negotiation." I mean those encounters where the participants negotiate over unessential matters in order to give even firmer footing to the tacit conventions on which orthodoxy is based. And here I am referring to the socio-economic orthodoxy of the modern status quo, which thus functions as absolute truth.

Obviously there is no direct line between Protestantism and the modern world, since the former never refers to such issues directly. Here we have two discourses that are totally distinct on the semantic level. This distinction and separation dissolves, however, to the extent that RDP discourse is *functional* for the modern world and its status quo. This functionality can be noticed on two levels.

First, as I noted earlier, the doctrine of divine providence *sacralizes* existing structures as products of divine causality. Believers must adapt to those structures with patience and submission, knowing that *God placed them there*. They are not objects to be altered or transformed; indeed that would be rebellion against divine providence. Existing structures are the *locale* where the believers work out their salvation, and even unjust structures have a place in God's plan of salvation. Note the significant remark by Calvin himself: "No tyranny, therefore, can exist which does not in some respect assist in protecting human society" (Lehmann b: 42).

Second, the Protestant ethic is one of repression of the body. As suggested by Max Weber and analyzed in this book, this ethic disciplines individuals to transform them into a *function*. The Protestant ethic is *an ethic of the civil servant*. It could not be otherwise, given the fact that existing structures are sacred and that believers must adapt to them. Since the logic of behavior is determined by the functional needs of the socio-economic system, the task of individuals is obedient submission to existing structures rather than criticism of them. If there is to be a metamorphosis of structures, it will come magically insofar as individuals undergo conversion.

Here one might note a significant difference between Protestants of the

RDP variety and Brazilian Catholics. RDP establishes a total, universal rationality. God is the Big Eye who follows believers in everything they think, say, and do. It is imperative to be consistent because cheating is impossible. We find something very different in popular Catholicism in Brazil, which of course has little to do with official theological formulations. The world of popular Catholicism is divided between two opposing rationalities. This is clearly evident in the *use* which Catholics make of the name of God as opposed to their use of the names of patron saints. If both sets of names had the same function, it would be hard to explain the dual-usage.

Protestants, for example, can only call on the name of God. And God represents inflexible causality, fated providence, the reality principle! The Catholic saints, by contrast, are friends: sensitive to the logic of the heart and the imperative of desire. They are powers on the side of the pleasure principle, which is totally repressed in the world of RDP. Thus the spirituality of popular Catholicism shows up as a technique for *cheating*, and I do not use that term in a pejorative sense here. One must appease the Lord of Fatality so that he will leave room for the game of life. Popular Catholicism is a spirituality for taking chances and letting loose now and then. In so doing, one is saying that what is in fact is not what ought to be. In the conflict between the indicative and the imperative, the latter takes axiological priority in this case. Herein lies the seed of an ambivalent attitude towards existing structures: respect and fear on the one hand, denial of their ethical validity on the other. Perhaps this is one of the underlying reasons for the differences in sociopolitical behavior that are now evident between Catholics and Protestants. Catholics operate amid two conflicting rationalities, so their world is contradictory, dialectical, and without precise definition. Protestants live within a single, total, closed rationality which provides no way of *naming* contradictions; and what cannot be said, cannot be thought. The totalitarian nature of truth produces human character and behavior that is equally totalitarian.

Is There Any Way Out?

I need hardly point out that the temptation of absolute truth and its accompanying dogmatic and intolerant behavior are not peculiar to one or more versions of Protestantism. The biblical myth of the fall identifies the temptation of absolute knowledge as the universal foundation of original sin. Are these permanent tendencies of the human spirit? I am tempted to say yes. Dogmatism is not a monopoly of religion. We find it at every level and in every area of human life, ranging from ideology and science to home life and individual behavior. Indeed there is something tragic about heresies too. Once they come to power, they turn into new orthodoxies. Heretics, too, institute inquisitions. In the last analysis the decisive factor seems to be power, not ideas. The strong are condemned to absolute truth and intolerance.

Is there a way out? I don't know. As I have already hinted, I don't believe there is any escape from the inside of absolute certainty and absolute truth. How might we convince gods to turn themselves into human beings? How might we convince immortals to become mortals? Once the suggestion of the serpent is heeded, once the basic option is taken, its logic unfolds with syllogistic precision.

To that extent I can affirm a twofold predestination. Those who already possess the truth are predestined to become inquisitors. Those who have only doubts are predestined to tolerance and perhaps to the burning stake. That is why I see only one way out. We must consciously and deliberately reject truth and certainty before they take possession of us. We must make our own the sentiments of Lessing:

> Suppose God held all truth in his right hand and, in his left hand, only perpetual striving towards truth. Suppose further that I were destined to err always and eternally. Still, if he were to say to me, "Choose," I would choose his left hand and say: "Give me this one, O Father. Pure truth, in truth, is for you alone (Kierkegaard a: 97).

NOTES

1. Otto here is evidently rejecting the animist explanation of religion, which viewed the idea of the soul as the origin of religion.

2. One of Nietzsche's aphorisms, collected in *The Will to Power*, is pertinent here: "Against that positivism which stops before phenomena, saying 'there are only *facts*,' I should say: no, it is precisely facts that do not exist, only *interpretations* . . ." (Kaufmann b: 458).

3. *Translator's Note.* No serious attempt is made here to reproduce the rhythm and rhyme of the Portuguese hymns cited. It is the content expressed that is relevant to the author's analysis here.

4. Protestant hymns in Brazil make extensive use of these idioms or languages. Here I can offer only a few samples:

> I will sing to Christ
> Who fulfilled the law for us!
> His mantle of justice
> I will happily don [HE, n. 257].

> The work is already completed!
> The debtor is free!
> Jesus paid the price,
> He, the just one and savior [HE, n. 259].

> There is no condemnation!
> For before the tribunal
> We have the Eternal Bailsman! [HE, n. 260].

> In that fountain I will wash
> My black heart,
> Never will his blood
> Lose its high appraisal [HE, n. 261].

> The punishment of the criminal world
> He took wholly upon himself,
> And at a grievous price ensured
> Eternal happiness for the believer [HE, n. 267].

He was our substitute
And our Bailsman
Crucified for us,
The holy Redeemer [HE, n. 32].

Blessed be the Lamb,
Who died on the cross for us.
Blessed be his blood,
Shed there for us.
Lo, in that blood washed . . .
Whiter than snow!
Yes, in that blood washed,
There I will remain, O Jesus [HE, n. 36].

He is, yes he is,
The medicine that cures every ill [Children's hymn].

If perchance one were to be wounded [by the snake],
Don't forget the powerful antidote: Jesus Christ
[OP, May 10, 1954, p. 4].

Jesus Christ is the penicillin of the soul
[Statement of an Elder in a Sunday School class].

5. For the book under review see the entry under Read, William, et al. in Secondary Sources Cited in the Bibliography at the end of the book. My citation from Goff is from a mimeographed copy of his review.

6. In the passage cited Bonhoeffer is referring explicitly to "the secularized off-shoots of Christian theology, the existentialist philosophers and the psychotherapists" (Bonhoeffer: 196). His point is to show that their procedure is identical with the various techniques used by the Church to "make room for God."

7. When the context is that of RDP, we shall often be using simply "Protestant(s)," or "Protestantism," to mean RDP.

8. I owe this suggestion to Dr. Elter Dias Maciel. He is currently exploring the problem by analyzing Protestant novels and fiction.

9. In his book on the social frameworks of knowledge (*Les cadres sociaux de la connaissance*, 1966), Georges Gurvitch devotes a page and a half to "The Reformed Churches and Their Cognitive Systems." His treatment is grossly in error, in my opinion. He begins by noting that it is based on "observation of the different Protestant Churches," thus erroneously equating Protestant Churches entirely with the Reformed Churches of Calvinist derivation. Furthermore, I don't think his conclusions are solidly based on observation at all. He considered Protestantism as a whole, ignoring completely the profound differences between various types. For example, he cites the Quakers to substantiate hypotheses about the "Reformed Churches." Writes Gurvitch: "The Protestant Churches leave no room for any specific knowledge about the external world. Being lay and profane, that world is not recognized as an object worth knowing by them." Such a statement is false insofar as it purports to be valid for all Protestantism.

Gurvitch also cites Kierkegaard as a typical representative of the subjectivist tendency in Protestantism. Now even the most cursory reader of Kierkegaard cannot fail to notice the polemical nature of his writings; Kierkegaard is constantly talking against the objectifying tendencies in the type of cognition which prevails in the Protestant Churches. In short, he sees himself as a radical departure from their epistemological orthodoxy.

Finally, Gurvitch is also mistaken, I think, when he writes that Protestant commonsense knowledge has no specific quality of its own, that it runs together with that "of the bourgeois class. . . ." It is one thing to say the Protestant cognition *functions* in harmony with bourgeois cognition—though even here reservations are in order. It is something else again to equate the two as identical, which is what Gurvitch does. For and English translation, see Gurvitch in Secondary Sources Cited in the Bibliography.

10. To the extent that believers make the church community their "significant other" and restrict outside relations to a minimum, their knowledge will tend to remain stabilized and unquestioned. RDP realizes this, so it tries to minimize contacts between members and other groups. That is why mixed marriages with "nonbelievers" are strongly discouraged, for example.

11. Note that before the conversion-experience death is presented in terms of its terror; after conversion it is transformed into a matter of heavenly glory.

12. For a discussion of the Hebrew concept of time in comparison with the Greek concept of time see Cullmann in Secondary Sources Cited in the Bibliography.

13. This message is hammered home incessantly, as the following excerpts from a pamphlet on dancing by João Conrado Wey make clear (*O Baile*, 1949):

> Young men, too, have gone to the doctor in a weakened state that made them unsuited for marriage. One of the questions they are asked by clinicians is: "Have you been dancing?" Dancing, you see, does harm. It interferes with the nerves and upsets the organism. Dancing kills slowly.

> A somewhat frail young man went to the doctor and found he had tuberculosis in the early stage. The doctor noted that his patient went to dances and drank a bit. He pointed out to his patient that he could get well only by avoiding dancing and drinking. But the young man could not overcome temptation. He went back to dancing and drinking. He died a sad death some months later.

> A famous old painting presents us with two paths, two ways: the one, to the right, is narrow, and is the road of salvation; the other, to the left, the wide, spacious one, leads to perdition. Along the one on the left we note the café, the person drinking, and the bordello, the theater, and the night club, flying the banner of worldliness; then the big casino, the lottery, and so on. . . . No one can walk with his or her feet on both roads. Either people keep them on the narrow one, the road to salvation, or they set them on the broad one and enter perdition.

The same basic sentiment was expressed by Dr. Flamínio Fávero in a lecture:

> Today I want to speak to you about dancing, to impress on you the principle that dancing and the believer are absolutely incompatible. They cannot live together. They cannot have mutual ties. They are mutually repugnant. There-

fore they need to be in a state of constant war, concerned for their own respective, indomitable, ever-waxing energies: believers, on the ascent of salvation, are bound for heaven, imitating, with dedication and perseverance, their Savior and Master, whom they ought to serve ever more and more with sincerity of heart; dance heads down the shameless slope to hell, for it is in the service of the prince of darkness, whose loyal servant and vassal it is, and charged with the destruction of deluded innocence by dragging it into the maelstrom of its most skillful seductions.

And finally, from a booklet claiming to analyze dancing from the viewpoint of depth psychology:

If the law we have from psychoanalysis is certain, and all human creations are related to interior energies which determine and explain them, the question arises spontaneously in our minds when we are speaking of dance: To what intimate, interior disposition is the pleasure produced by dancing tied? . . . Hence we conclude that the disposition which impels couples who come together for dance is above all the natural inclination which the members of one sex have toward those of the other [Rizzo: 12–13].

BIBLIOGRAPHY

Primary Sources Cited

BP   *O Brasil Presbiteriano*. São Paulo: Casa Ed. Presbiteriana. Official organ of the Presbyterian Church of Brazil. Successor to OP, and founded in September, 1958.

HE   *Hinário Evangélico*. Rio de Janeiro: Confederação Evangélica do Brasil, 1966.

LC   *Livro de Confissões*. São Paulo: Missão Presbiteriana do Brasil Central, 1969. English citations come from the *Book of Confessions*, 2nd edition, Philadelphia: The Office of the General Assembly of the United Presbyterian Church in the United States of America, 1970. This volume is Part I of the Constitution of the United Presbyterian Church in the United States of America. It should be noted that sections of the 1647 Westminster Confession of Faith have been amended (e.g., n. 6.130), and that the original text appears in footnotes in the American edition.

MC   *Manual de Culto*. São Paulo: Casa Ed. Presbiteriana, 1969.

MP   *Manual Presbiteriano*. São Paulo: Casa Ed. Presbiteriana, 1951.

OP   *O Puritano*. Rio de Janeiro, Rua Alzira Brandão 35. Founded on June 8, 1899, succeeded by BP in September, 1958.

Secondary Sources Cited

Alves, Rubem A. "The Case Against the New Roman Catholic Spirituality," in James F. Andrews, ed., *Paul VI: Critical Appraisals*. New York: Bruce Publishing Company, 1970.

Augustine. *The City of God*. New York: Modern Library Giant, 1950.

Bainton, Roland. *Hunted Heretic: The Life and Death of Michael Servetus*. Gloucester, Mass.: Peter Smith.

Barth, Karl. *Church Dogmatics I/1*. Edinburgh: T & T Clark, 1936.

Berger, Peter L. *Invitation to Sociology: A Humanist Perspective*. New York: Doubleday, 1963.

Berger, Peter L., and Luckmann, Thomas. *The Social Construction of Reality: A Treatise in the Sociology of Knowledge*. New York: Doubleday, 1967.

Bonhoeffer, Dietrich. *Letters and Papers from Prison*. New York: Macmillan, 1962.

Borger, Robert, and Seaborne, A. E. *The Psychology of Learning*. Baltimore: Penguin, 1966.

Brown, Norman O. *Life Against Death*. Middletown, Conn.: Wesleyan University Press, 1959.

Buber, Martin. *The Prophetic Faith*. New York: Harper & Row, 1960.

Bultmann, Rudolf. *Existence and Faith*. New York: Meridian Books, 1960.

Camus, Albert. *The Myth of Sisyphus and Other Essays*. New York: Knopf, 1955.

Carroll, Lewis. *Alice's Adventures in Wonderland—Through the Looking Glass*. New York: Random House, Modern Library Edition, 1971.

Cassirer, Ernst (a). *An Essay on Man*. New York: Bantam, 1969.

—— (b). *The Philosophy of the Enlightenment*. Princeton: Princeton University Press, 1951.

Castaneda, Carlos. *Journey to Ixtlan*. New York: Simon & Schuster, 1972.

Cullmann, Oscar. *Christ and Time*. Philadelphia: Westminster, 1950.

Dias Maciel, Elter. *O Pietismo no Brasil: um estudo de Sociologia da Religião*. Doctoral thesis, University of São Paulo, 1972.

Dewey, John. *Reconstruction in Philosophy*. Boston: Beacon Press, 1948.

Dostoyevsky, Fyodor. *The Brothers Karamazov*. New York: Signet Classics, 1958.

Durkheim, Emile (a). *The Elementary Forms of the Religious Life*. Glencoe, Ill.: The Free Press, 1954.

—— (b). *The Rules of Sociological Method*. Glencoe, Ill.: The Free Press, 1938.

Feuerbach, Ludwig. *The Essence of Christianity*. New York: Harper & Row, 1957.

Findlay, John N. *Hegel: A Re-Examination*. New York: Macmillan, 1958.

Freud, Sigmund (a). *Civilization and Its Discontents*. New York: W. W. Norton, 1962.

—— (b). *The Future of an Illusion*. New York: W. W. Norton, 1961.

—— (c). *A General Introduction to Psycho-Analysis*. Great Books of the Western World, vol. 54. Chicago: Encyclopaedia Britannica, 1952.

—— (d). *Totem and Taboo*. New York: Vintage, 1946.

Fromm, Erich. *Psychoanalysis and Religion*. New York: Bantam, 1967.

Gerth, Hans, and Mills, C. Wright. *From Max Weber: Essays in Sociology*. New York: Oxford University Press, 1958.

Gouldner, Alvin. *The Coming Crisis of Western Sociology*. New York: Basic Books, 1970.

Gurvitch, Georges. *The Social Frameworks of Knowledge*. New York: Harper Torchbooks, 1972.

Hegel, G. W. F. (a). *Phenomenology of Spirit*. New York: Oxford University Press, 1977.

—— (b). *The Philosophy of History*. Great Books of the Western World, vol. 46. Chicago: Encyclopaedia Britannica, 1956.

—— (c). *The Philosophy of Right*. Great Books of the Western World, vol. 46. Chicago: Encyclopaedia Britannica, 1956.

Hendry, G. S. "Reader's Response." *The Christian Century*, March 5, 1975, p. 31.

Holl, Karl. *The Cultural Significance of the Reformation*. Cleveland: World Publishing, 1962.

Huizinga, Johan. *Homo Ludens*. Boston: Beacon Press, 1968.

James, William. *The Varieties of Religious Experience*. New York: Mentor, 1958.

Jespersen, Otto. *Language: Its Nature, Development and Origin*. London: Allen & Unwin, 1922.

Kaufmann, Walter (a). *Hegel: Reinterpretation, Texts and Commentary*. New York: Doubleday, 1965.

——— (b). *The Portable Nietzsche*. New York: Viking, 1968.

Kierkegaard, Soren (a). *Concluding Unscientific Postscript*. Trans. D. F. Sevenson and W. Lowrie. Princeton: Princeton University Press, 1941.

——— (b). *Fear and Trembling* and *The Sickness Unto Death*, bound together. Princeton: Princeton University Press, 1954.

Kolakowski, Leszek. *Toward a Marxist Humanism*. New York: Grove Press, 1968.

Kuhn, Thomas S. *The Structure of Scientific Revolutions*. Chicago: Chicago University Press, 1970.

Kuncewicz, Maria, ed. *The Modern Polish Mind*. Boston: Little, Brown and Company, 1962.

Laveleye, Emile de. *Do Futuro dos Povos Católicos*. São Paulo: Casa Ed. Presbiteriana, 1950.

Lecky, Prescott. *Self-Consistency: A Theory of Personality*. New York: Island Press, 1951.

Lehmann, Paul (a). *Ethics in a Christian Context*. New York: Harper & Row, 1963.

——— (b). *The Transfiguration of Politics*. New York: Harper & Row, 1975.

Luther, Martin. *Three Treatises*. Philadelphia: Muhlenberg Press, 1943.

Malinowski, Bronislaw. *Magic, Science and Religion*. New York: Doubleday, 1954.

Mannheim, Karl. *Ideology and Utopia*. New York: Harcourt Brace Jovanovich, 1955.

Marcuse, Herbert. *Reason and Revolution*. Boston: Beacon Press, 1960.

Marx, Karl. *Early Writings*. New York: Vintage, 1975.

Marx and Engels. *The German Ideology*. New York: International Publishers, 1970.

Mayer, Antônio de Castro. *Carta Pastoral e Catecismo de Verdades Oportunas que se opõem e Erros Contemporâneos*.

Merton, Robert K. *On Theoretical Sociology*. Glencoe, Ill.: The Free Press, 1967.

Morris, Desmond. *The Naked Ape*. New York: Dell, 1970.

Myrdal, Gunnar. *Objectivity in Social Research*. New York: Pantheon, 1969.

Natanson, Maurice, ed. *Philosophy of the Social Sciences*. New York: Random House, 1963.

Orwell, George. *1984*. New York: Harcourt, Brace & World, 1949.

Otto, Rudolf. *The Idea of the Holy,* 2nd edition. New York: Oxford University Press, 1950.

Perls, Frederick, Hefferline, R., and Goodman, P. *Gestalt Therapy: Excitement and Growth in the Human Personality*. New York: Dell, 1965.

Polanyi, Michael. *Personal Knowledge: Towards a Post-Critical Philosophy*. New York: Harper & Row, 1962.

Popper, Karl. *The Logic of Scientific Discovery*. New York: Basic Books, 1959.

Rauschenbusch, Walter (a). *Christianizing the Social Order*. New York: Macmillan, 1912.

——— (b). *The Social Principles of Jesus*. New York: Association Press, 1916.

Ricoeur, Paul (a). *History and Truth*. Trans. C. A. Kebley. Evanston: Northwestern University Press, 1965.

——— (b). *The Symbolism of Evil*. Trans. Emerson Buchanan. New York: Harper & Row, 1967.

Rieff, Philip. *Freud: The Mind of the Moralist*. New York: Viking, 1959.

Rizzo, Miguel. *Dança e Psychanalyse*. São Paulo, 1929.

Rückert, Hans. "Die geistesgeschichtliche Einordnung der Reformation," in *Zeitschrift für Theologie und Kirche,* 1955, pp. 43–64. For an English translation see

Hans Rückert, "The Reformation—Medieval or Modern?" in Rudolf Bultmann et al., *Translating Theology into the Modern Age.* New York: Harper & Row, 1965.

Schleiermacher, Friedrich (a). *The Christian Faith.* New York: Harper Torchbooks, 1963.

—— (b). *On Religion: Speeches to Its Cultured Despisers.* New York: Harper & Row, 1965.

Schutz, Alfred. *Collected Papers.* The Hague: Martinus Nijhoff, 1971.

Schweitzer, Albert. *The Quest of the Historical Jesus.* New York: Macmillan, 1964.

Stark, Werner. *The Sociology of Knowledge.* Glencoe, Ill.: The Free Press, 1958.

Suzuki, D. T. *Zen Buddhism.* New York: Doubleday, 1956.

Szasz, Thomas. *The Manufacture of Madness.* New York: Harper & Row, 1970.

Tillich, Paul (a). *The Courage To Be.* New Haven: Yale University Press, 1952.

—— (b). "The Person in a Technical Society." In *Christian Faith and Social Action.* Ed. John H. Hutchinson. New York: Charles Scribner's Sons, 1953.

—— (c). *The Protestant Era.* London: Nisbet and Co., 1951.

Toffler, Alvin. *Future Shock.* New York: Bantam Books, 1971.

Troeltsch, Ernst (a). *Protestantism and Progress.* Boston: Beacon Press, 1958.

—— (b). *The Social Teaching of the Christian Churches.* New York: Harper Torchbooks, 1960.

Unamuno, Miguel de. *The Tragic Sense of Life.* New York: Dover Publications, 1954.

Van der Leeuw, Gerardus. *Religion in Essence and Manifestation,* 2nd edition. London: Allen & Unwin, 1964.

Weber, Max (a). *On Charisma and Institution Building.* Chicago: University of Chicago Press, 1968.

—— (b). *The Protestant Ethic and the Spirit of Capitalism.* New York: Charles Scribner's Sons, 1958.

Wittgenstein, Ludwig (a). *The Blue and the Brown Books.* Also known as *Preliminary Studies for the "Philosophical Investigations."* Oxford: Basil Blackwell, 1964.

—— (b). *Tractatus Logico-Philosophicus.* Atlantic Highlands, N.J.: Humanities Press, 1961.

Secondary Sources Consulted

Alves, Rubem. "Is There Any Future for Protestantism in Latin America?" *The Lutheran Quarterly* 22 (February 1970): 49–59.

——. "Protestantism in Latin America: Its Ideological Function and Its Utopian Possibilities." *The Ecumenical Review* 22 (January 1970): 1–15.

Araújo, João Dias de. *Inquisição Sem Fogueiras: Vinte Anos de História da Igreja Presbiteriana do Brasil: 1954–1974.* São Paulo: ISER, 170 pages, mimeographed.

Braga, Erasmo. *The Future of the Church in Latin America.* Manuscript in the Presbyterian Archives of Campinas, circa 1930.

——, and Grubb, Kenneth. *The Republic of Brazil: A Survey of the Religious Situation.* London: Dominion Press, 1932.

Camargo, Cândido Procópio Ferreira de, ed. *Católicos, Protestantes e Espíritas.* Petrópolis: Vozes, 1973.

César, Waldo A. *Para uma Sociologia do Protestantismo Brasileiro.* Petrópolis: Vozes, 1973.

————, ed. *Protestantismo e Imperialismo na América Latina*. Petrópolis: Vozes, 1968.

Costa, Esdras Borges. *Religião e Desenvolvimento Econômico no Nordeste do Brasil*. Louvain: Feres, 1968.

Ferreira, Julio de A. *História da Igreja Presbiteriana do Brasil*. São Paulo: Casa Ed. Presbiteriana, 1960.

Franca, Leonel. *A Igreja, a Reforma e a Civilização*. São Paulo, 1958.

————. *O Protestantismo no Brasil*. São Paulo: Liv. Agir Ed., 1937.

Gates, C. W. *Industrialization, Brazil's Catalyst for Church Growth: A Study of the Rio Area*. South Pasadena: William Carey Library, 1972.

IBGE. *Estatística do Culto Protestante no Brasil*.

Léonard, Émile. *O Protestantismo Brasileiro*. São Paulo: ASTE, 1963.

Ludwick, Robert E. *The Significance of the Church-State Relationships to an Evangelical Program in Brazil*. Cuernavaca: CIDOC, 1969.

Maurer, Theodoro H., Jr. "A Cultura Protestante no Brasil," *O Estandarte* (December 1954), pp. 39-42.

Pereira, Eduardo Carlos. *O Problema Religioso da América Latina*. São Paulo: Brasileira, 1920.

Pierson, Paul E. *A Younger Church in Search of Maturity: Presbyterianism in Brazil from 1910-1959*. San Antonio: Trinity University Press, 1974.

Ramalho, Jether Pereira. *Prática Educativa e Sociedade*. Rio de Janeiro: Zahar, 1976.

Ramos, Jovelino. "Protestantismo Brasileiro: visão panorâmica," *Paz e Terra*, no. 6 (April 1968).

Read, William R. *New Patterns of Church Growth in Brazil*. Grand Rapids: Eerdmans, 1965.

———— et al. *Latin American Church Growth*. Grand Rapids: Eerdmans, 1969.

Rossi, Angelo. *Diretório Protestante no Brasil*. São Paulo: Paulista, 1939.

Sinclair, John, ed. *Protestantism in Latin America: A Bibliographical Guide*. Revised edition. South Pasadena: William Carey Library, 1976.

Souza, Beatriz Muniz de. *A Experiência da Salvação—Pentecostais em São Paulo*. São Paulo: Liv. Duas Cidades, 1969.

Willems, Emilio. *Followers of the New Faith: Culture Change and the Rise of Protestantism in Brazil and Chile*. Nashville: Vanderbilt University Press, 1967.

————. "El Protestantismo y los Cambios Culturales en Brasil y Chile." In *Religion, Revolución y Reforma*. Ed. William V. D'Antonio (Barcelona, 1967), pp. 165-98. Eng. original: "Protestantism and Cultural Change in Brazil and Chile." In *Religion, Revolution, and Reform*. Ed. William V. D'Antonio (New York: Frederick A. Praeger, 1964), pp. 91-108.

Other Orbis Titles . . .

WHAT IS RELIGION?
by Rubem Alves
What is the meaning of religion in a world come of age, in a world in which, some claim, God is dead? In this profound and lyric essay, a Brazilian theologian addresses this question. His carefully wrought work will be valuable for classroom use in introductory courses on religion and in study groups.

ISBN 0-88344-705-3

96pp. Paper

HERALDS OF A NEW REFORMATION
The Poor of South and North America
by Richard Shaull
Foreword by Paul Lehmann
   Richard Shaull interprets Latin American liberation theology for first world Christians and shows how it relates to our situation. The one-time Princeton Professor of Ecumenics includes a moving account of how his own life plan and faith have been altered by his encounter with the poor of the Americas over four decades.

ISBN 0-88344-345-7

160pp. Paper

CHRIST OUTSIDE THE GATE
Mission Beyond Christendom
by Orlando E. Costas
"Solidly theological, amply historical, thoroughly ecumenical, and remarkably current, *Christ Outside the Gate* is the most succinct, yet comprehensive analysis of the missiological issues facing the church and the churches that has appeared in many years."
        Alan Neely, Southeastern Baptist Theological Seminary, Wake Forest

ISBN 0-88344-147-0

256pp. Paper

SALVATION AND LIBERATION
In Search of a Balance Between Faith and Politics
by Leonardo and Clodovis Boff
   After an introduction to the basic propositions of liberation theology, the authors discuss their stance on the relationship between faith and politics, salvation and libera-

tion. The expositional chapters are rounded out by a lively, imaginary "conversation" among a parish priest, a theologian, and a Christian activist confronting the challenges posed by the present social reality in Latin America.

ISBN 0-88344-451-8   *128pp. Paper*

THE LORD'S PRAYER
The Prayer of Integral Liberation
by Leonardo Boff

A scholarly yet inspirational reflection on the Lord's Prayer by one of Latin America's outstanding liberation theologians. First of all, the thinking and life experience of Jesus is explored. Second, the author outlines a way to pray the Lord's Prayer in "the context of the oppressive forces that weigh down upon contemporary humanity and make it unhappy."

"Boff discusses each supplication in the Lord's Prayer, carefully analyzing the words for their meaning when Jesus spoke them and their meaning in our modern world. This is a helpful and insight-provoking look at Jesus' own prayer—and ours."

Spiritual Book News

ISBN 0-88344-299-X   *144pp. Paper*

HOPING AGAINST ALL HOPE
by Dom Helder Camara

Powerful prose and poetry from the Brazilian archbishop internationally known for his advocacy of the poor and oppressed.

"Dom Helder is living daily with one of the most excruciating problems of our time: What are the grounds for hope for those who are powerless and know only one defeat after another? There are no clear rational answers to these questions today that make much sense to us, but there are a few people around the world who keep going—and help keep others going—hoping against hope. Dom Helder is one of these."

Richard Shaull

ISBN 0-88344-192-6   *illus., 96pp. Paper*

JESUS OF NAZARETH YESTERDAY AND TODAY
Vol. 1: FAITH AND IDEOLOGIES
by Juan Luis Segundo

In his monumental 5 vol. series, Segundo attempts to place the person and message of Jesus before us all, believer and unbeliever alike. He shakes off the christological dust of previous centuries so that we can hear the words that Jesus spoke.

"*Faith and Ideologies* continues to develop the key concepts that Segundo had previously analyzed in *The Liberation of Theology*. He does this with great incisiveness and profundity both on the anthropological and the theological levels. A must for those exploring the frontiers of contemporary theology." *Alfred T. Hennelly*

ISBN 0-88344-127-6 *368pp. Paper*

BASIC ECCLESIAL COMMUNITIES
The Evangelization of the Poor
by Alvaro Barreiro

"Inspired by his experience with the basic ecclesial communities of Brazil, Alvaro Barreiro has written a simple yet succinct synthesis of the biblical foundations for the evangelical option of the poor as manifested in this movement. These communities are shown to be truly the church itself at its basic level, seeking 'to rediscover what is most central to Christianity and to put the Church back into the life that is lived daily again.' " *International Bulletin of Missionary Research*

"This book offers one of the few sources of solid information on base communities in English." *Today's Parish*

ISBN 0-88344-026-1 *96pp. Paper*

A PLACE IN THE SUN
Liberation Theology in the Third World
by Theo Witvliet

Liberation theology is often perceived simply as a Latin American phenomenon. In this insightful study by Dutch theologian Theo Witvliet, however, the sundry manifestations of liberation theology throughout the Third World are explored, revealing a richly diverse and truly global theological development.

The author examines the bitter roots of liberation theology—economic exploitation, the identification of mission with imperialist expansion, the transition from slavery to racism—and demonstrates how the Christian peoples of the Third World, drawing from their unique contexts, have developed a theological approach radically different from that of their more affluent partners in faith.

ISBN 0-88344-404-6 *208pp. Paper*